LIFE AND DEATH MATTERS

LIFE AND DEATH MATTERS

Seeking the Truth about Capital Punishment

ROBERT L. BALDWIN, M.D., M.A.

NEWSOUTH BOOKS
Montgomery | Louisville

NewSouth Books
105 South Court Street
Montgomery, AL 36104

Copyright © 2009 by Robert Baldwin.
All rights reserved under International and Pan-American Copyright Conventions.
Published in the United States by NewSouth Books, a division of NewSouth, Inc.,
Montgomery, Alabama.

Library of Congress Cataloging-in-Publication Data

Baldwin, Robert, 1943-
Life and death matters / Robert Baldwin.
p. cm.
ISBN-13: 978-1-58838-234-4
ISBN-10: 1-58838-234-6
1. Capital punishment—Alabama. 2. Discrimination in
capital punishment—Alabama. 3. Baldwin, Robert, 1943- 4. Prison chaplains—
Alabama—Biography. I. Title.
HV8699.U6A3 2008
364.66092—dc22
[B]

2008031045

Design by Randall Williams
Printed in the United States of America

AUTHOR'S NOTE: With the exception of my physicians, the names of friends, acquaintances, students, and inmates mentioned in conversations throughout the book have been changed for the purpose of anonymity. Names of actual court cases, and personal communications cited and referenced, are real.

To my dear wife and confidante,
whose example, dedication, and love has sustained and guided me
throughout my life and the lives of the other wonderful members of
my family. I needed look no further than what she represents to find a
shining example of the innate goodness of humankind, manifest not in
the least by the understanding, respect, and service that she provides to
others, and in particular those families seeking wholeness through the
process of adoption.

A special thanks to all the inmates I have come to know
and call "my brother," bound as such as one under God. These men,
both in the general population and on death row, have given me the in-
sight to what it is like to be on the "inside" of a prison and have fostered
my understanding of the many travails inherent to that environment.
May they find peace and a pathway to that ultimate "freedom"
that only God can offer.

TABLES

CONTENTS

ACKNOWLEDGMENTS

First and foremost, let me thank my wife, Pat, for the support and example that she has given me through our lives together and particularly during the long hours spent "closeted" my study preparing this book. Being both the "rock" and the "rose" of the family, she also provides an example of the innate goodness of all humanity. Thanks also to her and my entire family for the tolerance and understanding of the lost family time inherent in this pursuit.

Second, without the teaching, guidance, and support of my original thesis committee at Birmingham-Southern College, from which this project emanated, neither the knowledge required nor the proper presentation of the data contained would have been possible: Dr. Ed Lamonte, professor of political science and chairperson of the thesis committee; Dr. Bill Myers, chairman, Department of Philosophy, Religion, and Ethics, and Dr. George Klersey, professor of accounting/statistics. It is a tribute to the academic excellence of Birmingham-Southern College, to which I am grateful for offering the Masters of Arts in Public and Private Management, and the professors they have provided to accomplish this degree.

Dr. Lamonte first exposed me to a serious examination of the issues surrounding crime and punishment, and the death penalty in particular, during his course on "Public Policy Process." He inspired me to more in-depth study of the topic, which led to my complete 180 on the issue, particularly when learning of the death penalty's lack of deterrent value; its indiscriminate application to blacks, other minority groups, and the poor; the exorbitant costs of prosecution; and the inadequate representation that these individuals had during their trial proceedings. Dr. Lamonte is well recognized for his teaching excellence, his personal attention to his students, and his advocacy for the under-served populations in our community and our nation. He is also an inspiration to his students and highly respected among them, as well as by his colleagues and certainly by me. I learned a valuable concept from Dr. Lamonte: "the common good."

Dr. Meyers may be described as philosophico exemplar in the discipline of philosophy and well-defined by his own. His personal convictions, study, and understanding of ethics, history, and religion, and his ability to relate what may be foreign concepts to the neophyte attempting to gain some comprehension of philosophical principles, history, and ideals, are unique. He also provides an excellent sounding board for those students interested in delving deeper into philosophical study and serves as an excellent mentor for discussion and argument (scientific), as well as an altruistic advisor. I was introduced to a valuable concept by Dr. Meyers: "the universal moral."

Dr. George Klersey is an analytical genius from my perspective and from the perspective of my fellow students, but with a multiplicity of graduate degrees and by using his unique talents as a communicator and teacher, he makes the study of quantitative analysis and statistics not only understandable but also practical and even fun.

And I give a very special tribute to Lynne Glasner, my adviser, researcher, editor, and a multi-talented individual, without whom this project would not have been possible. Her time and dedication over the last four years has added immeasurably to the authenticity, quality, and readability of this manuscript. I am deeply appreciative of all her efforts.

One is what one is, with God-given talents innate. But talents unrecognized, ignored, or under-utilized are nothing. Fortunately, one is given parents, extended family, friends, pastors, and professors to nurture these talents so that one can become the "best one can be." Thank God for the blessings, and family, friends, pastors, and professors for pushing us toward "perfection," an admirable goal that although not achievable by mere mortals in this life, will serve us well in another. John Bate stated that "We are given days by him to whom belong days. We are free to do with them what we will. We can travel twenty-four hours nearer to Heaven or nearer to Hell. Yesterday is gone. Tomorrow is not. Only today is ours." Remember to cherish every day, even every moment that one is allowed in this brief wisp of the ages called mortality, as stated so eloquently by the poetic phrase from unknown lips, "How quickly the tender flower fades, and like a moonbeam from this earth does disappear." ⌒

LIFE AND DEATH MATTERS

PROLOGUE

Tuscaloosa, Alabama, June 11, 1963. The day is seared into my memory, much like the heat of the summer day. I watched in awe ten to fifteen yards from where Governor George Wallace literally stood in the schoolhouse door, fulfilling the pledge he had made to his white constituency: there would be no integration of any of Alabama's public schools. He stood outside the auditorium on campus where registration was in progress. Flanked by Alabama state troopers, the crowd gathered. I was among them. I had come to register for my summer classes at the university and also to see what would happen.

Excitement was in the air. I was unaware of history in the making, yet it was hard not to know something big was happening. The media was in attendance—the national media—as this was no longer just local news. We considered this a local issue and the attention brought to bear on it only served to engender more distrust and anger. I had walked from my dorm to the auditorium where registration was being conducted, as originally directed in my student information packet.

The campus was abuzz with apprehension of the governor's appearance. In keeping with my apolitical lifestyle, I had come as an observer not a participant. But it was impossible not to get caught up in the heat of the moment. I hadn't anticipated that the whole campus would be blocked by barricades and encircled by the police and security agents to prevent unauthorized entry. Crowds were forming all around. I was furious. I just wanted to go to school and get an education, do the things that college kids do. In their attempts to integrate the university, these civil rights groups were interfering with my rights, too. I resented all of the people who were involved in these events and the disrupting effects they had on the peaceful society that I knew and loved.

I watched as U.S. Deputy Attorney General Nicholas Katzenbach and some other federal officials approached Wallace. By this time, I had inched up close enough to hear them. "I just want to abide by the federal court order," Katzenbach said when Wallace refused to step aside to let Vivian Malone and James Hood enter the auditorium and register with the rest of us. The tension created by this clash of political wills was as thick as the gathering crowd. We waited silently, dripping in the heat, uncertain of Wallace's response, hoping he would win this battle without violence. But we were not sure. The ghost of the Klan filtered into our collective consciousness. Surely, many of those in the crowd knew first-hand of the KKK's extra-legal activities; they had been witness to some sort of related violence or at least knew others who had. My stomach was tight with fear, fear of the dreaded integration and its inherent evils that would shape my future as well my position front and center in the possible physical violence that could erupt at any moment.

Even then, I recognized that this showdown was different: Would the Klan dare to confront federal forces? We so badly wanted Wallace to succeed and despised the presence of Katzenbach who was there under federal order of the Kennedys. But I don't think most of us grasped the enormity of the moment and the possible changes that would follow depending on which way the dice were thrown. We barely noticed the presence of the big news cameras that rolled around to record this slice of history. Were Wallace and Katzenbach playing to the cameras even then? I don't know; certainly it was not a thought that would have occurred to me at the time. My ears were tuned to their conversation.

Wallace read from a prepared speech and cited states' rights in declaring his authority to operate public schools and universities as he saw fit:

> I stand here today, as Governor of this sovereign State, and refuse to willingly submit to illegal usurpation of power by the Central Government. I claim today for all the people of the State of Alabama

those rights reserved to them under the Constitution of the United
States. Among those powers so reserved and claimed is the right of
state authority in the operation of the public schools, colleges and
universities.[1]

Katzenbach stepped inside to phone President John F. Kennedy, who
then authorized the federalization of the Alabama National Guard. It wasn't
long before the troop carriers rolled down the road, stopping in front of the
auditorium building entrance where I stood with the crowd. With bayonets
affixed to their M-16s, they left their vehicles and headed toward Wallace,
who for a second time now took position behind the lectern. This time he
surrendered and stepped aside so that the two black students could enter
and register for classes. The cameras flashed again, freezing the frame of
another event that would change the South forever.

We silently watched Wallace climb back into his limousine and leave the
scene, rolling down his window to give his last wave. The students, myself
included, thrust our clenched fists into the air and broke the tense silence
with loud cheers of support for his efforts. We loved Wallace and we were
greatly distressed by the imposition of federal rule.

WEST JEFFERSON, ALABAMA, OCTOBER 10, 2006. After clearing the metal
detector and a body search, I signed into the prison and walked to the prison
chapel where I waited with about forty others in the volunteer group. By
prison standards the room is cheery. Natural light escapes through small
windows almost at ceiling height and glass doors, rather than the standard
thick metal ones securing the entryways, give the appearance of normalcy
and civility. Plastic molded chairs face the front of the room where a small
podium serves as pulpit and lectern. A small, back-lit stained glass enclosure
on the wall behind the podium glows dimly and several pieces of inmate
artwork bearing themes of God and redemption adorn the plain white walls.
A seldom-used piano sits on the side.

The fluorescent lights buzzed over the muted conversations as we waited.
We were slightly startled when a loud male voice boomed above the static
of an intercom to announce a delay in the arrival of the inmates because the

"count" was not correct. At this maximum security facility, physical inventory of the inmates is taken every few hours. More waiting. More time to think rather than do. I had been looking forward to today's activities and I felt ready, but the waiting gave me time to doubt myself.

"Here they come," someone yelled. And then they filed in, one-by-one, each entering the chapel only after his name had been called. Neatly dressed for the occasion in freshly washed and ironed prison whites, the men gleamed although a few looked apprehensive.

I heard them call Wendall Brown and I rose from the bench to greet him. Wendall entered the room with a grin so infectious it was easy to forget where we were. I thrust out my hand and then had to stop myself from embracing him. Still following the proscribed routine, I asked and received his permission to pin on his nametag. I reached up to do so and he chuckled shyly as I stretched to reach the lapel on his six-foot, four-inch frame and fumbled with the pin, trying to adjust my glasses so I could see it better. We exchanged small talk, mostly mine, and walked to a table in the back of the room where a coffee machine, provided by the ministry, had been set up. I poured him a cup and one for myself.

"Cream and sugar?" I asked.

"Oh, yeah. Man, cream and sugar!" he exclaimed.

I suppressed my surprise, later learning that cream and sugar, salt and pepper, and other condiments were not part of the normal prison cuisine. The ministry had also brought in platters of home-baked cookies, another cause for hoots of delight. These too had restrictions: no fruit, powdered sugar, or nuts. It was thought that the inmate entrepreneurial spirit might lead some to the production of alcohol by the clever use of such ingredients. It was hard to fathom, yet most of the rules were a response to some elaborate inmate scheme, and there is no shortage of creativity among inmates.

It had been two months since I first started prison visits as part of the prison ministry program. In one of my first meetings with a small group of inmates, we discovered some shared roots, and it became a homecoming of sorts. Out of a group of fifteen inmates, one was from my old home town, Toulminville, and another from the adjacent town, Prichard. The men could hardly believe it, but it sure tickled them. I wasn't sure how I felt at the moment; so much was new to me in this role. "You the first white boy I ever met from Toulminville," one of them grinned. I smiled in recognition.

Prichard and Toulminville were, and are still, poor suburbs of Mobile. Though both towns had small areas where the color lines overlapped, during my formative years Toulminville was largely white and Prichard mostly black. The town lines also served as the racial divide and everyone knew where the boundaries were. During my childhood, Toulminville was considered a step above Prichard economically and of course, socially. No longer segregated by law, both towns are now largely black, with a small number of whites, Hispanics, and others. The laws have changed and the towns have grown and developed, but the poverty in some parts has grown worse over the years, at least worse than I remember it.

I haven't been back to that part of Mobile in many years and of course it has changed significantly since my days. The geographic markers of my youth had mostly vanished by the time these men were growing up. But there were some things that remained intact and that commonality helped us start to form a bond.

I had been assigned to work with Wendall a couple of weeks ago. He seemed to really look forward to our time together and in truth, I enjoyed it, too. Wendall grew up in Prichard and it was sobering to think how different my life would have been had I been born on the other side of that color line.

Today Wendall told me a bit about his childhood. He learned early on that if he wanted anything, he would have to find a way to get it himself; his family was barely able to provide bare necessities for any of the four children. Wendall started lifting things from local stores at the age of ten, petty stuff—candy, small toys, socks—the kind of things you could stick in your pocket. But he soon graduated to bigger-ticket items and had already been introduced to the world of drugs by the time of his first arrest. He had just turned twelve. I knew the streets he described, even one of the stores, and the location of the booking station where he had been taken. It was home turf.

We had been instructed to be very cautious about allowing ourselves to be privy to information about an inmate's crimes, lest we become a possible witness in some legal proceeding. These particular crimes had occurred so long ago that it was hardly an issue, but being one who had always gone by the rules, I steered away from the details. It wasn't difficult. Wendall suffered tremendous guilt about how badly he had hurt and disappointed his mother, who had tried to help him in those early years but didn't have the means to hire an attorney who might have been able to get him another chance to change paths. At each turn, Wendall kept getting in deeper, winding up in a prison where he found that drugs were easy to come by. He was hooked quickly and continued this pattern of drugs, arrest, rehab, release, drugs, re-arrest, prison, escape, re-arrest, until finally he was sentenced to life without parole. Wendall's mother died while he was being held in maximum security, where he was informed of it after the fact.

"I felt so bad for hurting my mother all those years. I never got to tell her that before she died. I just got really angry and ended up in trouble again," he told me. But Wendall was now realizing that there was a power greater than himself.

Wendall and I talked a bit about his feelings and prayed. Our mission was to help the inmates understand themselves, recognize their sins, and seek forgiveness through redemption. They did not understand that prison walls and razor-wire fences cannot keep out the love of God or the people who make it known to them. We wanted to help bring some sense of inner peace to the inmates. That this usually meant the inmates were easier to manage and less prone to take exception to the rules made the Department of Corrections glad to see us, too.

Later, on my first day of teaching a class in the biblical perspectives of tough social issues, I decided to use Martin Luther King's "Letter from a Birmingham Jail" as a springboard for talking about racism and justice. Most of the inmates in the class had never heard of the letter, although they all knew of Dr. King.

"April 16, 1963," I started. I glanced around the room at the roughly two dozen men, all listening attentively. About three-quarters of the group were black, about the same proportion as in the prison. Most had not even been born during King's activist era; none would have been old enough to have any memory of it. I continued reading:

You express a great deal of anxiety over our willingness to break laws. This is certainly a legitimate concern. Since we so diligently urge people to obey the Supreme Court's decision of 1954 outlawing segregation in the public schools, at first glance it may seem rather paradoxical for us consciously to break laws. One may ask: "How can you advocate breaking some laws and obeying others?" The answer lies in the fact that there are two types of laws: just and unjust. I would be the first to advocate obeying just laws. One has not only a legal but a moral responsibility to obey just laws. Conversely, one has a moral responsibility to disobey unjust laws. I would agree with St. Augustine that "an unjust law is no law at all."

I stopped there and looked up to gauge their response. I repeated the line, "One has not only a legal but a moral responsibility to obey just laws" and asked what they thought about that statement. This opened up an interesting discussion about responsibility, morality, and justice. It was a more intelligent conversation than I had anticipated, in fact more thoughtful and provocative in some ways than conversations I've had with friends and colleagues who have more formal education than all of these inmates combined. I noted how eager the men were to hear what I thought and tried to be conscious of leading them to their own conclusions rather than adopting mine. Several of the men talked about how they had broken laws and broken their trust with their families. They were sorry, they said, for their sins.

I injected a story about Jesus and how he forgave the sinners who had betrayed him and explained the unconditional love that is God's gift if we are redeemed. "God always takes you back when you fall by the wayside of his path to salvation," I told them. "In fact, he created us with the free will to choose between right and wrong, good and evil." A few of the men grew solemn; some seemed like they wanted to believe me but weren't quite there yet. I knew they would be as I led the group in prayer. It was just a matter of time.

I had been warned about how easy it was to become "addicted" to pursuing this mission of prison ministry, but I had dismissed it. By this time, however, it was apparent that my addiction was as strong and as rapid as Wendall's had been. Though the nature of the addictions is admittedly very different, with far different consequences, I knew I would be back very soon. This was now my path.

I

GROWING UP SOUTHERN

Mine doesn't seem an extraordinary story, yet it is a story of radical change against what was and still is in many cases, the norm among my family, peers, and community. My evolving transformation feels quite ordinary, though I am told it is not. I don't feel like a radical or a traitor to my Southern upbringing or culture or friends. I am still much the conservative on fiscal matters. But on social issues I have become more the liberal, if labeling is appropriate. This in itself has made me the object of derision and scorn on more than one occasion. Regardless, I now feel like I am being true to my own values and belief in justice and fairness.

When we are faced with our own mortality, as I have been several times in the last decade, we often look inward. In my case, I looked for answers and turned to religion to supply them. In this process, I felt enlightened as I sought out a truer calling. I discovered that meaning and happiness for me had to come from giving back to the community that had supported my family and me, and helping those who had not been as fortunate as I had been. My material gains had been important, but as I turned inward, it was the spiritual gains I was seeking. What kind of life do I want to have lived? How can I apply the teachings of Jesus Christ and Christianity to my everyday existence to make me a better person and the world a better place? These were the questions I had to ask myself in order to attain peace when facing death.

When facing my own death it also became clear that the death machine we use to punish those guilty of the most egregious crimes is fraught with racial inequality. The facts forced me to look at the issue in a different light and reexamine my belief system. It felt like a natural transition, perhaps at least in part because of my own parallel changes of attitude about race, though I can see now why others thought it radical.

I was born and raised in the Deep South at a time when segregation was the law and KKK meetings did not raise any eyebrows. There were lots of rules governing behavior in polite white society, and mostly I lived within the rules and did what was expected. That's just the way it was. No one questioned our language or our values or our standards of behavior. My family attended the local Methodist church every Sunday, said grace at our table every night, and then went about our business—daddy went to work, mummy stayed home and kept the house and looked after the children. We led very typical lives in the post-WWII white South.

My hometown, Toulminville, is a suburb of Mobile, but at the time it was quite rural in nature although only a few miles from downtown Mobile. The church was a center of our family life: Sunday mornings and evenings and Wednesday nights were times for church and church activities, though other nights were added for special activities, which were frequent. My sister and I attended Sunday school, where much of our thinking was shaped; we were taught the values of a life patterned after that of Jesus Christ through sermons, Sunday school lessons, Bible stories, songs, and parables. These were the beginnings of a strong foundation that helped me understand at an early age the difference between what was good and what was not. We learned how the Christian life included a strong and enduring love for God, as well as the caveat to love your neighbor as yourself. But I must admit that being exposed to such doctrine and living it were not mutually inclusive; often they were not. I did not figure out until much later how to live a life that is consistent with these Christian principles. Often they seemed theoretical rather than practical. But I really admired those who did live them.

Growing up, it was my mother and others in her family who reinforced my Sunday school lessons and church teachings. It was her parents who exemplified the concept of "good" people for me. They walked the walk, so to speak, laying the foundations for a strong belief in the inherent good of humanity that was personified in the teachings of Christ. My mother worked hard to ensure that my sister and I always looked our best, often sacrificing her own needs. She was always the first to volunteer to help out at the church and was definitely a role model for being charitable. Since my mother's parents lived close by, my sister and I spent a lot of time with them, visiting them almost daily, especially during the long summer days in a Southern childhood.

These grandparents in particular greatly influenced my development and outlook. Their home was pleasant and serene, which was not always the case in my own childhood home. They were gentle and kind and were reverential with each other as well as with others. They always seemed to be there for counsel and advice, and were instrumental in mediating the sometimes violent fights between my mother and father. My grandfather had a positive outlook that always found answers to life's troubles in and through the scriptures. He studied the Bible daily and was devoted to the church. He stood apart from most other family members because his general comportment was more in keeping with Biblical teachings. He lived his religion and it showed. He was so committed to religion that after retiring at age sixty, he signed up for a correspondence course, became a Methodist minister, and "rode the circuit" in south Alabama, serving churches for whom a preacher was not always available.

I was in college when he started his course and once in a while when I was home, he would talk to me about it. During one of my home visits, he loaned me one of his books, a very complex book as I remember it, which he wanted to discuss when I finished it. Being immersed in my own studies, I did not have much time to spend reading it and never completed it. In truth, I was not that interested in either his book or religion in general, being a sophomoric student and a bit full of myself. Subsequently I felt badly about it, and I know it disappointed him, though he was never critical. We continued to enjoy a good relationship throughout his life. I learned only after his death that he had not always been so pious; he found God after a significant heart attack when he was in his forties. When my own prostate cancer prompted me to look into my family medical history, I also discovered that he had had prostate cancer, as did both of my uncles.

Growing up, my grandfather was my role model; I wanted to emulate his kind and generous spirit.

My grandfather was ordained as a lay minister of the church late in his life, but it had been ordained since before I can remember that I would become a medical doctor. While I never objected—I certainly liked the idea of self-sufficiency, the respect and status of a medical career, and, remotely considered, a healthy income—I was never consulted, either. An important part of my education was a deep respect for authority, including parents, teachers, and just about all elders. As a child and even as a teen, it did not occur to me to question what people told me, especially if it came from a minister or pastor. I was no different from most people in that I adopted the beliefs of my parents and teachers and peers and went about my life. There was no underlying cognitive dissonance in a world that accepted what was as if it had been that way for eternity.

Like all white families in that era in the South, I lived in a homogeneous community. Neighborhoods, then as now, were determined by income level, and minorities didn't mix regardless of income. I don't remember anyone ever questioning separate rules for blacks and surely no one among the people I knew at the time questioned the premise on which such rules were based: blacks were biologically and intellectually inferior to whites; social inferiority went without saying. The main purpose of blacks (yes, we used the term "niggers") was to serve the white ruling class. Everyone knew their place in my ordered world and no one questioned it. It's just the way it was.

Perhaps this underlying attitude was a remnant of post-Civil War Reconstruction in which the rules from the North had been imposed. The South had to obey, but that imposition hardened old attitudes rather than opening avenues for new ones.

After high school, I enrolled in a local Jesuit-run college not far from where I lived with my family in an upper-middle class white enclave in Mobile. Like other institutions of the time, Spring Hill College was all-white save for the blacks who served as janitors, workers in the cafeteria, or other such positions. The only dark faces here lurked in the background of where we went to class, worked, and socialized with our own. I don't remember anyone questioning the disparity. Even though Spring Hill was and still is a Jesuit school that advocates equality and the inherent goodness of the human spirit, I have no recollection of any campus talk about the issues of civil rights and segregation that were beginning to surface in other quarters. But as a biology major and a chemistry minor, with an eye toward medical school, most of my time was spent buried in my books, not in the news. No one I knew thought segregation was odd or unjust. It was part of our heritage. It was how we lived our lives.

During my first year at Spring Hill in 1961, the then-fledgling civil rights movement was beginning to grow. Although my mind was mostly on my studies, which included no references to current events or racial issues, it was still hard to avoid the topic altogether. My opinions had already been formed much earlier.

One by one, the bricks of segregation were being removed. When Rosa Parks first defied the white rules by refusing to give up the seat she had taken on a Montgomery bus, I was just twelve years old, and the public buses were our main mode of transportation. I have a vivid recollection of discussing it with one of my friends as we walked around downtown Mobile, having arrived there by bus. It was simply unheard of that blacks would be seated up front in the "better" seats. We thought it was awful for her to disobey the law; it was just inconceivable to us. We couldn't imagine anyone being so defiant. The only explanation we could fathom was that she must have been put up to it by others.

Looking back now, I have to assume that we picked up that explanation from hearing adults discuss it, or perhaps from local news that may have framed it that way; at twelve, we did not have the sophistication of thought to have arrived at that conclusion by ourselves. Had someone asked, we could not have answered just who might have been behind such a scheme or why. I'm not sure that even my parents and relatives, who had similar thoughts, could have answered that either.

In spite of the precedent Parks set and the furor and tension her defiance created, I don't recall any real change in the fabric of our lives. We continued to ride the public buses as we always had and for as long as I was still riding the buses, blacks in Mobile remained in the back. Eventually, of course, they moved up to the front, but by that time, I was driving and no longer noticed.

What I remember with much more fear and trepidation from that era was the possibility of a nuclear bomb attack. After the Soviet Union detonated their first atomic device in 1949, the hopes for post-War peace went up in smoke; fear of attack was everywhere. There were many discussions about taking cover under our desks at school for such an event, which of course seems ridiculous now. But at the time, adults and children alike took it very seriously. We had bomb drills in school every Friday at noon; the siren atop the grocery store just across the street from the building would blare and we would jump under our desks. I clearly remember the first one, which for some reason we were not told about in advance. I thought that the sirens were planes dive-bombing our city and it scared me to death.

We also were required to wear "dog tags," just like the military, for identification purposes if we were killed, injured, or lost in an attack. It made us feel grown up and proud and definitely "cool"; but it also served to make our fears that much more real and vivid. That fear, transferred from the adults to the children, was connected to the fear people harbored about integration and it was all mixed up in one big stew pot. Many adults, particularly in the South, attributed the new activism of the black community to communist agitators who wanted to disrupt our way of life. It was an easy nexus, helped along by the local news media and politicians who were happy to draw imaginary lines separating Mason and Dixon as well as "us" and "them," blacks and whites, and Americans and "Commies." The communist threat was exacerbated and exploited to garner support from the post-War nascent international community for the U.S. policy of containment. It would have been difficult to defend a United States that stood for justice and freedom that also denied basic rights and freedoms to black Americans at home. That official policy change was inevitable, but Southerners didn't see it that way.

The rise of the communist movement in the U.S. was rooted in the labor movement, where race and class issues merged. Although some of the early civil rights leaders had started out associating with its tenets, by the early 1940s, when the horrors of Stalinism became clearer, most had abandoned their affiliation. But that didn't dissuade the segregationists from using the issue to further divide North from South and to inject a "red scare" into the civil rights movement.

Bayard Rustin, who had once been a member of the American Communist Party, later became a key adviser to Martin Luther King Jr. Though Rustin had long ago disassociated himself from the party, this past affiliation became a cause célèbre for casting the civil rights movement in the red shadow of doubt. At that time (and in some quarters even now), any association with a "communist" meant being labeled subversive and a threat to the U.S. King was placed under FBI surveillance and his activities were closely monitored. As an anti-war activist, he was that much more desirable as a target and as the anti-war movement grew, so did the list of "subversives" who had their phones tapped. Ironically, King was a staunch anti-communist though he was also critical of the shortcomings of capitalism. He believed that there was a link between poverty and racism and he had called attention to the economic inequalities in the United States, which he felt threatened freedom for all races. The politics of the South as played out during the peak of the civil rights movement, however, happily connected the infiltration of Northern civil rights workers in the South with bogus infiltration of international communists in the civil rights movement itself, an association that served to keep both concepts on the list of things to fear.

Bear in mind, many of our parents and relatives had fought in WWII not all that long ago. They were proud of their service and our victory, as they should have been, but they were also quick to follow without much thought about who was leading and what they were actually following and defending. They knew they were defending their country again, and perhaps even more importantly, their way of life. Instead of looking inward, they needed to find something bigger than themselves to blame for the inevitable changes.

Although I was still a pre-adolescent at the time of the 1954 *Brown v. Board of Education* Supreme Court decision, it had created a lot of tension and resentment, not only at the mere thought of going to school with blacks, but also at the accompanying busing rules that would serve to dismantle our school system.

Although my family was generally apolitical, all politics is local, and no one could avoid being affected by the changes. They were clearly upset by the upheaval. Their responses became more evident as television began to play a more prominent role in disseminating the news. We acquired our first TV in 1956 and while our local newspapers mostly supported continuing the fight for local control and segregation, it was harder to ignore pictures of angry whites trying to keep black children out of school. Everyone seemed to feel betrayed by President Dwight D. Eisenhower who finally in 1957 called out the National Guard in Little Rock, Arkansas, to enforce integration orders there.

By our reactions, you would have thought the world was coming to an end. My friends and I were shocked at the impudence of President Eisenhower, our war-hero-turned-redcoat. We could hardly believe such a thing was possible. We not only resented his actions, but we feared for our lives. As a young teen I had adopted the stereotypes and the accompanying fear of integration of my environment. Too young and timid to actually participate in any public outrage, I admired at a distance the hecklers and others who tried to thwart the efforts of those sent to force integration. Friends and family alike, we all belittled and berated both the officials enforcing the policy and the blacks trying to better their education.

Although I now cringe at the recollection of those conversations with my peers, goading each other on in the epithets of righteous hate, at the time we saw nothing immoral about them. We repeated the refrain of "send them all back to Africa," hopelessly ignorant of the history of that failed controversial policy that had been advocated and unsuccessfully implemented prior to the Civil War as well as more recently. To us, it was one of many slogans that were hurled in defense of our lifestyle, a simplistic solution to a complex problem.

Along with our other hateful misconceptions, we thought integrated schools would pose unspoken dangers for white girls sharing close contact with blacks. Budding adolescents, eager to assert our Southern, white gentlemanly place in the world, we couldn't even fathom that a white girl would give a black boy the time of day, much less have a relationship with one, even just a friendly one. The thought of interracial dating outraged us, and interracial marriage was so beyond the pale that it wasn't even considered.

These kinds of pervasive attitudes naturally become part of your character; it's not a conscious choice. It's like cancer cells that lie dormant for years and then are suddenly triggered by something in the environment. Then they multiply and become invasive, taking over the rest of your being, unless they're consciously excised. I can clearly recall my initial revulsion at seeing racially mixed couples (especially if the woman was white) after the Civil Rights Act and on into the 1970s, as it became less and less taboo and therefore more public. I didn't think about it at the time; it was merely a passing thought upon noticing it. Part of the shock was in the oddity; it simply wasn't something I had seen before. But it also touched off my somewhat buried belief that this kind of racial mixing was wrong and somehow dangerous, and it made me uncomfortable. It wasn't until much later in my life that I came to recognize how deeply woven into the fabric of Southern culture my attitudes really were.

I know now that the perceived danger was derived from the clear prohibition of miscegenation, both social and legal. The rationale used for miscegenation was the Biblical "separation of the races," which was quoted all the time throughout my childhood. So ingrained was this concept in that it wasn't until 2000 that Alabama finally rid itself of the invalid language in its Constitution banning racially mixed marriage.

Anxious to escape the "evils" of integration, my father was determined to get out of the old neighborhood, where blacks encroached upon our "domestic tranquility." Our new neighborhood and larger, more upscale house was actually beyond our means at the time but my father managed to make it possible by doing much of the work himself on weekends, with assistance from his brother and me. Through his sheer will and hard work, the house was finally completed. But even in the fancier neighborhoods, by this time the public schools included some black students.

By the time I was ready to enter high school, my father had worked his way up the ladder in a steamship company based in Mobile. With a rising income, he was able to afford to send me to a local all-boys private military academy where the curriculum was more challenging and I would get more careful supervision and preparation for college and the med school track he had decided upon for me. My sister was sent to the affiliated girls' school.

Our mother had died a year earlier and in truth, I'm sure it had been a difficult time for my father, who had not been the primary parent in charge of child rearing and was surely overwhelmed. I was left to cope with my own grief and had nothing but disdain when he started dating the woman he would subsequently marry some months after my mother's death. I'm sure he remarried at least partly to provide a mother for me and my sister. But I would have none of it; I resented it all and was glad to focus on school and stay away from the household as much as possible.

That the private school was all-white goes without saying; that we would "not have to go to school with the niggers" was said loud and clear. Although I was proud to attend such a well-respected school, I missed my friends who continued in the public schools that were now succumbing to the unthinkable, but unstoppable integration. While they didn't seem to be in any danger, they continually plied me with tales of how stupid and unworthy the "niggers" were. True to form, my friends were in awe of the athletic ability and alleged sexual prowess of the blacks—stereotypes that we all subscribed to without questioning. As much as I liked hearing about their exploits and of course believed in the truth of their perceptions, I was grateful that I didn't have to deal with it in my new school, where most of the students were from the more privileged families of Mobile. They, of course, had been completely sheltered from even the discourse, and the focus on academics didn't include what was going on outside the walls of the insular campus. Although I got along with the students at the school, and did well academically, I was never entirely comfortable. On the other hand, the more distance I had from being in the public school, the more distant my old friends became.

As much as my father derived satisfaction from protecting his family from integration, he also enjoyed the status attached to his ability to send us to private school. But it was not without a struggle. He worked extra jobs to send me to college, not an insignificant expense even then. Eventually, it became too burdensome and my sister had to switch to the public high school not far from our home, where there were only a few blacks in attendance and only a couple in her graduating class. That didn't stop my father and stepmother from continually expressing concern for her welfare and safety there, however. I suspect they were more intent on garnering support for the horrors of integration foisted upon them than they were truly worried about her safety. Primarily, they feared the possibility of her "getting mixed up" with one of "them"—"them" of course being a black boy. I have to assume that in spite of the "dangers," they didn't believe that it was quite as bad as they said, else they probably would have found the financial means to keep her in private school.

As a rebellious teen, I didn't understand the depth of my father's commitment and didn't really appreciate the sacrifices everyone made until much later. What I did understand was the threat to our lifestyle. While I grumbled and complained at the physical labor I had to contribute as part of my father's plan, there was no counterweight to the heavy acceptance of the doctrine of hate.

So when the Freedom Riders drove through Birmingham and Montgomery in their first invasion of the South, I had nothing but contempt for their actions. I thought it most disrespectful that these troublemakers were invading our state and disrupting our system. How dare they! I had nothing against blacks, mind you, and certainly not against any particular black person whom I knew.

I was a product of an environment in which blacks simply didn't belong in the same social strata as whites. In my world, blacks were inferior beings and not entitled to the same privileges as the whites who made the laws and built the schools. If the blacks were going to allow themselves to get roused up by a bunch of Northern commies and act so disrespectfully, well then, so be it, I thought. They deserved to be beaten back by the likes of Bull Connor. Someone had to do it and who better than he? I was outraged by all of the people in the civil rights movement, who as far as I was concerned, were fomenting revolution. This attitude extended to everyone in the movement—Martin Luther King Jr., Ralph Abernathy, Fred Shuttlesworth, the Kennedys, sympathetic judges, and others. With the luxury of history, I can now reflect on the error of my thinking. I'm sorry to say that I didn't question my belief system until much later.

The underlying hatred was beginning to surface. Not that I was aware of hating anyone; after all, my Christian upbringing didn't teach me to hate, at least in theory. Weren't we all God's children? Equally loved by him? I didn't see the disparity. Didn't the Bible say that the races should be separate? All of my role models, from Sunday school teachers to ministers and family members, had instilled in me that "fact." What I felt was the threat to the stratified and peaceful society that we lived in, where everyone knew his or her proper place and good behavior in the here and now would be rewarded in the hereafter. That precept applied to blacks and whites alike. So what was the problem? I didn't think about why blacks might not have thought it was such a great deal, or that their idea of what was good in the here and now might be radically different from mine.

The problem with hating is that it eats away at your soul without conscience and leaves no internal trace, though the external ones are visible. When hatred is subsumed in the culture, we often are not aware of it; it seems normal and even righteous, especially because we associate with others who are in accord and prop up the hatred, making it feel legitimate. In fact, anyone in my early environment who didn't feel and express hatred of those who carried the flag for the civil rights movement was out of sync with the norm at the time and was met with the same scorn as the objects of the hatred. It's always so much easier to go along with the majority and not think about it further. I certainly did not, even when I was old enough to think independently. As with most of us, I was too busy with my own life and it was not a priority. Besides, I didn't think there was anything wrong with my thinking.

2

COMING FULL CIRCLE

M r. Holland replied rather emphatically: "Don't talk to me about what Bull Connor did with his police dogs and hoses. Don't tell me what Martin Luther King did or said or about racism in prosecuting criminals. I don't care." I stammered, unable to think of a quick response to his diatribe about the plight of blacks. That Holland is a black man made my task even more difficult.

I was leading the discussion in a graduate class on Public Policy Process at Birmingham-Southern College, where I had earned my master's degree in 2003. It was almost exactly six years ago that I had sat in this very class as a student, and now I was filling in for the instructor, Dr. Ed LaMonte. I was honored that Dr. LaMonte had asked me to fill in for him; it was in his class that I had first discovered that my own ideas about capital punishment were indefensible. It had been an enlightening experience, though a difficult process. But I had emerged stronger and determined to make a difference in the movement to abolish the death penalty. I had spoken to many people since that time but to no blacks who were as adamant and outspoken as Mr. Holland.

"It's the drug dealers that are killing our families and our children, ruining the neighborhoods, and until they venture out of the neighborhood and kill a white person," Holland went on, "they don't get prosecuted."

Holland was obviously caught up in the emotion of the argument and I knew that no rational comment or data I could summon would change his mind. He was not hostile, but the issue clearly triggered a lot of anger and resentment. Ironically, in a class of fifteen, the majority of them black, he was the only one who expressed this viewpoint. The others were either on the fence or in favor of abolition of the death penalty. The class had engaged in a productive discussion of the issue that included refutation of some of the major arguments put forth by those who support the policy: deterrence, safety, accountability. But when the discussion got to race, Holland started to object.

"The data clearly show the racial disparity," I explained. I supplied some data, adding that more than 80 percent of the U.S. population in 2006 was identified as white and less than 13 percent as black, but the death row population was 45 percent white and 42 percent black.

TOTAL NUMBER OF U.S. DEATH ROW INMATES[2]

RACE OF DEFENDANT	# OF INMATES*	% OF TOTAL
White	1512	45.22
Black	1396	41.75
Latino/Latina	358	10.71
Native American	38	1.14
Asian	39	1.17
Unknown at this issue	1	.03
Total	3344	

Holland questioned the integrity of the data. He didn't see how it could be true and wouldn't concede that it was possible. I didn't take it personally. I couldn't assign him with the task of refuting it for the next meeting of the class as I was the guest instructor, not the teacher. Was it my job to try to convert him, as was my instinct, or was my role here merely to clarify the issues and help the students think for themselves? This course was elective. These were adults interested in the subject, in a program designed specifically for returning students looking toward a career change or toward enhancing the career they were in; many of them worked in non-profit organizations or public institutions. I welcomed the opportunity to hear their views and lead a discussion with them, but I didn't know how to handle the likes of Mr. Holland.

Some of the other students chimed in. They objected to his broad rejection of data without any supporting evidence. Given that most of the students were black, they were sensitive to the race issue, and they were upset and frustrated with Holland's obstinacy. Although many in the class opposed the death penalty, overall they did not have a working knowledge of the specific issues and supporting data. Many felt the practice was immoral and most were troubled by the number of inmates who had recently been proved innocent. Some were aware of the racial issues raised by the policy. I gave the students some resources and encouraged them to do further research and gather more data to test and confirm their views.

It was a lively and interesting discussion and I enjoyed being part of it. The students seemed genuinely interested in what I had to say. They were particularly interested in my own conversion.

"Six years ago," I told them, "I would have sounded much like Mr. Holland, although I don't know if I would have been brave enough to express it." I watched for Holland's reaction as I spoke. I did not want to antagonize him but I did want the class to understand the depth of my change. A few students nodded and smiled; Holland shrugged but was stone-faced.

I explained that my earlier opinions had been formed without consideration of facts. We discussed the importance of facts and I encouraged the students to evaluate how they arrived at their views and to find support for their opinions in facts that are verifiable. This was after all, a class about public policy and public policy ought to have roots in the relevant facts. On that everyone seemed to agree.

As I related the chain of events set off by the research and paper I had completed as a student in Dr. LaMonte's class, I had trouble imagining how I could have held my earlier views about the death penalty. "I had never given it much thought," I confessed to the class. "It just seemed right. In my youth and throughout most of my adult life, I believed what most of my peers believed: punishment should fit the crime, capital punishment deterred further crime, and the government has the right and the duty to mete out justice accordingly."

I noted heads that were nodding. These were the standard arguments and everyone had heard them in some form. Holland seemed to be on board too, but probably for different reasons.

"My outlook didn't change until I found myself in this class, wildly trying to defend the policy," I continued. "When I looked at the facts, I couldn't find any that actually supported those arguments."

The class was fascinated. "There must be some data that support the opposing side," one student ventured.

"There's some," I told him, "but not any that holds up if you really analyze it. Much of it is anecdotal. The biggest 'factual' argument is about deterrence. Most people think that the data show that capital punishment acts as a deterrent. But it really doesn't. You have to analyze the data and not take things at face value."

I explained how I thought that deterrence is the issue that most people have a hard time overcoming. It makes people comfortable with their views if they think that the data support them. "It's these 'facts' that made at least some of the others in my class rethink the issue. I did my final paper on it and when I did my presentation, I found that it truly did have an effect."

Unlike my former classmates, most of the students in this class already agreed with the policy, but they were fascinated by how the facts had persuaded me so effectively. "I didn't set out thinking that I was going to change anyone's mind," I said. "My presentation wasn't very long, as I remember it. But I did point out the weakness in the deterrence argument rather quickly. The general public will simply say it deters crime and leave it at that." I then briefly explained the "academic" argument: punishment is an effective deterrent only if it is severe, swift, and certain. It is always severe, but it is never either swift or certain. Again, I could see heads nodding. "So, some of my classmates changed their minds about the policy when they were able to look at the facts more objectively," I said. "I don't think I really convinced anyone. I just let the facts speak for themselves."

I fielded several questions and then described how surprised I was when I discovered the contrarian facts, and further that I was able to convince others by using them. Several students brought up the issue of safety and law and order, which are part of the deterrence argument. "We assume the facts are on the right side of deterrence because so many people say so," I said. "It's repeated so often that we don't even question its validity."

I had decided that this was a good place for confession. In a group in which a large majority was black, I thought my story would resonate. I took a breath and recalled my support of segregation as a young man. "It took many years of being immersed in an integrated culture to realize that my 'facts' were wrong. So be wary of the intrinsic value of 'facts.' Look at the source and think for yourself," I cautioned.

"What 'facts' supported segregation?" a black woman challenged me.

"Well, there was the Biblical 'fact' that the races were supposed to be separated," I replied indicating the quotation marks for "facts." "And there were also supporting myths that were passed off as 'facts.' Things like 'blacks are inferior.'" Several people looked around a bit uncomfortably, but I continued.

"I know you're thinking that's an opinion, and of course it is. But people back then would supply accompanying 'facts' to support that opinion—like statistics that 'proved' that blacks had lower IQs, higher school drop-out rates, higher rates of illnesses, etc.," I pointed out. "All of these kinds of things were supposed to emanate from the genetics of the race, an inferior gene pool, if you will. Of course it's all nonsense and it's easy to refute now that we're looking at it from a different perspective."

Although the students in this class were well into adulthood, some were just young enough that their experience had not included segregation. Certainly they had been touched by it, but not overtly. It was something to reckon with, and my comments set off a broader discussion. Besides capital punishment, the overall class syllabus included a range of social issues from racial bias, affirmative action, and health care systems, to the legislative process and interest groups. There was lots of material and many related issues were touched upon. After a while, I brought the conversation back to the death penalty. I didn't know if anyone was having second thoughts about their stated views at this point, but I wanted to wrap things up before our time was out. I emphasized that using facts to defend any policy is mandatory, and facts can be fungible.

"It seems so simple because it's so reasonable," I explained. "But most people, and I include my former self here, want to fit the facts to the policy, and they are able do so because people find it hard to refute things that they consider basic and fundamental. So they find themselves supporting data even if that data is bogus." We discussed this concept in the remaining class time.

There was some further discussion of fact-based judgments as well as deterrence and safety. I had been quite flattered when some of my classmates had changed their view based on my presentation. Now that I was acting instructor and not fellow student, I hoped that I could continue that pattern. But at this point, I knew better than to push when someone is clearly coming from their emotions. So it was when Mr. Holland vented: "I just do not want the death penalty taken off the table. We need something to deal with the John Gacys, the Jeffrey Dahmers, the Ted Bundys, etc. Now, I can differentiate between these types and the guy that gets mad in an argument and kills someone out of character and regrets it," he admitted. "But we have to have some way of punishing these evil characters."

I let the defense rest. It seemed to me that Holland had softened a bit, though I don't know that he would have agreed. Clearly he had not changed his mind.

Of course I remembered how being in Dr. LaMonte's course had opened my mind to other truths. I had been looking for answers, but I had had the wrong questions. By the time I found myself in that class, I was ready to examine facts and separate them from the emotional home we often give them. I was at a point in my life in which I could be comfortable with self-examination. I had already been through major life traumas and had come out of the experience with renewed strength. In this process, I had had to do a lot of soul-searching to acknowledge my own truths.

My relationship with God, also newly discovered at the time, allowed me to approach things with the innocence of a child: "Truly I tell you, whomever does not receive the kingdom of God as a little child will never enter it" (Mark 10:15). At that time, I was still involved in a thorough reading of the Bible and was discovering new strengths. I believed that God was guiding me so I could let down the old defenses and strip away the social platitudes. I admit my habitual competitiveness made me think about grades. I did want to get all A's, but my primary interest was in learning. The intrinsic rewards in this process were, in fact, much more satisfying than all the A's I had ever earned over a lifetime.

I had approached the material with great fervor. When confronted with facts that contradicted my own belief systems, I had to reexamine my thinking. Instead of feeling threatened by it, I found it interesting and it forced me to think in new ways about issues I hadn't really given much previous thought to. Perhaps as a college-age student my reaction would have been totally different, but at that point in my life I was excited by the challenge of thinking in new ways. Having had a late introduction to Plato and other great thinkers, I found myself seeking a more examined life. Socrates faced a death sentence but stood his ground, opting for truth and the right and responsibility of citizens to engage in critical thinking, regardless of the consequences. So now I was poised to use the same kind of critical thinking to wipe out forever that archaic sentence.

Of the many topics covered in Dr. LaMonte's public policy course, I was particularly drawn to the issue of capital punishment. Perhaps this can be attributed to the wide gap between my beliefs and the facts regarding this issue and because of my own experience with confronting death. On the surface, it may seem odd; I did not feel like my illness was punishment for any of my past sins, although the thought had occurred to me during the worst periods of my various medical crises. I certainly didn't identify with criminals. But reading the materials on the subject engendered a different kind of wake-up call.

I do believe God allows certain things to happen to help "show you the way." The discovery of facts and critical thinking during my course of study with Dr. LaMonte was a lightning rod, shining a light on the "road map" that I knew I would follow for the rest of my life. The process of confronting my past, owning up to errors in judgment, and reaching contrition didn't come easily, nor was it swift. But it was part of a process of self-examination and reflection and I was compelled to use whatever time I had to lay out the facts and help others to see the light, too.

Often, the facts challenged my views, and being at the crossroads of my own life allowed me the comfort of examining the issues in new ways. I don't think that before this class I had ever really examined social issues using fact-based research. I had never really probed my thoughts to assess how I had arrived at many of my opinions. Nevertheless, I acted on them, voted my conscience, and then went back to my life. In this conversion, my change of attitude felt quick and severe, though the outcome was by no means certain. Yet it is one fork in a road that I took, and it changed everything.

3

FACING MORTALITY

I n 2007, forty-two persons were executed in the United States; all but one by lethal injection. Of the forty-two, fourteen (33.3 percent) were black and twenty-eight (66.6 percent) were white.[3] An additional three executions had occurred by June 1, 2008.[4] Meanwhile, the U.S. population as of July 1, 2007 was 81.3 percent white; 13.5 percent black; 5 percent Asian; and 1.8 percent other.[5]

"Court Stays Execution of Mobile Man,"[6] screamed the headline from my hometown newspaper, which I still read on occasion. I scanned the article with my morning coffee. Though I didn't expect to recognize the name of the condemned man, I was always relieved to confirm that information.

I read further and got chills, though the day was not cold on this temperate January morning. My body was reacting to the brutality of the case described in the article, bringing into focus all of my feelings about the death penalty, which at this point run deep.

It was several years since my complete turnaround on this issue, but I had spent many years in transition, in preparation for that change, though I didn't know it at the time. If you are attuned to them, there are frequent reminders of the problems and issues involved in capital punishment, and here again was another example of how immune we have become. Like the Klan in the South, the death penalty is a sad anachronism that never quite dies with its victims. I glanced at the small photograph of the inmate. Confirmed. Another black man—no one will care except the usual advocacy groups whose outcry is generally dismissed by the average citizen.

The condemned inmate, Clarence Hill, was literally seconds away from being given a lethal dose of drugs when the Supreme Court intervened. I winced as I read about how he was strapped to a gurney with intravenous lines in his arm when the prison warden rushed in to stop the clock. It's a patient's worst nightmare: not being able to move while hearing the sounds of frantic medical workers and seeing their shadows hovering over your body. I can easily imagine the IV lines in Hill's arm, similar to those I had experienced not that long ago, his bringing a cocktail designed to wipe out his life, mine a cocktail designed to wipe out the threat of death brought about by my disease. In both cases, the intent was that the drugs would have a permanent effect, or at least a reprieve; his reprieve was granted by the Supreme Court, mine by modern medicine. It's hard to imagine a more stark contrast. As I read the story, what I couldn't imagine was the indifferent treatment of the person on the gurney about to die.

The more I read, the worse I felt. It's impossible to imagine what would go on in someone's mind under those circumstances, and Hill never discussed it afterward, refusing all interviews. Hill was finally executed nine months later; my reprieve has lasted much longer, and my empathy for Hill and others like him has continued to evolve.

I understand quite well the anxiety produced in anticipation of medical procedures. I have been on both sides of the table. As a surgeon, I have stood by thousands of times while anesthesiologists prepared my patient for surgery. But I must confess that it did not feel routine when I was the one receiving treatment. Nowhere is the old axiom "it is better to give than receive" more true than on an operating table. No matter how much you trust the doctors taking care of you, it can still be a frightening experience to know that your life is in the hands of others. Ultimately, we are all in God's hands, and at the moment you are about to be put under anesthesia, it is comforting to know that spiritual truth. Trusting in God gives you the "faith-strength" that things will turn out okay.

Physicians are charged with the maxim of "first, do no harm." For most surgical procedures, an anesthesiologist (or nurse anesthetist) first administers an IV line to infuse tranquilizers, which allay the natural fears one has of the procedure and make it easier to administer the actual anesthesia. Then the anesthesia itself, which keeps the patient unconscious during the procedure, is added. It is not until I am reassured that the patient will neither feel nor remember the surgery that I begin to operate.

Although this works fine in the vast majority of cases, there are still no guarantees. It is rare, but I have had patients partially awaken from their anesthesia during surgery. One time, a patient suddenly sat up in the midst of a complex microscopic ear operation. Another related remembering in detail what went on during the procedure, even recalling some of the conversation among the doctors. It is also the physician's nightmare when the end result is painful, frightening, and/or harmful rather than healing. It is not uncommon for physicians to dismiss patient's descriptions of such incidents; you really do not want to admit that something was not just right under your watch. Under the "captain of the ship doctrine," the operating physician is the one in charge. This applies not only in the operating room but in the courtroom as well; the operating physician is the one held responsible for any unfortunate result, although everyone including Adam's house cat may be sued.

While some medical procedures are uncomfortable, even painful, doctors try to shield the patient from as much of the pain as possible. We weigh the risks of the procedure/surgery/treatment against the chances of success in curing or at least alleviating the disease. Whatever the available medical options, we are mindful of restoring health and avoiding pain and discomfort. Of course, the patient can still hurt. But we swallow that hurt in the knowledge that it is temporary, or that it will lead to reducing other pains or conditions that are worse. That knowledge is what allows us to inflict pain and let others inflict it upon us. It may be gently administered, but it still carries a sharp edge. I have borne my share of pain, both physical and psychic, in the last ten years as I grappled with reconciling my mortality and coming to terms with my own history and legacy. It is that history that brought into focus what is cruel, though hardly unusual.

The Supreme Court issued its ruling on Clarence Hill in order to further deliberate on the issue of the use of lethal injections in death penalty cases. Hill's attorneys had argued that the lethal dose of the drugs that were scheduled to be given to him can cause great pain and are therefore in violation of the Eighth Amendment which bars the use of "cruel and unusual punishment" on those accused of a crime.

Execution in itself is not particularly unusual in this country, but Hill's experience certainly was: he was physically prepared for death and then was granted a reprieve only to have it rescinded again; it was also cruel. While I can't know what Hill felt or thought, having experienced my own reprieve, for entirely different reasons and under greatly different circumstances, I can attest to the toll such experience naturally takes.

One February morning in 2003, I found myself lying on the bedroom floor unable to move. I was laboring to breathe when my wife found me and called 911. I was rushed to the emergency room at the hospital where they started IV lines to give my body needed fluids and medications and put me on a ventilator so I could breathe. After a few hours, I was able to breathe on my own, but it was a humbling and frightening experience. It took five days of IV treatment with various chemical infusions designed to counter the effects of my Myasthenia Gravis. For each of those days, I lay tied to an IV line, knowing that without it I would already have found my permanent resting place. The fear of a recurrence of this sort of crisis is with me all the time. You see, I know a little bit about living with reprieves.

Much like a medical emergency, when an execution date is given, often the inmate is informed only when the officers show up in his cell block to take him to the prison where the execution takes place. Recently, while I was meeting "one on one" with a death row inmate, I was suddenly and very stridently told to "get on out now." I found out the next week that it was only fifteen minutes later that an eleven-year veteran of death row, with his appeals in progress, was transported to the prison that is home to the death chamber. That was the first he was told that he had been assigned an execution date.

It seems ironic that Hill's on again/off again date with death was imposed by none other than our own court of last resort in an effort to assure pro-scribed humane treatment. Hill's treatment was far from humane, whether or not that was the intent. In the interest of jurisprudence, the court pulled the plug on his death, debated the legal theory, and then threw his case back to the state to determine how best to kill. While we have theoretical discussions of ethics and how much pain is acceptable on a sliding scale, real people are subjected to a painful demise, sanctioned by a sanctimonious public that thinks it's all right to kill in the name of their own self-defined justice. As Winston Churchill once said, "When you have to kill a man, it costs nothing to be polite."

LETHAL INJECTION EXPOSES THE odd contradictions inherent in capital punishment; in a strange way it is the zenith of the evolution of the practice. As of February 2008, nineteen states stopped executions pending legal decisions concerning lethal injection. While the "experts" in the criminal justice system argue over the specifics of the death cocktail to be used in capital punishment cases, the medical community cringes in distaste. We can see how the conflict is building between the medical community and the state in a 2007 court ruling in North Carolina which prohibited the state medical board from punishing doctors who participated in executions.

This pits the legal system against the medical community, and physicians have begun to react. Most of those doctors who support the death penalty don't want anything to do with administering it. A few participate, but they do so at the risk of losing their medical licenses, not to mention a stigma or censure from their fellow practitioners. To get around this, some states offer legal immunity and a promise of anonymity.

In fact, on the occasion in 2001 of the first execution in forty-five years in New Mexico, the state had to import a medical team from Texas to carry out the execution; none in New Mexico would volunteer. And even then, the state had to agree to keep secret the names and identities of the participants. Some states provide legal immunity to participating physicians; some promise anonymity, though that has been compromised in court challenges.[7]

What does this say about the policy? How can an elected government carry out the will of the people if the people who have the best knowledge about the effects and process, people who are trained and experienced in actually performing it, refuse to be party to it? Perhaps execution is only what we want in theory, so long as we don't have to look at it.

The ex-governor of Illinois, George Ryan, who was one of the first politicians to oppose the death penalty, had been a proponent of capital punishment. Then at a meeting before he became governor, he was asked during a debate on the policy if he would "be willing to throw the switch."

He replied, "It was a sobering question and I wish now that I could swallow the words of unqualified support for the death penalty that I offered." Once he assumed the responsibilities of governor and was in fact the one who had to "throw the switch," the issue was no longer theoretical. It was then that he began looking into the disparities in errors in the criminal justice system and capital punishment in particular, and started on the path that was instrumental in imposing a moratorium on it in Illinois.[8]

Although it would seem that doctors should be more comfortable with death than others might be, I don't think this is the case, the few exceptions perhaps being oncologists and certain other specialists who deal with terminally ill patients every day. But even these doctors are affected by the stark reality of death and are not always comfortable with it. As a society, we readily pass off terminal patients to others for their care. Fortunately hospice facilities nowadays do a wonderful job. Doctors deal with disease every day, not death. In fact, we (and I include myself here) rarely have to deal with death; most doctors have no training and little or no experience in dealing with the dying patient.

I do not think many if not most doctors know how to handle dying patients or their families any more than anyone else. They do not know what to say. It's the same with people going to funerals and talking with the family of the deceased. Some are natural at it, but most people are extremely uncomfortable and avoid funerals if they can. We don't want to deal with the ugly façade of death, whether by natural causes or other. Too often, we let others take care of it for us, removing the human part of "humane." Instead, we send flowers.

SO WHY THEN HAS the criminal system called upon the medical community for help? The answers to this question are complex and require taking off the rose-colored lenses as we hold the issues up to the light of day. The majority of Americans are still supportive of capital punishment while at the same time are uncomfortable with the process. That dichotomy and the overall discomfort with the subject of death make for a contradictory system.

Doctors are trained to be healers, not killers. Killing another human pits us against our own instincts and throws us into a gray area of ethics. Most doctors genuinely care for and sympathize with their patients. They are not only concerned about the health of their patients; they are often invested in the outcome of treatment. Like others, doctors enjoy success. When a patient dies, the discomfort about the death is upsetting because of the doctor's empathy and compassion for the patient. But for the doctor, death can also be interpreted as a defeat; it can feel like both a personal and professional failure. This is true even when the doctor knows the patient has little chance of survival. When asking doctors to help kill, it is also asking them to fail. They have spent years devoted to doing just the opposite.

Though a majority of the population favors euthanasia in certain situations, the American Medical Association (AMA) has been unwavering in rejecting it on ethical grounds. The official AMA position, which has not changed in the last decade, is that "euthanasia is fundamentally incompatible with the physician's role as healer." In spite of the polls, however, most people reject the modus operandi of Dr. Jack Kevorkian, who attempted to make a career out of euthanasia. I can't judge whether his intentions were "good," but I don't believe it is a doctor's moral or practical role to help end a patient's life.

There isn't a great deal of popular support for Kevorkian, who eventually wound up serving jail time for his actions. But while we punish Kevorkian for his efforts to kill people who say they want to die, we continue to support our government in killing people who are healthy and do not want to die. We ultimately reject the methods of Dr. Kevorkian as inappropriate and immoral but apply the same standards to a criminal and call it justice. Both are seen by their supporters as "noble" ends that justify the means; both are immoral taking of life that is not ours to take. "The Lord gave and the Lord has taken away" (Job 1:21).

In these days of modern medicine, we continue to be faced with more and more ethical questions that affect the practice. These are issues that doctors need to give more than passing thought to and perhaps provide some leadership. Although the AMA does provide guidance, most doctors are not members of the organization, and in any case, the AMA lacks the means to enforce any of its policies. Nevertheless, the AMA has been clear in stating that physician participation in the use of lethal injections in administering the death penalty is unethical. This position holds whether physicians are directly administering drugs or designing the specific dosage that is used. Priscilla Ray, head of ethics at the AMA has said that even "formulating a way to kill somebody would violate the spirit of the policy."[9]

So if as a society we want to continue to impose the death penalty, how do we do it? It is easier to support the issue of capital punishment if we don't have to deal with the messy parts—like death and dying. Given the general consensus that lethal injection is more humane than other methods, 99 percent of all executions in the U.S. since 2001 have been via lethal injection.[10] As we move into more modern techniques, we must understand that a humane method of execution is an oxymoron. Deliberate killing of a human being is by its very nature a brutal and violent act. Looking at it close up and personal might force us to reexamine not just the process but the underlying premise as well.

We've come a long way from the age of the public guillotine, which was particularly messy. History recalls rivers of blood running down the streets of France. Though that device seems crude by current standards, at one time it was considered "state of the art" and was reserved for use with royalty because it was thought to be swift and therefore painless. Though decapitation devices had been in use for several centuries, the Age of Enlightenment brought with it some new perspectives about ethics and human rights. At the end of the eighteenth century, a physician and a member of one of the early French revolutionary groups, Dr. Joseph Ignace Guillotin, recommended an improved decapitation device, one that he thought would ensure a quick and therefore painless death. (Guillotin's name became associated with the device, although he was not its inventor.) Guillotin believed that such a device would reform capital punishment as it was then practiced. He advocated its use for all social classes, in keeping with the revolutionary concept of equality for all, a stark beginning to the enlightened idea of human rights.

After the French Revolution, indeed, the guillotine became the device of choice for all and was used for regular civilians, not just for the royalty as had been the case. The new penal code was rewritten to say that, "Every person condemned to the death penalty shall have his head severed." This was progress and a positive development considering the brutal and tortuous methods of execution that preceded it. It was also egalitarian; punishment would be the same for everyone, regardless of their station in life.

Cliché as it may be, it's hard not to see how the more things change, the more they stay the same. Even 250 years ago, some people were concerned about intentionally inflicting pain during the administration of the death penalty. The guillotine continued to be perfected, making it more certain and quick; a painless demise was the goal. In fact, its use was continued in France and other parts of Western Europe until later in the twentieth century when capital punishment itself was abandoned by most Western European countries; it was no longer considered to be an appropriate way to deal with crime in the modern world.

Here on the other side of the Atlantic, Americans didn't adopt the guillotine; as policy we mostly stuck to the more bourgeois practice of hanging. (We had no royalty to worry about killing.) As in France, we were concerned with equal justice, sharing some of the same constitutional concepts. Everyone here slated for the "ultimate" punishment was subject to the same treatment, however crude or inhumane. Although the guillotine was never actually used here, it was considered as an option before the advances of electricity brought with them the electric chair at the end of the nineteenth century.

The electric chair became a popular alternative to hanging or a firing squad, and its wide use in the U.S. became a symbol of the death penalty here, much as the guillotine had been in Europe. As recently as 1996, Georgia state legislator Doug Teper proposed that the state use the guillotine as a replacement for the electric chair. He reasoned that the electric chair prevented inmates from being organ donors. His proposal never passed muster in the state legislature, but it does indicate the degree to which we have removed the concept of human from those whose killing we sanction. Kevorkian has also long been an advocate of using inmates for organ donors. As well, in China close to one-half of the transplanted organs are taken from executed individuals. The AMA seems to agree with

Kevorkian, or at least there is no official policy that prohibits the practice as long as certain parameters are followed.[11]

China and some other countries have been accused of killing to sell body parts and we generally reel at the notion; we don't want to put ourselves in the same category. But how far removed are we really? These are not questions that are easily answered but they need to be debated and analyzed so that at least we will know when we have descended down that slippery slope.

As the United States evolved, so did our methods of capital punishment, moving from public hangings to more private forms of execution held in an enclosed chamber, farther away from public eyes. Horror stories of burning skin and hanging eyeballs eventually forced a search for a more "humane" method, though the reality is that there is none. In the last twenty years, the use of lethal injection has gained favor and is now the most common form of execution in this country. It is thought to be painless, at least by the civil servants and non-medical personnel who mostly are left to administer it. It is but another of the myths we tell ourselves to soothe our conscience and look the other way. We have become hardened to those on death row, humans being killed by the state, by choosing not to see.

Just twenty-five years ago, Governor George Wallace refused clemency for an inmate whose botched execution horrified those who witnessed it. The inmate's attorney, outraged and sickened by the spectacle, got the governor on the phone, but Wallace ignored his pleas and refused intervention. Though the brutality of the process of execution was clear in these circumstances, the Court continued to refuse to ban the practice (*Glass v. Louisiana*, 1985).

In 1983, the electrocution of John Evans in Alabama was described by his attorney, who was an eyewitness, as follows:

> At 8:30 p.m. the first jolt of 1,900 volts of electricity passed through Mr. Evans' body. It lasted thirty seconds. Sparks and flames erupted from the electrode tied to Mr. Evans' left leg. His body slammed against the straps holding him in the electric chair and his fist clenched permanently. The electrode apparently burst from the strap holding it in place. A large puff of grayish smoke and sparks poured out from

under the hood that covered Mr. Evans' face. An overpowering stench of burnt flesh and clothing began pervading the witness room. Two doctors examined Mr. Evans and declared that he was not dead.

The electrode on the left leg was refastened . . . Mr. Evans was administered a second thirty-second jolt of electricity. The stench of burning flesh was nauseating. More smoke emanated from his leg and head. Again, the doctors examined Mr. Evans. [They] reported that his heart was still beating, and that he was still alive. At that time, I asked the prison commissioner, who was communicating on an open telephone line to Governor George Wallace, to grant clemency on the grounds that Mr. Evans was being subjected to cruel and unusual punishment. The request was denied.

At 8:40 p.m., a third charge of electricity, thirty seconds in duration, was passed through Mr. Evans' body. At 8:44, the doctors pronounced him dead. The execution of John Evans took fourteen minutes. (*Glass v. Louisiana*, 471 U.S. 1080 [1985].) Afterwards, officials were embarrassed by what one observer called the "barbaric ritual." The prison spokesman remarked, "This was supposed to be a very clean manner of administering death." (*Boston Globe*, [April 24, 1983]: 24.).[12]

THE ISSUES RAISED BY use of the electric chair are not that different from those raised for lethal injection; neither is painless and neither is pretty. In both, doctors are on hand to ascertain and certify death. Yet in both, the objections seem to focus on the superficial characteristics of pain and appearance rather than the policy itself.

We want to believe in our better selves; so we don't want to impose a painful penalty, just one that will do away with those who we judge as evil, guilty, lesser, or "other." We want to be protected from not only their actions or potential actions, but their very existence. We don't want to see them as human and we certainly don't want to be reminded of their humanity by hearing screams of pain. So we wall ourselves off from the reality and try to bring in the doctors to devise a way of getting rid of our guilt without pain.

The cocktail of drugs used in lethal injections often includes pancuronium. This drug prevents the movement of the major muscles; the condemned can't grimace or cry out, which is a common response to cardiac arrest. This drug does not kill; it merely paralyzes the body, masking any semblance of suffering. In surgery, it is used to make sure the patient doesn't move while a surgeon is operating. Yet even in these controlled conditions, I have known patients who gained consciousness during surgery but were paralyzed by that drug, unable to move or speak, but feeling the pain of the surgery. It was a horrifying experience. With doctors on hand and watching, quick changes in the IV infusion can sedate the patient again and avoid further pain. In executions, however, the drug is included as part of the lethal cocktail to ensure that those observing the execution will be free of pain. As long as there is no appearance of pain, then it is so.

Controversy over the administration of a lethal injection as a means of execution has heated up in the last several years as objections were mounted about the procedure. In reality, lethal injection is no less horrifying than other methods of killing and it is especially problematic when things go awry, as they often do. The expectation is that the process will be painless and quick; often it is not. Lethal injection conjures up images of the serenity surrounding the euthanasia of our beloved pets. In fact, the formula used by most states and the federal government is specifically banned by veterinarian organizations because it does not meet their standards in preventing pain.

Death via "the needle," as it has come to be called, became the most desired form of execution after 1977 when Oklahoma mandated its use in capital cases. Since then, other states followed suit, though the formula proscribed then has been copied with little change. There are currently thirty-five states (in addition to the federal government) that favor its use and in many of them it is now the sole method of execution.

However, there remains a reluctant medical community at odds with the policy, and state laws differ wildly. A number of states require some degree of physician participation in the process of administering lethal injections, while Illinois, for example, specifically bars doctors from participating. In California a capital case was put on hold in 2006 because of the court order requiring use of a medical professional to administer the drugs for the execution. The state's court-appointed anesthesiologists withdrew, leaving the state out of compliance with the law. Michael Morales was granted a stay of execution, still in place while the state grapples with trying to figure out how to comply with the state laws regarding the protocol and medical personnel.

As state courts were faced with legal challenges, stays of execution mounted. It was inevitable that the Supreme Court would again get involved in this issue and in September 2007 the Court agreed to hear the case of *Baze v. Rees*, a case brought by two inmates in Kentucky. Kentucky had been using lethal injection since 1998 when the state mandated its use for all executions. *Baze* was not a challenge to the constitutionality of capital punishment; rather, the case revolved around the specific drug protocols being used by the state. Other states that used the same protocol also halted scheduled executions as they awaited the Court's decision.

The plaintiffs claimed that the specific three-drug protocol violated the Eighth Amendment because the formulation constitutes cruel and unusual punishment. They argued that the specific drugs and the way they are administered posed high risk of unnecessary and excruciating pain because there are alternatives available. If the Court ruled in their favor, it would render the specific protocol unconstitutional; it could however, call into question whether the death penalty and humane treatment can be reconciled.

Different states have somewhat varying rules regarding the procedure, including the specific combinations of the drugs, order of delivery, dosage, and whether or not the inmate is given anesthesia prior to the lethal injection. There is no uniformity; each state has cobbled together its own rules and regulations. The Court ruled on *Baze* in April 2008, in a fractured decision that did little to put the issue to rest. Chief Justice John Roberts, writing for the majority, declared that the plaintiffs did not show any "objectively intolerable risk of harm." The majority opinion concluded that pain-free is not a Constitutional requirement.

The barn door is still open. Within the opinion the justices, including those in the majority, allowed that some methods could be considered unconstitutional, particularly if it was found that there are methods that could ensure a more humane rendering of capital punishment. Justices Scalia and Thomas argued that the constitutional standard is not met "only if it [the lethal injection protocol] is deliberately designed to inflict pain." I have to wonder how my patients, and others undergoing medical treatment, would feel about that standard. Although the Constitution is not posted on the walls of the operating room, the Hippocratic Oath is, and it presents a real conflict for medical professionals. While the courts continue to press their cases, within a month of the *Baze* decision, there were three executions—one in Virginia, one in Mississippi, and one in Georgia.

In some states, the condemned is also administered tranquilizers or anti-anxiety medication prior to execution. In Alabama (among several other states), sedating the condemned is not allowed. Much of the argument centers on differences in how the inmate will look during the process and how this might affect those who are watching as well as the time needed for the wardens to oversee the whole process. "Quick" applies to prison personnel as well as the executed, and in an odd way, so does "painless."[13]

The controversy over the exact measurement and combination of drugs illustrates the complexity of the problem. The formula can't be prescribed by law or decree. Anesthesiology is both science and art. Each patient has very specific needs and is closely monitored during surgery and it takes knowledge and skill to do this job competently. In addition, the practice of medicine is constantly changing and doctors update their knowledge as it does, applying new drugs and medicines to their practice. "The science has evolved on this as medical science will," says Richard Dieter of the Death Penalty Information Center. "Things go out of the operating room in twenty years. But they haven't left the execution chambers."

It is not surprising that studies have found victims of lethal injection to have blood levels of the drugs that are lower than what would be required for surgery. Translation: the inmate was probably fully aware of what was happening but could not communicate it. This is what we are calling humane. Just who is it we are protecting? There is also a "culture of secrecy" that surrounds lethal injection, making it difficult for lawyers to dispute protocols. Fordham University Professor Deborah Denno, an expert in the study of lethal injection in capital cases, determined that nineteen states make the protocols of their lethal injection formulas available to the public; twelve states allow public access under specific conditions; and in five states the information is completely confidential.[14] In Alabama, the formula used and the dosage is "privileged information" according to Brian Corbett at the Alabama Department of Corrections.[15]

Some drug combinations are more toxic, faster-acting, and less painful than others. Do we really want to debate this? The medical community does not, at least not in this context. Trying to enlist physicians in the procedure is an attempt to sanitize the process and make it more acceptable. As we push the death penalty further and further from its reality, stripping it of any emotional content and making it into a medical procedure rather than a criminal one, we fool ourselves into thinking it is painless and simple. What we are doing, however, is anesthetizing ourselves, not the condemned. We don't want to look at the horror that is killing. Like closing your eyes during a particularly brutal scene in a movie, we choose not to see. I cannot help but be reminded of Psalms 102:19-20, ". . . he looked down from his holy height, from heaven the Lord looked at the earth, to hear the groans of the prisoners, to set free those who were doomed to die . . ." And in Hebrews 13:3, "Remember those who are in prison, as though you were in prison with them."

We pretend "lethal injection" is a mere medical procedure, recalling the made-for-TV image of a hospital gurney in which a dying patient is administered emergency treatment, the tubes and bottles and mechanical devices mere props that are part of the drama. That image has become so much a part of our consciousness that it is easy to forget: those in charge are executioners, not doctors and medical personnel trying to save a life. "The problem with lethal injection is that it's a medical charade," explained Dr. Jonathan I. Groner, an associate professor of surgery at the College of Medicine and Public Health of Ohio State University. "It's set up to look like a medical procedure, but it's not."[16]

Though the AMA prohibition of physician participation in the execution process can result in license revocation, in fact, the policy has not been implemented; no one has been censured thus far, though that could change as more doctors speak out. This is due to the weakness of the AMA as a self-monitoring organization as well as the controversial nature of the issue. The AMA is primarily a reactive organization and is not one to readily get involved in significant political issues, especially if the issue is likely to be controversial. Although the majority of physicians do not belong to the AMA, the organization has a variety of interests to protect so it is unusual for it to take a proactive stand. Perhaps because politics has drawn in the medical community, the AMA has been forced to clarify the origins of medical care in the "First, do no harm" precept. I am pleased that it has done so.

For the small number of physicians who have agreed to get involved in execution procedures, it is often easy to get pulled in and start crossing boundaries without realizing it. Typically, a doctor would be asked to act in an advisory role; for example, to pronounce death. Later, the doctor might be called upon to perform a medical procedure; for example, properly inserting an IV line, sometimes after many failed attempts by prison personnel, because no one else who was on hand could to do it correctly. Dr. Atul Gawande, a surgeon at Brigham and Women's Hospital and an assistant professor at Harvard Medical School and at the Harvard School of Public Health, Boston, interviewed some of the limited number of doctors who do participate in the capital punishment process; most were uncomfortable and had ethical reservations about their role.[17]

ON THE OTHER HAND, Dr. Carlo Musso, an emergency care physician in Georgia, disagreed, up to a point. Musso explained that he feels obligated to assist inmates in their dying moments, likening his role to that of a doctor caring for a terminally ill patient. "[A death-penalty] patient is no different from a patient dying of cancer—except his cancer is a court order," he said. Although Musso is against the death penalty, he said, "It just seems wrong for us to walk away, to abdicate our responsibility to the patients." However, he did add that if he were asked to actually administer the lethal cocktail, he couldn't do it.

Musso sees his role as that of making the process as painless and easy as possible for the condemned. He reasons that since he had no role in making the decision to terminate the inmate's life, he shares no responsibility for it. In fact, he feels good that his participation can make it easier and less painful. Ironically, these are identical rationales to those used by Kevorkian.[18]

By conflating patient and condemned inmate, Musso does a disservice to both; they are not the same. Patients seek medical help to eliminate or at least alleviate disease or injury, and that's what their physicians try to do. The condemned are healthy to begin with; they are not patients in need of medical intervention to restore health. To refer to a condemned inmate as a patient is a dishonest euphemism. Presumably, when Musso administers emergency care in his practice, his objective is not to kill the patient. Ironically, given his role, it is likely that he often takes extraordinary measures to do just the opposite.

If Dr. Musso is sincerely interested in alleviating the possible pain and suffering of condemned inmates, perhaps he should bear in mind that what causes the pain is the process of execution, to which he is voluntarily a party. While it is true that he had no part in the legal decision to execute the inmate, and he alone cannot change that policy, his participation allows it to continue smoothly and gives it the appearance of being humane, civil, and medically and ethically acceptable. It is none of these. Although Musso says his actions are benign and are carried out in an effort to help the inmates, his actions facilitate a system that is unjust and do nothing to alleviate that injustice. As Martin Luther King Jr. said, "An injustice anywhere is a threat to justice everywhere."[19]

Drawing an arbitrary line at not actually pushing in the lethal dose neither serves the condemned nor those who oppose the policy, the very people Musso says he agrees with. Rather, his actions enhance the injustice by supporting the system. The fact of execution doesn't change because we remove some of the pain in the process of dying. The Nazis who performed medical experiments on human prisoners in the name of advancing medical knowledge used the same rationale, as did those SS officers who alleviated their consciences by sneaking some morsel of fresh food to the Jews lined up to be taken to the gas chamber.

"[Lethal injection] subverts medical technology and medical expertise— designed to bring comfort and healing—into instruments of killing," said Dr. Jonathan Groner, trauma medical director at the department of surgery, Children's Hospital, in Columbus, Ohio. "This medicalization of killing originated in the atrocities of Nazi medicine during World War II . . . Furthermore, lethal injection is a stain on the face of medicine because it defiles not only those physicians who participate, but all physicians as well. Doctors have a responsibility not only to heal and comfort, but also to be a morally protective force in society."[20]

Ethics aside, if the doctors felt sure that they were doing the right thing, why would they hide their identities by wearing hooded masks and goggles at the execution? Who are they hiding from? Professor Deborah Denno, who has studied the lethal injection procedure and involvement of doctors in executions, found that states closely guard the identities of these doctors, citing security concerns. These concerns, she said, are unfounded. Denno stated that she's never found anything but minor threats against doctors involved in executions. "You're talking about a country where most of the public is still in favor of the death penalty," she noted.

We don't like to use the word executioner to describe those who do the final killing, but this is just another way of distancing ourselves from the reality. The trend is toward more sanitized forms of execution; since 1999 most executions have been via the needle. It looks better from the outside, lending a veneer of medical respectability to a process that is counter to what the medical community is all about. Yet this is exactly what Groner was referring to: "The Nazis used the imagery of medicine to justify killing, and they corrupted doctors and, ultimately, an entire nation. Capital punishment in the United States now depends solely on the same medical charade. Without the respectability that lethal injection provides, capital punishment in the United States would probably cease."[21]

CLARENCE HILL WAS CONVICTED of a brutal killing, but my reaction wasn't only about Hill and how he was treated in the process of capital punishment. I was also reacting to the arcane system we have created in which we impose death to punish those members of society who are least likeable. The flaws in the criminal justice system shine a light on we the people and measure who we are and what standards we accept to measure justice, fairness, and equality. Until a few years ago, I too would have shrugged. But now I could no longer just look the other way.

Some might argue that people like Clarence Hill, a convicted murderer, don't deserve humane treatment, don't deserve to live out their natural lives even in a prison, don't deserve to be free of physical pain during their last moments of life. After all, look at the suffering he had caused. There are some who might even relish the cruelty of his punishment. But how can we presume to know his history and legacy and that of others like him? How can we judge others while we are but imperfect beings? "Do not judge, so that you will not be judged. For with the judgment you make you will be judged, and the measure you give will be the measure you get" (Matthew 7:1–5). In killing Hill we become that which we condemn. Even the stroke of an artist's brush cannot change the picture this paints of us. We must rid ourselves of the canvas.

We still like to believe in the power of doctors to fix every ailment and are confident that those charged with carrying out our criminal justice system will take care of it efficiently, and for the most part fairly. Having experienced both the face of my own death and the face I once painted on my own life, I think I can understand the need to look with a blind eye.

Nevertheless, when it comes to the death penalty, we hardly give it a second thought. Executions routinely inflict pain; the intent is to kill not to heal. To a naïve and ignorant public, lethal injection seems like the best solution—a painless death so we don't have to feel guilty about executing people. We show more concern and spend more money on euthanasia for our pets than we do for people on death row.

It's important to look at ourselves in the context of our own history, both personal and political. We like to believe that we have evolved to become a more civilized and enlightened society and in some ways, per-haps we have. We are more discreet; we no longer think of going to the public square to watch someone die as entertainment; we debate the ethics of the use of video cameras in the execution chamber. Regulations about who may watch an execution vary from state to state. Some states allow at least the families of the victims of the crime to observe. None would call it entertaining but of those who voluntarily watch, some say it makes them feel better; others feel great pain and sadness at the loss, regardless of their relationship to the inmate.

On the other hand, millions of us go to the local movie theater and watch death on the big screen, once removed from the real world that is us and our own inventions of ourselves. We are simultaneously attracted and repelled by death and dying. Perhaps it is human nature to be compelled to observe what we fear. We close our eyes and turn our heads, but we peek anyway, like slowing down to catch a glimpse of an automobile accident. We know that death is not pretty but we wince and look away, silently giving thanks that it is not us, at least not this time.

Hill was at the mercy of the courts and the criminal system. I was at the mercy of the medical care available. We are all at the mercy of God, the ultimate judge. Death would take this victim of capital punishment and nothing I could do either as a doctor or a fellow human being would bring him back. I knew what it was like to face my own death and I knew first-hand the fear produced from its anticipation.

I also knew that I was not the same young man who had stood with George Wallace and cheered; nor was I among those who could shrug at the execution of Clarence Hill, a forty-seven-year-old black man. Recognizing that personal history made me feel worse when reading Hill's story, at least I knew I was now doing the right thing. It was my mission to move through my "penance" to achieve atonement for my previous sins. Now that I had concluded that the death penalty was wrong, that process included whatever I could accomplish to abolish it. Sitting still was no longer an option.

4

It's All in the Family

The social and racial changes in the South evolved around me. I was a bystander; I didn't participate in actively defending or opposing segregation, though my instinct was certainly to defend it. It was the system in which I had grown up and as a young man, I couldn't imagine a different way of life—not that I tried.

I hadn't anticipated a politically active campus when I made my decision to transfer to the University of Alabama; it was purely a move to save money and get on the right career path. My private high school had sheltered me from the depth of the growing conflict. I had stumbled into the confrontation at UA and though it contained an element of excitement, I also found it frightening. I couldn't help but to have an opinion, but I never got actively involved in the Southern resistance to the civil rights movement.

While my friends and I stewed over what was happening, we were too bent on our studies to be politically active. Perhaps that was a blessing. However, it was too hot an issue to ignore completely and my friends and I certainly expressed our feelings openly. It was clear that none of us wanted to share the campus with the blacks who we thought were being rebellious in their efforts to integrate it. Although we were several years past integration orders, this was my first exposure to it and I didn't like it. The first few blacks in attendance were mostly symbolic, and none were in my pre-med classes. The effects were more theoretical than practical, though I don't think I made any distinctions. I was upset mostly by the imposition of the rule.

Though I continued to support Wallace, segregation, and states' rights in theory, I was too focused on my studies to pay more than cursory attention to these issues. Once the inevitability of integration was recognized, the process was fairly smooth and the early days of turmoil evolved to business as usual. The black students were still taunted on occasion, but the riots and demonstrations had passed their prime. I paid little attention to any of it, particularly since there were no blacks in my classes. Even then, I don't think I would have openly taunted anyone; my objection was more theoretical than practical. I recognize now, however, that without the vote and allegiance of those of us who supported Wallace's agenda, the inevitable changes in the South would likely have come much earlier and perhaps without the same degree of violence and angst. Hanging onto our past gave the civil rights movement a continued raison d'être and exposed to the world the anachronism of segregation.

My father's family was generally more hostile and resentful and the integration at the University of Alabama fed their prejudices. When I would return home for weekends or holidays, my paternal grandmother kept asking me if "the niggers are staying in their place up there." Ironically, I was a bit agitated at her blanket belittling of an entire race. I even thought she was a bit misguided.

Perhaps it was part of my own small way of rebelling, though it was not particularly overt and didn't feel like rebellion at the time. It was a way to take the high road and show some one-upmanship with my new independence and my version of college-induced enlightenment. I was hardly enlightened, but I suppose it's relative. Their obvious and deep-seated prejudices allowed me to feel better about my own, which were certainly strong but not quite as firmly rooted as theirs. As the years went by and my views were softening from exposure forced by integration, I grew increasingly annoyed by my grandmother's repeated reference to the problem of the "niggers." She became the brunt of a family joke one year when she sent me a Christmas card that displayed an image of a black Jesus. Because of her cataracts, she had no idea of what she had done, but my father and uncle kept reminding her. They thought it was hysterically funny.

Of course my father had grown up in a totally segregated environment and his father was a product of the Reconstructed South, and such ideas about race continued to be passed down. He was hard-nosed and determined and change was not something he was going to take to easily. His strong hand in determining my medical career as well as other aspects of who I was and who I would become left its imprint. This is not unusual, of course, but the helping hand he offered in education was the same hand that had turned violent on occasion in my earlier years. Once I was no longer living in his home, I was not subject to either his physical or verbal hostility and I was free to examine my own hostility toward him, which was formidable by that time. My list of grievances was long and included his marriage after my mother's death as well as his disparaging attitudes toward me, toward blacks, and toward anything and anyone else who happened to cross his path the wrong way. After the absence of such talk, his racist ramblings became more noticeable. I also couldn't help but observe, conscious or not, that the dreaded integration that he and the community so violently opposed had not had the disastrous consequences he had warned about.

On the other hand, my maternal grandparents seemed more resolved about the whole issue. They didn't complain much and were more accepting. They felt that God loved everyone and they didn't pay much attention to politics and the like. Their attitude of "Well, we will just have to get used to it" prevailed, as it did in most things. Perhaps they were more open to change, believing it was God's will; we never discussed it.

My maternal grandparents remained in the same house, befriending their new black neighbors, long after many others had fled the neighborhood as it integrated. Although the family had some trepidation about their safety, they were adamant about staying. Part of their reasoning was financial, but it was also because they just didn't want to leave their home and saw no reason to. They didn't feel threatened; it was other members of the family who feared for them. The presumption of guilt was widely cast, though never borne out by the reality. I remember my grandmother, in particular, commenting about how nice their neighbors were. It was only after my grandfather died that her children insisted that she move to quarters closer to their own "safer" and whiter neighborhood.

It would take years before history could distill those fears. The clash of ideology kicked up layers of latent dust. As the South heated up, so did the flames of hatred, practiced without a trace of irony by many churchgoers who on Sunday prayed to Jesus for guidance and talked of love thy neighbor and then on Monday felt totally justified in participating in or at least condoning violence against the blacks who sometimes waited on their tables, shined their shoes, and tended their children. I was among them.

I not only believed that foreigners from the North should leave us alone, I was adamant in defending my stake in the Southern portrait of a white genteel society. I believed integrationists were dead wrong. While I resisted the overt racism in my family, I saw no incompatibility between my criticism of them and my support of the foundation of their racism and the very tenets of what I had been taught: blacks were not equal so how could they have equal rights? This attitude was deeply ingrained in Southern society and I strongly believed it. Although it was one hundred years later, many in the South still subscribed to the views put forth by the vice-president of the Confederacy, Alexander Stephens: "Our government is founded upon exactly the opposite idea [opposite from the idea that all men are created equal]; its foundations are laid, its corner-stone rests upon the great truth, that the negro is not equal to the white man; that slavery—subordination to the superior race—is his natural and normal condition" (March 12, 1861).

Although my father's racist remarks were frequent and were an integral part of my home environment, at times I resented his comments. Particularly as I got older, they seemed more and more uninformed and mean-spirited. As a child, they had confused me since they didn't always seem to apply to the blacks who were in our life. My early environment was filled with examples of African Americans who were wonderful people. But it was also filled with contempt for any alternative viewpoint from the stereotype that I had been handed, for that might have threatened the status quo. The stereotype where I cut my teeth was that blacks had smaller brains than whites, had excessively strong sexual urges that were often uncontrollable, had no ambition, were happy with their lot, and were driven by only animal instincts.

These ugly and bogus "facts" served as the underlying rationale for their treatment by the white ruling class. As a child, I didn't question the "facts" and by adulthood, they had been sufficiently ingrained that it didn't occur to me to question them. Our maid, Rosie, who cared for me and my sister like her own after our mother died, was surely an example of a good, kind

African American, and typical of her race. Though I really loved her like a mother, it didn't occur to me that she could want anything for herself other than what she already had. Or John, the man who worked at my grandfather's shoe shine store—kind and nice to me as he was, it didn't occur to me that he might have had other ambitions. I assumed that he was both lucky and happy to have a job where someone treated him well. Or "Rosy," the muscular black man so named because of his rosy outlook, hired by my father to help him with "manly" labor needed for his various extra jobs to support our family. As a teen working out with weights, I was in awe of Rosy's muscular build and was always amazed that he had never worked out with weights. "They just come natural," he would tell me when I asked about his big muscles, allowing me to continue my stereotype. It didn't occur to me that his muscles might have been developed through laboring in menial jobs like the ones my father had hired him to do in the fields.

There were no animosities whatsoever; in fact, just the opposite. At least it seemed that way to me. Looking back, it may well have been that my family was just "accommodating," to use a description coined by Diane McWhorter in her book, *Carry Me Home*, describing race relations of that period. We were "nice to our niggers" and even friendly with them, but no way did we see that they should think about going to our schools, or our clubs, or theaters.

THE FREEDOM RIDERS REPRESENTED a real threat to the psyche of the white South. The visceral reaction, I think, was related to how it struck at the core of the belief system that was in place and the threat to its being dismantled. Most white Southerners assumed that their belief in segregation was sanctioned by the Bible. "From one he made all nations to inhabit the whole earth and allotted the times of their existence and the places and the boundaries of the places in which they would live" (Acts 17:26). According to this interpretation, the races were to live in separate places, and the boundaries were not to be crossed. Those separate places included the whole continent of Africa, which bred the "savage" uncivilized peoples who comprised an entire race.

Though the rationale for segregation and prejudicial views was not uniform, whatever the basis, the influence of religion and the Bible was strong. Whether it was using specific passages like the above while ignoring others that were contradictory, or a belief in a God whose will dictated who would be rich and who would rule, the white power structure did not take kindly to any efforts to undermine its authority or its justification for that authority. Like most entrenched political power throughout history, giving it up is a struggle. Sometimes it comes with a revolution that involves war and violence and sometimes it is more peaceful, but it is never without conflict. The threats to the white supremacists were across the board, from schools to voting to public train stations. Rulers invested in maintaining their own power inevitably do so by keeping others powerless.

At the time of this social upheaval, I certainly knew right from wrong and good from bad, and my maternal grandfather had become a role model for living a life based on the Scriptures. But I also lived in a community that rationalized the status quo and didn't question anything. While I was young and impressionable, I was determined to follow the life plan that had been put in front of me. I did not want anything to interfere with completing my education and having a successful career in medicine. Disrupting the status quo had the potential to do that—at least that's how it felt. So as far as I was concerned, these invaders were both wrong and bad. If they got hurt in the scuffles during their invasion of my home, well, they deserved it. I didn't think about the harm done to the "outside agitators." They had no business stirring up trouble in the first place, I reasoned. And furthermore, they were being naively driven by the communists who had infiltrated their ranks. How could anyone entertain their support?

As I look back at that period from my current, more enlightened social perspective, the parallels with issues of capital punishment are palpable. When I supported the death penalty, I certainly thought that it was giving the criminal the punishment he/she deserved. The criminal on death row, to my mind at the time, was no less deserving of being eliminated than those who invaded the South in the civil rights era and were met with fists and the barrel of a gun. While I didn't want innocent people getting hurt in the process, there was a part of me that rationalized that it was the price we had to pay as a society to defend us from people who are out to do us harm.

We can argue, of course, that the times are different now and the circumstances were different then, etc., and this is true. On the other hand, the hunger for retribution is the same. All the arguments for capital punishment can be boiled down to one word: revenge. There is no other rationale for killing than to punish the perpetrator—whether guilty or not. Though a life sentence serves the same purpose in terms of punishment and removal of the person from society, those who support capital punishment insist that it's not enough; death is the only proscribed punishment that makes capital punishment advocates feel like justice is served. But is it?

Those same people who in the 1960s stood on the streets cheering for George Wallace and Bull Connor, glad to see the Freedom Riders hauled off to jail and beaten up en route, are now cheering for the demise of those criminals who await their fate on death row. If someone innocent is killed by mistake, well, again, that's the price we have to pay to defend ourselves. The thinking (or non-thinking) that accompanies this strongly held belief is exactly the same as that which supported segregation and fought against those who wished to end the institution. I can only say this with the hindsight that comes from someone who once lived in that thought-bubble, endorsing Wallace and segregation as well as capital punishment with enthusiasm, certain that my views were right, moral, and even supported by the Bible.

Although the University of Alabama had been forced to integrate, once the cameras left campus, the token blacks on campus faded into the background and campus life went back to "normal," much like the formerly all-white high schools. While there was some resentment, there was little change. And the med school was still de facto white. Few blacks had the college pre-med requirements, so restricting admission to whites (and mostly males in those days, too) was easy to do without violating any of the newly established civil rights laws. The initial shock of integration had passed and by this time, I didn't think much about race. It wasn't something we talked about; med students were simply too focused on our own futures.

There was one black fellow med student in a later class of eighty students, and I'm sure he took his share of taunting. I always found him to be personable and friendly. If anything, I felt rather proud of my acceptance of the policy and of the student himself. In addition to allowing me to falsely feel that I was now free of all racial prejudice, it also served as another way to subtly flaunt my hostility to my father. As hard as he had tried to keep my school environment "white only," he had no control over the barriers that were being torn down. As the racial barriers eroded on campus, the construction of thicker walls between my father and me began at home. Those barriers took even longer to remove and it would be years before I could come to terms with who he was and reconcile my hatred toward him.

Of course one black student, and no minority faculty, doesn't exactly demonstrate integration, but this wasn't terribly apparent since I don't think I made the distinction. When I began rotations in the university hospital, I sometimes worked in the clinic and would treat whoever came in. The clinic served the poor, which more often than not meant the blacks and other minorities of the population of Birmingham at the time. I had no qualms about giving medical care to whoever needed it. I didn't think much about race; all blood is red. I did notice that there were no black doctors on the staff, and few in the community. But the majority of the hospital workers—nurses, RNs and LPNs, assistants, lab workers, etc.—were black. We worked side-by-side as was expected.

I can't speak for other whites, but it certainly didn't occur to me that the black staffers were inferior or less able than anyone else. We were all working toward helping patients and race wasn't an issue. The pecking order was really determined by education and skill rather than race. However, by being involved in working together and sharing goals, I began to recognize that the blacks in my environment were no different from me, they just had different opportunities and interests. On the other hand, it didn't occur to me to befriend any of them outside of the workplace.

THOUGH OUR PATIENTS WERE frequently minorities and we were obliged to treat everyone, the vestiges of ugly prejudice were still on the surface. That doesn't mean blacks were treated any differently, at least medically. But the attitudes and presumptions made about their particular circumstances showed the underlying racism. My department chair during my residency was a typical old-time Southern physician. When discussing a stabbing incident involving two black men whom we had admitted from the emergency room one night, he unabashedly made disparaging racial jokes.

We all laughed. I ignored his comments, as I did any others who made similar remarks. But even internally, I didn't refute them. It didn't feel like racial jokes were a big deal or that they demonstrated prejudice. I hadn't really evolved enough in my thinking at that point to recognize the underlying message in them. Although this physician was well-known for such commentary, he also probably dispensed more free care for blacks than anyone else on the staff.

After sharing the joke with the others in the group, we went back to work. I was simply too busy to give it any further thought. I was more focused on learning the ropes and providing good medical care. Residency requires grueling hours, and my wife and I were trying to make decisions about where we would live, work, and build a life. Race was not a problem, at least not for me.

We finally settled down in Birmingham and I joined an ongoing practice and worked in my otolaryngology-head and neck surgery specialty (ear/nose/throat doctor/surgeon). We had started a family and eventually I started my own practice, which I limited to otology (ear disorders). It was a busy time and a challenge, but one I loved and enjoyed. Life was full and rewarding; I had fulfilled my family's dream for me and in an odd way, it turned out to be the life I really wanted, too.

Given my still-unresolved anger at my father, I didn't visit very often, and phone calls were often perfunctory. I was busy with my own life, which he had had an important role in shaping, but I was still resentful of his other sins. I didn't want reminders of either his temper or his bigotry. My prejudices had softened over the years, but his had not and I think it embarrassed me. His racist commentary was a dialogue that ran through his side of the family like a string of DNA. I was always particularly bothered by it from him. I had learned to expect it, but it never really sat well; it always felt like a thorn in my side. As I got older and was more removed from his bigoted views, it made me even more uncomfortable.

He was not part of my daily life though he was still my family. When my wife and I decided to adopt a racially mixed child, he was never privy to the decision-making process. At first, he was shocked by his new granddaughter, who is not African American but is nonetheless "dark" by Southern white standards. But he wouldn't admit to his disapproval and discomfort. By then, even he knew that the kind of deep-seated prejudice represented by his views was socially unacceptable. Besides, he liked the idea of another grandchild, and it was difficult to reconcile it all. As Anne got older, he did get more accepting and eventually not only accepted her but loved her dearly. I'm not sure that he connected her with his racial views, however, even as time marched on. Interestingly, as he grew to love her, he didn't see her as "other" so she didn't count as one of "them." He was still wedded to the concept of black inferiority; Anne was simply not black in his eyes, as she was in the eyes of other bigots of the time.

On the occasional family visits to see my father and stepmother in Mobile, I would notice my father's grumblings about the "low-life blacks" and "niggers" in the community, not much different from his standard repertoire that I had grown up around; the difference was that now it sounded discordant. Mostly, however, I ignored it and eventually matured to the point that I could tell my children to do the same. I was pleased that I had risen above the kind of bigotry represented by his rants.

After our visits, we'd go home and return to our lives that were de facto segregated, although I hardly noticed. We lived in an all-white neighborhood, having moved to a more upscale home as our income rose. The reality is that on each step of the economic ladder, there are fewer minorities on the next rung.

THERE WERE A FEW black professionals I would run into from time to time and talk shop with, and about 20 percent of my practice was minority patients. My patients came from all economic strata. My main concern had always been to give quality care; that I was financially comfortable as a result of that policy was a wonderful bonus. The economic disparity is a difficult obstacle that affects all aspects of heath care, from access to physicians, to hospital admission, to the race of the doctors.

It seemed normal and appropriate to me that people would "seek their own kind" for medical treatment whenever possible and studies have confirmed that people are more comfortable with physicians of their own ethnicity and race. That said, there are proportionally fewer minority physicians and even fewer black doctors than other minorities. The U.S. physician workforce does not reflect the racial/ethnic composition of the general population, although their numbers are growing. Blacks represent only 3.5 percent of all physicians and Hispanics 5 percent, as of the last survey taken by the AMA, although these groups in total make up 24.7 percent of the general population.[22] There are simply not enough black physicians, even now. Only 3.3 percent of all medical school graduates in 2004 were black. The color barriers have started to erode somewhat by other ethnic immigrant groups: Asian physicians, a category that includes Chinese, Filipinos, Koreans, Japanese, Vietnamese and Indians/Pakistanis, represent 5.7 percent of the total number of doctors.[23]

Many of my referrals came from primary care doctors whose practices were mostly white, too. It's a cycle that will be difficult to break because black and Hispanic physicians are grossly underrepresented. This won't change any time soon given that these minority groups are still disproportionately represented in medical schools both in the student body and faculty.[24]

Studies have indicated that ethnic minority physicians have more difficulty obtaining medical services for their patients. They are also more likely to experience problems when trying to admit patients to hospitals for non-emergency conditions or referrals to specialists. These differences could not be systematically explained by other factors: payment methods, location of office, age of physician, etc.[25]

Long gone is the old-fashioned family doctor (stereotypically male) whose office is located in a section of his clapboard house. Today's physician offices are in more commercial parts of town or near the hospital in which they practice. Even so, family/general practitioners often draw their patients from the surrounding neighborhoods, and minority physicians are more likely to practice in locations where greater numbers of minority patients reside. Often, it's a matter of access and familiarity with a particular neighborhood.

My own practice was growing and successful and I felt comfortable treating whoever needed care, regardless of race. I didn't think about the racial composition of my practice or minorities or about race in general. I was content with my life and felt no need to look beyond or ask questions about such matters. If I did think about race, it was to tell myself how enlightened I was in contrast to my father and some other relatives who never let go of their bigotry.

I was not involved in politics, though I was a member of the Rotary Club of Birmingham and we did our share of charity drives and fundraising for various local organizations. Those had a lofty purpose and also allowed me to feel like I was doing the right thing. Though my views on race had shifted, my political views and beliefs were not far from where they had started many years earlier back in Mobile.

That said, the racial shifts were discernable, at least to me. I no longer thought that blacks were necessarily inferior or a danger to anyone. Many in my social circle still held more hostile views, but mostly race was not a subject that people raised much now that the violence and upheaval of the earlier years of the civil rights movement had subsided. My attitude had become live-and-let-live, more akin to that of my maternal grandparents. I saw no reason to prevent blacks from climbing the social and financial ladder as I had, but it also never occurred to me that they would have a more difficult time of it than I did. Not having come from a privileged background, and knowing what it was like to struggle financially to get through school, I assumed minorities would have the same struggle. I reasoned that they would have the same experience I had, and since I had managed to overcome the odds, so would they—if they really wanted to. I was not yet open to seeing the effects of racial bias—sometimes direct, other times more subtle—that could impede equal opportunity. I had not factored in the strong support that my father had given me to enable me to get through both college and med school. My resentment of his bigotry and of the way he had dealt with his family overshadowed how large a contribution he had made to my ultimate professional success. Not everyone is blessed with a family that has that kind of will. It served me well and I am grateful for it.

Seeing how many more blacks were now integrated into society fed into my misguided ideas that I (and most of the other white Southerners I knew) was free of racial prejudice and that race was no longer a big issue. After all, there was no more forced separation, and there were successful blacks in many professions, not only in the entertainment field and sports; there were even a few black doctors. I didn't see any problem. I accepted that African Americans were an equal part of the world I now lived in and thought of them no differently from my own peer group. That was what I told myself and anyone who might have asked, though no one did. It was the same defense I used to reinforce the sincerity of my beliefs: blacks were now equal participants in society—they went to the same schools, shopped in the same stores, went to the same doctors, drank from the same water fountains, and at least some lived in the same neighborhoods. It didn't dawn on me to ask myself the question: if blacks were really equal how is it that my friends were all white, as were my children's friends, and my neighbors? Once I had bonded with Anne, her skin color faded with my prejudices. I didn't see her as different or black or "other"; she was my daughter and I loved her. Period. I'm not sure that all of the remnants of my own old prejudices were unilaterally excised; they just didn't apply to her.

ONCE IN A WHILE I would work with a black physician in the hospital and there were blacks in attendance at seminars or medical conferences. Of course, they were a very small minority, probably 2 percent of the overall professionals, but I didn't think about the numbers much. The fact that there were still disproportionately fewer black physicians, mostly attributable to the obstacles in the way of getting into and through medical school, didn't register on my radar. If I noticed it at all, I told myself that there was progress and was satisfied at that. I certainly didn't think about the paucity of black faces among those at the Rotary meetings or country clubs or charity events or even professional associations. And certainly not on the golf course. After all, it's just the way it was.

I was as accepting of the new status quo as I had been of the old. When changes are radical and they make headlines, we sit up and listen. We may not react, but we are aware that a change is taking place and either we support it or fight it. But the evolution of race in the aftermath of the civil rights movement, once the smoke cleared, was evidenced by a slow progression of changes that were not noticeable unless you were consciously looking; most of us avoided the issue, thinking we had already made the transition and nothing more was needed. Of course it was the whites who were most likely to believe that, but most of those in my professional and social circles had very little contact with minorities. When we did, we surely didn't talk about race; we were still living in a polite society. Friends and acquaintances would just comment about our cute new baby and leave it at that. Some, I am sure, were appalled, though they would never have said so; others more accepting. Of course it was the latter group who continued in our social circle.

It was only when I attached meaning to the word "equality" that I began to recognize the social hierarchy that I was a part of. Over time, the more exposure to blacks and minorities who were on equal footing in my own environment, the less strange racial mixing seemed, and whatever irrational fears there had been fell by the wayside. Eventually, I lost sight of skin color. And once Anne joined the family and we became the objects of occasional snide remarks about mixing races, my views came into focus and I had to face my past.

Although I now know how misguided my early anti-integration viewpoints were, at the time they were reinforced by those around me and they drove my thinking. My defense of the segregated South was two-fold: a defense of the system that I had grown up with that assured me a comfortable path to a better life, and a defense of the American system against the threat of communism. I believed that both dangers lurked inside the civil rights movement and therefore vehemently opposed both. In truth, I was also afraid of both, though neither was reality-based.

Those who support capital punishment also have a built-in defense system. They believe that the community is safer if criminals are put to death; that the friends and families of the victims of these crimes feel vindicated; that the policy itself is a crime deterrent, enhancing public safety from further threats; that society should not have to pay to feed and house these criminals; and that the practice is sanctioned by the Bible and is therefore morally justified. As we will see, these arguments are as vacuous as those once used to defend segregation as a policy of the state.

5

THE STUBBORN STAIN
OF BIGOTRY

As I grew more successful, I also lost interest in the church of my youth. I was secular now, more intellectually inclined, and content to reap the rewards of my newly acquired station in life. I saw no need for the church and religion in general; it seemed small and irrelevant to my life. My wife and I had become too intellectual to accept the Christian way and had more or less proudly reasoned God out of existence and out of our lives. When a close friend suggested that we come back to church for the sake of the children, I responded that I did not want them to be ruined by it.

At the time, I thought religion was all a psychosis of sorts. My rejection was really a compensatory action knowing full-well that I would be unable, and unwilling, to give up the "good" life of material pleasures. These were more important to my self-image and self-esteem than living the really good life in a spiritual sense. I felt it was sufficient that we were giving back to the community by my service in positions of leadership in medical organizations and hospital activities and through our heart-felt contributions to other community organizations.

Looking back on this period, I have mixed feelings. It was a good time for me and my family in many ways. I had climbed the ladder to success and was proud of my achievements. I felt good about being able to provide for my family in ways that my father had not, and I certainly didn't harbor his kind of prejudice. Compared to him, I was prejudice-free, although I recognize now what a poor barometer he provided. Unaware as I was of my own brand of bigotry, perhaps less overt and less hostile than his, I convinced myself that I was not cut from the same cloth. I learned later that was simply not true.

While I can attribute some of my early lack of awareness to the innocence of youth, as I grew older I thought I was making amends simply by not demonstrating the hatred that had been part of my family's heritage. I regret how unaware I still was. How easy it is to ignore what's in front of your face!

My illness had propelled me to seek answers to spiritual questions, and so I turned back to the church. In that search I discovered Canterbury United Methodist Church. Here, I felt welcomed back into the folds of religion in a new way. Though the church of my childhood was also Methodist, it was small and had a poor and largely uneducated congregation. Canterbury, on the other hand, boasts a 4,750-member congregation that is generally well-educated and affluent. This in itself doesn't make it superior. However, it is full of kind, caring, and generous people, making the whole atmosphere warm, friendly and welcoming. It is where I now feel at home.

I was also attracted to Canterbury because of the opportunities it provided to learn more about the Bible and Christianity and because it offered the camaraderie of many people I already knew and respected from various community activities. Sharing one's spiritual growth with others is rewarding and I have found great solace in coming back to religion in general and this church in particular.

Part of my regular Sunday routine includes participating in a Sunday school class, one of many offered by the church. One Sunday a few years ago, the gentleman who usually conducts my class was out of town so I sat in on another one. This was a much smaller group comprised of only six men, somewhat younger, and decidedly more conservative than the class I was used to.

Knowing some of the group members from other social venues, I welcomed getting better acquainted. On this bright morning, the class discussion was about doing good works. We each took turns sharing our recent contributions to good works and how we felt about the activities and ourselves, as such the works of Christ.

Some of the group already knew a little about the work I had been do-ing for the past decade with the Alabama Ear Institute (AEI), a nonprofit organization I had founded in 1991, which offers various outreach programs to serve children and adults in Alabama who are deaf or hard-of-hearing. Throughout my medical practice, I had treated people from all racial groups, but the majority of my patients were whites from the local community. For the most part, I didn't give much thought to this either way. My referral policy was set up to include patients who could not afford to pay, some of whom were on Medicaid. I always factored in the ability of a patient to pay when I considered fees, and would charge, not charge, or reduce fees accordingly. Many of those who fell into the latter categories were minority patients. I felt a sense of obligation to serve these populations but I also liked the experience; the vast majority of them were truly appreciative of the policy and my services. I also felt a bit of sorrow for the children of parents who were not able to afford their medical care.

While my objective was to provide an underserved part of the community with needed medical services, this work acted to distance me from my past stereotypes. I had come to realize that people were the same, regardless of race; some were wonderful and kind, others harbored anger and hostility. Race had little to do with their outlook and how they treated others. Rich or poor, black or white, we all have the same needs for love and acceptance, for taking care of our basic needs for ourselves and our families, including our health.

During the course of developing the outreach programs for the Institute, I had further opportunities to work with minorities in the community, including Latinos and African Americans. By the time I found myself in this small Sunday school class, it had already become my habit to make a conscious effort to mend fences and find ways to bring people together to foster better race relations and bring down the barriers. I often looked for ways to atone for my past. Accordingly, I was feeling rather pleased to be able to tell the group about a recent local event the Institute had orga-nized which was sponsored by the Tiger Woods Foundation. When it was my turn, I explained my role in taking a group of hearing-impaired black children and their parents to the event and how much fun it had been for everyone involved.

Tiger himself was in attendance. He did a short golf demonstration and interacted with the group. I described how impressive Tiger was in person and how the kids loved it; they reacted as if it had been Coach Paul "Bear" Bryant of Alabama fame out there with them on the greens. It was an opportunity these children never would have had without the sponsorship of AEI and I was proud of my role in the event. Given the more informal nature of this particular class, I was enjoying the opportunity to share my own pleasure from the experience. In my regular class no such discussion would ever have taken place since it is usually held in a lecture format.

While most of the men concurred that this was a genuine example of spreading good works, there was one fellow who rather gruffly remarked, "Well, I don't know what's so great about seeing Tiger Woods. I sure wouldn't want to see him."

I was a bit taken aback, but at this point in my life, I was not timid about confronting people who might disagree with me. I asked a couple of questions to try to clarify what he was saying. "You don't like golf? What is it about Tiger Woods that you don't like?" I asked him.

"Well, I question the intentions of people like Tiger," he replied. "But as far as those kids are concerned, you would have done much better for them if you had gotten them a job!"

I had learned not to respond in anger to this sort of baiting. Holding my ground, I calmly replied, "Would you have felt the same way if the visiting golfer had been Arnold Palmer or Jack Nicklaus?"

It was easy to spot his prejudice; after all, I had once subscribed to it myself. I was hoping to make obvious what was underlying his caustic attitude, perhaps even help him recognize it and consider the callousness of his feelings. I was being overly optimistic. Instead, he grew increasingly hostile as he correctly interpreted my implied accusation of racism.

I explained that I was just trying to offer these kids an equal opportunity to participate and perhaps even develop an interest in golf.

"Them folks get up, pull up their pants, and put their feet on the floor just like I do each morning," he responded, as if he too had once experienced worry over basic needs and a stable income.

When I pointed out that equal opportunity was more equal for some than others, I was next accused of being "a bleeding heart liberal." "Why don't you just go and join the Communist Party?" he said angrily.

Why is it that discussions of this sort always seem to get reduced to these kinds of rejoinders? It was clear that there was no substance to his argument and that racism was at its core. Yet I felt helpless and diminished, my intentions totally misunderstood.

An uncomfortable silence followed. A few people interjected conciliatory remarks and tried to refocus the subject back to the dialogue about good works. But others stood silent in the face of the confrontation, afraid to offend either party, both of us being active members of this church.

I am increasingly disappointed by this type of silence; it reinforces to the offending party that his views are acceptable and mainstream. I don't believe the others in the group were in accord with this man, but they were unwilling to articulate that position. It was the group who should have spoken out, silencing the offender instead of the reverse. Though the offender didn't threaten anyone, it felt as if he had. His hostility created a cloud that hung over the class, obscuring any disagreement from others in the room and allowing the offender to continue to believe that he was on the right side of the argument; the silence condoned the outburst. By allowing him to play bully, it turned the rest of us into victims.

Fear makes us act in odd ways, ways that can be inconsistent with our conscious values and who and what we think we are and want to be. Sometimes speaking out means exposing our beliefs and I understand how much courage that seemingly simple act can take. I can only speculate on how people really felt at that moment in the class and what their real fears were. Most of us dislike confrontation and would rather avoid it, so we close the circle rather than open the wound.

I can only project from my own history what fears might have been at play: fear of anger—your own or the other person's—fear of taking sides and losing friends, fear of disapproval, fear of being misunderstood, fear of being exposed as a racist (even in Alabama, no one wants to think they hold racist views, or at least they don't want others to think they do) and fear of being labeled a communist sympathizer (still a highly charged epithet in this state). Having been part of silent audiences in the past, I understand the reaction. You get frozen in time for a fleeting moment, and then the moment passes and the door closes; what might be on the other side of that door is forgotten. You breathe a sigh of relief as everything goes back to "normal."

While in the process of my re-education, I came across some of the writings of Dietrich Bonhoeffer, a Lutheran pastor best known for his resistance to Hitler. He spoke out when it was dangerous to do so, not merely unpopular. He was jailed for criticizing Nazi imperialism and refused to be silenced. Hitler eventually had him hanged. I admire Bonhoeffer and his courage; it sets an important example for us all. Not that my church group and its renegade parishioner is at all analogous to Bonhoeffer's plight, but it does serve as a lesson for what can happen when people are not willing to speak up for their beliefs. While I don't expect people to jump to my defense at every opportunity, it is only when people voice their opposition that bullies and people who harbor these types of hostilities become weakened. Breaking the silence is unlikely to make bullies change their views, but they are more likely to keep their hostilities to themselves and limit the damage they can do.

The uncomfortable moments in that class were short-lived, although the discussion had grown rather heated by the end of the class time. I had learned to break the silence and be heard: "For it is God's will that by doing right you should silence the ignorance of the foolish" (1 Peter 2:15). I was not totally willing to let it go, so I continued to engage him in what I still (perhaps naively) hoped was friendly persuasion, and it carried on into the hall. I surely didn't want to continue this pointless argument, but I do admit that the whole conversation made me feel sick. Recognizing his ugly prejudice was an unpleasant reminder of that part of my own past. I was also very frustrated by his arguments and couldn't help feeling that I was not being understood. I could not help but think about of Psalms 119:86: "I am persecuted without cause; help me!" But I knew from my own reading of the Bible and from other studies that God loves us all and forgives us, whatever the sin.

"Well, I love you, brother, in spite of our differing opinions," I told him as we separated paths. He didn't respond; in fact, he sneered at me as he left.

The small size of the class and its more conservative makeup, including one bigot, probably account for the situation that developed more than anything that I did or said. But I couldn't help analyzing it to try and figure out if there was some alternative way that I could have handled this man that would have made the situation less contentious. When I did run into one of the men from the group later in the week, he had moved on and written it off. To him, it was trivial and I doubt that he thought about it again. Although this singular incident is atypical of the behavior and attitudes of the members of this church, it nonetheless rankled me.

My wife astutely observed that this is just how older Southerners react to racial issues and that it was ironic that this conversation took place in church. Maybe so. I did take this man's response rather personally and felt rejected. What upset me the most was his dense attitude and total lack of sensitivity to others who are less fortunate. Here we were, in a beautiful church, among an "elite" congregation, the vast majority of whom have to worry about taking care of their basic needs. Yet there are still some within this churchgoing community who pay lip service to the tenets of Christianity embodied in the church while refusing to recognize how their own actions run counter to all that it stands for. Their concept of equal is unbalanced, with all the weight of their own convictions on their side.

I knew that this conversation, if that's what we can call it, however unpleasant, allowed me to experience what many blacks have lived with for years: prejudice, unfounded judgments, and hostility that didn't end with either the Civil War or the civil rights movement. Although I knew I was on the right side of this debate, it still made me feel badly, and this encapsulated incident paled next to the suffering experienced by blacks then and now. It made me feel awful not because of how I was being characterized, but because it once again reminded me of the depth of the persecution against blacks in this country. Perhaps what bothered me most was how such a shield of ignorance and hatred could prevent even the sturdiest arrows of truth to penetrate it and how the mere mention of racial issues can still touch off a firestorm that encourages people to withdraw from the discussion and pretend it never occurred.

As I reflect now on how my own views have evolved and the latent racism that is still rampant not just in the South but nationwide, I also recognize the impact of silence. I feel certain that there were others in that class who agreed with me and were upset by the tone and tenor that had overtaken the discussion. But as with most polite Southerners, they wouldn't express these views for fear of escalating the argument and rousing tempers—at least that is what they probably tell themselves. And certainly, they didn't want to inject themselves into it, much like those around my father whose silence condoned his violence and waited for him to "settle down." Not that it matters to me really; I have learned to defend myself and my views without any help, feeling comfortable with the knowledge that they are based on sound principle and in accordance with what I think is the will and wisdom of God. But it does matter to those still afflicted by the sharp tongues and passive-aggressive manners of the racists moving silently in their wake.

I know firsthand how cruel is the language of bigotry. I remember quite well the confusion created by the strange looks and occasional name-calling hurled against our daughter. Although she is not black, her contrast to those in her immediate environment was often enough to trigger the same automatic response. She was in kindergarten the first time she heard the term "nigger" applied to herself and she didn't know what it meant but she understood that it is not nice. Silence was not an option we would have considered.

My wife, being the maternal protector and strong advocate that she is, put an immediate end to the problem; the school couldn't and wouldn't tolerate such behavior. But being reminded of those Southern roots, those perennial weeds that take years to die, I knew I certainly had come a long way. I had cut off the tap root and my own bigotry had been starved, dying a natural death. But the roots of bigotry still run deep and can suddenly appear in unexpected places, cracking the sidewalk far from their origin. Some weeds can't be simply killed off; they must be crowded out by other plants that eventually take over.

My reaction to the deep-seated hatred in this man was partly an ac-knowledgement that I once harbored this type of vulgar and prejudicial hatred. I didn't like looking into that mirror. My illness had forced me to face many truths about myself and they were not always easy to reconcile. The man I was and the man I wanted to be were not the same. By the time of this incident, however, I had come full circle. I now had the benefit of hindsight; he didn't. It was that simple.

6

A TEST OF FAITH

The beginning of my spiritual growth came several years before I became conscious of any real change in my attitudes. It started on a sunny summer day in July 1997. I was on the golf course, playing alone as was my habit then to get in extra practice. I was on the fourth hole, feeling good about my progress so far. As I lined up my second shot to the green and looked up at the flag, I saw two flags about four inches apart. I blinked, adjusted my glasses and my stance, and drove the ball. The ball landed about 150 yards away and on the green but as I approached it, I saw two balls resting about four inches apart. Tired eyes, I told myself. At close range, it was hardly noticeable, but it was more pronounced at greater distances. It had been a hectic morning in surgery and being tired can play tricks on your eyes, I reassured myself. Anyway, it was hot—this was Alabama in the early afternoon in July. I continued to play and stubbornly finished all eighteen holes. I was concerned but tried to dismiss it and the double vision subsided once I got home.

Although my symptoms were gone the next morning, I was still a bit worried, especially since my wife and I were scheduled to leave for vacation the next day. Being a doctor, I was caught between the panic of self-diagnosis that included all the terrible things I knew could cause double vision, and the rational part of me that told me to stop getting caught up in textbook syndromes. I went about my day, seeing patients as usual, but the symptoms had returned by the afternoon. I immediately went to see an ophthalmologist whose practice was near my office. He carefully examined me but could find no reason for the double vision, though he did note that my glasses needed to be adjusted. Just the news I wanted. I took care of my glasses and admonished myself for getting all worked up for nothing. Then I went home to pack.

Still not totally convinced that everything was okay, I awoke the next morning with some trepidation. To my surprise and relief, my vision seemed normal—only one wife and one cup of coffee. I had told my wife of my experience but since the symptoms disappeared overnight, we both dismissed the whole thing. We got in the car and took off. I was confident in my denial and my wife was comfortable in her optimism, both of us looking forward to a relaxing week.

After a long drive to our destination, the symptoms returned and this time they didn't go away. Within twenty-four hours we found ourselves back on the road headed home, trying to allay fears of all the terrible possibilities. As a doctor I could count the ways—in gory detail.

On Monday, I saw my ophthalmologist. Although the exam still showed nothing to indicate anything awry, we were both worried. He ordered an MRI. A few hours later, I found myself immobilized in the noisy tube, trying to keep fear at bay. I tried to focus on good things: previous trips and vacations, great golf shots, memorable events. It didn't work. Somewhat distracted by the loud clatter of the machine, my mind kept running to the possible causes of double vision, including various types of aneurysms and multiple sclerosis. I cannot describe the relief I felt when the results came back negative. It was the most wonderful thing I had ever heard! To celebrate, my wife and I went out to dinner.

The next morning, my worry returned, however. Although the MRI ruled out some possibilities, I was still seeing double and we didn't know why. I went back to see my ophthalmologist who was also a long-time close friend and colleague. Dr. Tom McKinnon examined me and then called on his senior partner, an excellent neuro-ophthalmologist, to come in for a consult. After his exam, Dr. Elmer Lawaczeck adopted the prototypical physician pose; with his finger to his chin and arms folded, he looked directly at me for what seemed to me like several long minutes. I had to restrain myself from screaming, "Jesus Christ, man, tell me something!" But I wanted to be polite and appropriate, so I waited. He asked me some questions, which seemed irrelevant in my impatience. Finally, he concluded, "It sounds like myasthenia gravis." He suggested a Tensilon Test, which gives a fairly accurate diagnosis of the disease. The test was positive.

"Well, Robert," he said after looking at the results, "you have myasthenia gravis."

Wow, was I ever relieved! In my panic, I had culled a list of much more potentially serious and life-threatening diseases. MG was usually not fatal. Certainly it had an effect on your life, but death was not the usual outcome. It was only after being diagnosed that I recognized the definite weakness and fatigue I had been experiencing for a long time as part of a disease process.

Dr. Lawaczeck explained more about myasthenia gravis and the current treatments. I already knew a little about the disease, but he brought me up to speed. I discovered that there was a local expert on MG right in Birmingham and went to see him that week. Dr. Shin Oh helped me understand more about the disease, easing my concerns. He assured me that I was likely to do very well with treatment; but he also warned me that the disease could progress over the next two to three years and I could develop more significant problems from it. So far, the only noticeable symptoms were double vision. I felt lucky, and in my usual, optimistic mode I took the appropriate drugs and was determined not to let it interfere with my life. After a few weeks of medication, the extreme double vision improved. I still tired easily, even though my strength was reasonably good.

Part of my plan for management of my disease was to keep it quiet. Of course my family knew, and some of my close friends and my doctor partners, but I didn't broadcast the news. Like many people who live with debilitating diseases, we live in fear that others will look at us differently, that we will be stereotyped by an ill-informed assessment of our condition, that people will feel sorry for us, or think we are too weak to do anything. And I definitely did not want to be thought of as weak! None of these contribute toward better fighting the demons of the disease and they frequently add to the stress. I was also concerned that misinformation might jeopardize my practice; once my symptoms had improved, I could still comfortably resume my normal work schedule.

I was soon outed by a patient who had been at church when my name was included in a call for prayers. He was scheduled for ear surgery and was concerned because he thought I had MS (multiple sclerosis), not MG, myasthenia gravis. I don't think his hearing was remiss; it is easy to confuse the names of diseases when they are all rather unfamiliar.

I continued to keep my condition quiet, however. I didn't want to be the object of a different kind of prejudice. It was odd to acknowledge my own fears about being on the receiving end of prejudice. Discrimination takes many forms and often involves pigeonholing people according to their deficits instead of focusing on their assets. These distorted perceptions and expectations feed on themselves and make it more difficult for people to be comfortable exposing their deficits, as if human perfection were the norm. Typecasting makes a mockery of all human differences; perhaps that's why race plays such a large role in how we relate to one another. Race isn't something you can hide, and unfortunately, in this country and culture, all too often it is still considered a deficit.

Ironically, about a year and a half after my diagnosis a dear colleague and friend, who was also a patient, called me to discuss some of his medical issues. When he told me he had MG and wanted to make sure that the drugs I was treating him with would have no negative interactions with the MG drug regimen, I almost dropped the phone.

"Well, welcome to the crowd?" I said once I had regained my composure.

"What do you mean?" he asked me.

"I mean, I have MG too," I confessed.

I have known Ron Henderson since medical school, and yet he kept his disease a secret for three years, sharing the information with me only because he thought it prudent to ask about possible negative drug interactions. He was so fearful of having others know of his condition, he requested that I hold the information in strict confidence. I emphasize that he felt compelled to make this request even though we had a long history and he trusted me, and of course he knew that medical ethics would prevent my divulging the information anyway. Eventually we both became more comfortable talking about it more openly. He subsequently went so far as to publish a book about his experience and how he finally came to terms with the disorder.[26]

It was his confession, however, that allowed us to share confidences and form a much closer friendship. Of course I understood not only his specific issues with the disease, since by the time he divulged his to me I had already been living with MG for at least six months, but also the need to hide it from the world. We are so fearful of people knowing the truth about our condition that we hide it from those around us who could offer support. I say this not to judge him, but to remind myself of how I fell into the same trap. Whether we were protecting others or ourselves remains a question.

So often we know what the truth is and yet use self-deceit as ointment for our wounds, liberally applied while the wound festers under the skin. I found this to be the case in health issues, my own and others', as well as when seeking higher truths. In fact, I found it across the board when confronting all kinds of issues that one does not usually frame in terms of truth, like the things we tell ourselves we believe that are not quite true. Like the silence of those in the Sunday school class, we are afraid of exposing our views, foibles, and imperfections, whether physical or spiritual, lest we be ridiculed, criticized, or rejected. Sometimes it is just easier to ignore things than to confront them. Besides, we don't want to embarrass anyone, including ourselves; we want to appear to others as perfect, though we know that perfection is not human and is reserved only for God. Silence in the face of fear can be pernicious.

When first confronted with a serious illness, I tried to deny that it would affect me significantly and I was determined to live my life as I always had. That was a different kind of strength; perhaps some would call it stubbornness. My wife and children did! At the time, it was all I knew how to do. But as much as I tried to deny it, disease has a way of infiltrating your being and the struggle of who is in control is a difficult one. I was determined to conquer the disease but my overall strength and stamina declined and affected everything I did, from getting out of bed in the morning to seeing patients and even performing surgery.

First I referred the more complex cases to other surgeons in my group and limited the number of operations I would schedule on any given day. Gradually, I decreased my patient load and delegated more and more direct patient communication to my nurse and the more difficult cases to my younger partner. But when I experienced double vision in the OR, I knew I had to consider throwing in the towel. I was good at what I did and I derived great satisfaction from using my medical expertise to help people, but I had to come to terms with the fact that there were some things out of my control. I had good days and bad ones, but I had no control over their timing. I couldn't practice medicine on such an ad hoc basis.

Just contemplating the enormity of such a change felt at the time like one of the most difficult things I ever had to face, worse in some ways than the illness itself. Though years removed from my religion, I prayed for guidance but I was angry, too; I didn't want to be in this position. Of course I wanted to be healthy, but if I was going to have to live with disease, at least I wanted to be able to continue to work and feel productive. Although I had other interests outside of medicine, much of my self-image was tied to my career. While I understood the importance of my family and loved ones, and they are still my priority, my identity was primarily housed in my life's work. I had been groomed to become a doctor since childhood; it was almost as much a part of me as my name. If I gave it up, who would I be, what would I become? Of course, we never know what God has in store for us but it was difficult for me to imagine a different life.

My wife and I discussed my options. I guess she too had been waiting for my moment of recognition, but was wise enough not to say anything. She also was highly acquainted with my stubborn streak and did not want to give me more reasons to have to prove myself. Of course there were financial considerations, but the emotional fallout was more important.

Coming to terms with giving up a successful medical practice was not easy. I know I am not the first person to confront these issues, nor will I be the last; many people are joined at the hip to their work. But knowing about such things and experiencing them are two different things. I had been working in a field filled with daily discussion of various maladies and certainly I knew people who had been ill and had to deal with more than their fair share of disease. Until this point in my life, I had gotten a free ride; I had never had any serious illness.

As I gradually withdrew from my practice, I began to spend more time at the Alabama Ear Institute (AEI). The tasks at hand there were more manageable given my disease. My hours could be more flexible, I could do some of the work from home. I stopped taking night calls and eventually my patient load dwindled. At the same time, the AEI started doing more community outreach and adding programs for children with hearing loss and their families. I did gain some degree of satisfaction knowing that my efforts were making a difference in some people's lives. It was a start. In May 1999, after two years of struggling to maintain my practice, interrupted by prostate cancer surgery in the summer of 1998, I had to call it quits.

Being confronted with life-threatening illness eventually compelled me to look inward. First, I tried self-help manuals and books. They all said they had answers, but I found them lacking in terms of answering the questions I was asking: Why am I here? What is my purpose? I knew that my intentions had always been honorable and sincere, yet my life had been dominated by seeking satisfaction from external sources. I was searching for meaning, a way to fill the void of what's left when you strip a life of its material extremities. I was seeking alternatives. Where would I find the "truth" about life? "Dust to dust?" Was that all there was? I knew science; science failed me. I also knew God, but I did not know him well. Was he the answer?

I searched the Internet for resources on life, meaning, and purpose. No satisfaction there either. Google wasn't much help in finding God. I looked at Buddhism; I read Gandhi and Martin Luther King Jr., C. S. Lewis and Reinhold Neibuhr, Plato and Socrates, Tolstoy and Kant, John Locke and Charles Darwin. While all of this made for interesting reading and certainly kept me busy, I decided if I was searching for the Holy Grail, I should read the Bible in its entirety.

I came to understand that inspirational moments occur across all religions, but the profundity of the message is the same. In my case the minutes were many years, and I have found truth in the axiom that the greater the struggle, the greater and more gratifying the reward. Knowing that "obstacles are opportunities disguised in work clothes" (Henry J. Kaiser, 1882–1967), I thank God, the author of the book of good life, for granting me the grace, opportunity, wisdom, and strength to savor his love and his direction, and the wisdom to pursue it.

It had been a tumultuous two years and I thought I had emerged as a stronger person. I was closer to God than I had ever been; I was well enough to be more active in my role at the AEI; I had joined the church and become active, attending Bible classes and even singing in the church praise band group. In my search for meaning, I found new paths that had previously been blocked by my short-sighted vision. My double vision had improved, but the life I now visualized was on a singular but focused course. I was spending my time helping others in a very different way, one that was decidedly richer in spirit. As my physical strength grew, so did my faith and I was pleased with my new direction. However, I was unprepared for how I would be further tested.

Less than two years after retiring, I had another cancer scare. This time cancer of the larynx or lung was suspected. My vocal cord had become paralyzed, a condition with which I was familiar because of my medical specialty. I could barely whisper and any attempt at talking was very tiring. The condition also aggravated the muscles needed for breathing and swallowing, which were already weak because of the MG.

Just prior to this episode, I had been praying to God for the strength and wisdom to overcome what I felt was my primary weakness, or sin, namely that of pride. How else did you express your pride except through your ability to speak and make yourself notable? I felt that God had taken my voice for just that purpose: he quieted me so that my pride would go unexpressed. He took away my ability to say the things I needed to say during the professional lectures I was giving and the discourse I engaged in during Bible study groups or in the private conversations that enhanced my state of well-being or maintained my status. Perhaps some saw my inability to participate in church singing as a blessing, but I prayed a lot not just for my physical recovery but also for renewed faith.

Surely my will was being tested—again. I attempted to overcome this new obstacle; I bought a personal amplifier that had a speaker I could attach to my belt and a head set with a small microphone. This allowed my whisper to be loud enough for most in my immediate vicinity to hear me, although it was extremely tiring. I was determined not to give up. I tried to keep up with my activities and attended classes and church, tethered to the amplifier. People were extremely sympathetic, for which I was grateful.

After more tests, we finally ruled out cancer as the cause. The most common cause is a viral inflammation of the laryngeal nerve, which could be treated with cortisone. I knew recovery was possible in a large number of cases. I was determined to be one of them. But it took a full nine months.

In a strange way, a part of me had always felt that someday I would make the change to a life with and through God. The question had become not if, but when, and would I have the strength? Although I had once shunned the church and religion, I believed that once I had experienced all that the material world had to offer, there would be the time to turn back to God. Quite naïve and selfish, I know. It was my way of trying to control the path God had set for me. Although I really believed in the need for salvation, I thought I could determine the time frame. I had to learn to trust in God and allow him into my life. Ironically, now that I was lacking physical strength, I managed to find the mental strength to search for God and find out if he had the answers I was looking for. He did. And finding that truth gave me the strength to go on. Each time I was tested, I emerged stronger. When true life started, the past life seemed paltry in contrast.

When standing apart from one's life, a different picture emerges, one in which the "I" is not the primary player on the stage. It was with this third "eye" that I began searching for deeper meaning and this journey led me to the door of life and death issues. I believe that we are all God's children—all equal in the eyes of the Lord. Isn't that what the Bible says? "For all who are led by the Spirit of God are children of God" (Romans 8:14). Yet when taking the long view of how we live and how we treat one another, that concept isn't always so apparent.

My illness and early retirement forced me to rediscover myself and my life's purpose and brought me face to face with different truths. As I struggled with the ups and downs of illness and the inevitable emotional byproducts of the sum of all changes, I developed a new outlook and a different kind of empathy toward people who had not been able to overcome their own struggles. It was a different kind of transformation, but it was in its own way as radical as my illness. In the process of seeking my own truths, I discovered other truths outside myself. This too gave me purpose and meaning, for it laid claim to my rational self and my faith in humanity and in God and Jesus Christ as our Savior. My newfound relationship to God was surely being tested, but once I accepted Jesus Christ into my heart, I knew I would be okay, for my purpose became clear.

My transformation has been a painful, obstacle-laden journey leading me to the point that "I am." From a practical point of view, my struggle with illness, by its nature, had a great impact on how I looked at the world and examined what part I played in the bigger picture.

Although we all know we are mere mortals, it is not until we are faced with the reality of a finite life that we look toward the infinite love of God for answers in how best to live during the short time we have. This quest takes over your being and drives your life. My life as I knew it changed forever. I wanted to make more of a contribution in whatever time I had left here on Earth. I had read "Keep your sphere of concern within your sphere of influence"[27] and the resonance of that short but meaningful statement lifted a weight off my shoulders. I felt empowered. As I grappled with where to put my energies and how to put into practice my beliefs in leading a good life, I became a student again. Not just a student of religion and my own path to truth, but a student in the real-world community of Birmingham where I interacted with others at various stages in their own life journeys.

During the struggle to regain my health, I had done a lot of reading and I reflected on a quote from Henry David Thoreau: "I know of no more encouraging fact than the unquestionable ability of man to elevate his life by conscious endeavor." I was consciously looking for a new endeavor, one in which my values would finally be in sync with my daily activities and goals. This is not to say I had never been sympathetic to the plight of those less fortunate than I or had never donated to charitable organizations or given of my time to such activities. I had, and I was active in doing so. But the spirit of giving had taken a new turn. I was looking at making a change both for myself and for however much of the larger world I could influence. I wanted to take it beyond what I had been accustomed to doing.

I think of myself as a rational man, though some might argue differently.[28] My education and medical training taught me to look for reasonable answers to questions—fact-based judgment calls are part of diagnosing human illness. But I had never applied that same kind of thinking to the social issues of the day or even to my own opinions about broad social issues and politics. Although I had long ago completed college and medical school, I had had little exposure to non-science courses as part of my formal education. I suppose that accounts for my voracious appetite in seeking answers from the early philosophers and religious thinkers.

I had taken a course in nonprofit organization and management and even earned a certificate in the subject. I wanted to learn more and gain more insight and credibility as I continued to increase my work with the AEI. Having become more active as president and board chair in 1997, I was ready for more. I was interested in public policy and I wanted to learn how ideas get played out in the public arena. I also thought it would satisfy my desire to understand the humanities better, subjects to which I had had minimal exposure during college and med school, but that now were playing an ever-increasing role in my life.

Though I wasn't looking for a new career, I had become more and more interested in how government social policy affects people's lives. The idea of additional formal courses in the humanities appealed to me, so I looked into and then enrolled in the master of arts in Public and Private Management program at Birmingham-Southern College. I knew I had come upon a new path and now I just had to move forward.

In large part, I believe that through God's mysterious ways, he gave me the seeds of knowledge and the gift of reason. I didn't know exactly what to anticipate in this program, but I was enthusiastic about enhancing my people skills and learning more about the conceptual foundations for public policy, which were new to me.

One of my first elective courses was Dr. Ed LaMonte's class and it was in his class that my views about capital punishment made a U-turn. Certainly I was also interested in the other issues that were part of the course, but the issue of the death penalty resonated more than any of the others. It not only sparked my interest but it created a passion to become a voice for change. At the time, though the decision to act and become an advocate was conscious, the reasons why this issue resonated with me so completely were not.

I had selected the class because its content was interesting. I didn't know much about either LaMonte or the course at the time. Once in class, I discovered a gifted, deservedly well-respected teacher. One of the things I found most fascinating was his teaching style. I had never been exposed to Socratic methodology and I loved it. I had already been doing my own search and now I had a structure for it and broader resources. LaMonte encouraged us to form our own opinions, based on facts, and that approach was an eye-opener.

So many of my early assumptions were based on false or inaccurate information. I was ready to hear it now—the racial myths, the hypocrisy, the misleading data spun to garner public support. I no longer accepted "facts" on faith; my own faith had taken over and it made me angry that we are so often victims of this kind of politicization and so easily led. My anger was at myself for believing so blindly and also at the political will to mislead.

How easily I had fallen victim to George Wallace's appeal to populism. I was young and had no real political savvy, nor was I exposed to any for a long time afterward. Wallace had been a Democrat, a liberal one at that, who was sympathetic to blacks until he got "out-niggered" by John Patterson in the 1962 gubernatorial election. After losing to Patterson, Wallace became the leading segregationist of the times. Later, he would imply that if he had needed a different political position to get elected, he could have assumed it as easily as he had segregation. It has been noted by some that "he led us where we wanted to go, and when we got there we were ashamed." Had Wallace simply taken the segregationist position for political gain and power? It certainly never occurred to me at the time. What does occur to me is that we are seeing the same dynamic in terms of capital punishment today. In both cases, politicians prey on people's fears, silencing opposition both by decree and unstated agreement with misleading "facts."

While my own experience with violence and race is unique and others are not likely to share them in the same way, it's important to look at your own experience and how it impacts your views. I'd like to believe that my father's violent outbursts are unusual, but I have come to understand that they were not. Many people have had worse and more frequent experiences with family violence and uncontrollable anger. We suffer in silence as victims of such behavior. As children we are taught to believe that we somehow deserve it; as adults we assume that others who have done wrong also deserve it. When we are angry and/or feel victimized, the desire to lash out and take revenge is natural. We want to retrieve what has been hopelessly lost, whether our dreams, a loved one, stolen goods, our ideals, and perhaps most of all, our dignity. In that process, we perpetuate the hostility and the violence begets more violence. It gets passed down from one generation to the next, whether in the acceptance of a father beating his son in the name of teaching him a lesson or a prison official beating an inmate for the same reason. The personal so easily melds into the political.

7

THE TRUTHINESS
OF THE DEATH PENALTY

As I spend more time learning more about those behind bars, I find more commonalities with the "insiders" than one would reasonably expect. On examination, it is easy to see how little really separates us, other than the physical barriers. It was hard to read the below passage and not identify with the author, Frank Elijah Smith. Smith was on death row in Florida until recently, when his sentence was commuted to twenty-five years to life. He is still struggling to gain his freedom and as he does so, he continues to better himself through reading whatever limited materials are available to him in prison and by writing about himself:

I am simply a man, one whose life has been riddled with bad decisions and mistakes.

I have been no angel in my past, but I have been no murderer either. When I was first arrested and charged with a capital crime, I was merely nineteen years of age, poorly educated (sixth grade) and profoundly ignorant. After being convicted and sentenced to death I experienced a transformation, a kind of spiritual enlightenment. This did not occur overnight, it is a transformation that is ongoing.

Nonetheless, I have come a long way in many areas and have fully rehabilitated myself—socially, spiritually, psychologically and academically. It is ironic but true that I am the type of person that they look to release from prison, not to kill. But, what with politics, I fear that I may never be released from bondage. Yet I will not be dissuaded from trying to do something good with my life, and that good is helping to put an end to capital punishment.

Although I am incarcerated, that restriction only extends to my anatomy, my physical being, not to my mind. I may never have an opportunity to prove or share my true worth outside these fences. To those of you who believe that capital punishment should be abolished I urge you to embrace the principles that I have set forth in this manifesto. If you firmly commit yourselves to this cause, to this life or death issue, we can bring our nation into the twenty-first century with renewed hope.[29]

While the "bad" decisions I made in my own life and those of Smith in his are not directly comparable, that fact doesn't erase his humanity nor does it mean that God doesn't forgive him. His sentence and imprisonment are real. My own transformation and dance with death are no less real than his. In a way, we all live under a sentence of death. It is a truth of the human condition. Yet it is something only God has the power to control.

The only thing we can control is how we live the life we are given. We can choose to try to rid ourselves of hatred; we can choose to treat others, regardless of race and ethnicity, age or gender, with dignity and respect. This would be asking ourselves to examine our own actions and motives and act rationally and in accord with what we know is right. Supporting the death penalty is neither rational nor logical. Yet people who are rational and logical in most other areas of their lives have no problem whatsoever clinging to the irrational fears and feelings of insecurity, whatever language they may be couched in, and drawing opinions and forming belief systems from them.

It's hard to say whether political support for an issue is born from the people or if it's a response to political leadership. Perhaps there's no difference so long as the leadership and the people are a homogeneous group, but what happens when the power structure includes few if any minority voices? How does change take place when the only voices advocating it are outside of those homogeneous circles? Slowly, and not without a struggle.

I know what it takes to undergo personal change, having been subjected to my own radical "attitudectomy"; these changes were not easy and occurred over time. But changes that involve society in general have to come about top-down as well as bottom-up in order to influence sufficient numbers of people to garner political support. There was a time when local support for racial integration was negligible, at least among the Southern whites, but as history has demonstrated, attitudes do change. Then, as now, there were fault lines in the closed system that was the South of the 1950s and 1960s.

Will a voice like Smith's be heard by the politicians who write the laws that keep him imprisoned? Not likely. He can't even vote. Does it take a personal death threat for one to examine a policy that threatens the life of others? These questions haunt me because I know how difficult it was for me to come to terms with new information and change my former belief system. It didn't come from reading one book or one particularly convincing article or essay. I had been looking for answers to broader life-and-death questions and these questions were already being addressed by my church and my renewed relationship with God. I found myself in a new academic environment reading differing points of view. When I considered the actual data and facts, it was hard to reconcile the conclusions with my own basic opinions about social issues. I had to adjust my thinking if I was going to be honest, and if nothing else, my call to redemption and atonement mandated honesty.

While in medical school, my studies required fact-based learning; scientific study and medicine are full of facts that must be mastered to practice competent medicine. But the actual daily work with patients is guided much more by judgment calls, for example, in determining treatment options. It is only when judgment calls have to be made that anyone questions facts, and these questions are generally about what the latest research studies indicate.

When I returned to school for the master's program at Birmingham-Southern College, my perspectives about facts and ideas shifted. I began to understand how facts are used in persuasion and the formation of opinion. My opinions about medicine had rarely been challenged because I had always practiced "conservative" medicine, that is, a bit more cautious than average. I didn't consider surgery as an option unless it was clearly the only way to take care of a problem. Sometimes it might have been easier to just go ahead with surgery, but that was not always the best option in my judgment. I tried to look at each patient as a person and carefully analyze the specific problems and the subsequent management. Most of the time, this policy served me well (and I hope also served my patients' best interests), but on occasion, it presented conflicts.

In my field, it once was the prevailing wisdom that the "cure" for children's chronic and recurring ear infections was to insert tiny tubes in the eardrum to keep fresh air in and fluids and infection out of the middle ear. This procedure became one of the most common surgical procedures in the pediatric age group and was often recommended for children who had such infections. It was always a balancing act to determine if undergoing the surgical procedure was better for the child than frequent or prolonged treatment with antibiotics. I performed this procedure numerous times and had many, many grateful parents. Over the years, however, the indications for surgery were replaced by fact-based guidelines and surgery was no longer the automatic answer to a child's recurring ear infections. The same evolution takes place in other medical specialties, whether heart surgery or tonsillectomy. Guidelines for these medical protocols are developed by research and disseminated by professional organizations, and they impact how doctors look at and care for patients with these conditions. If a doctor keeps up with his or her specialty, a judgment call can be made with enough evidence to support the decision.

Throughout my years as a physician, I was making fact-based judgments and I prided myself on keeping up with my field and trying to give the best of care. That doesn't mean I was perfect, but I felt secure in most of my decisions and comfortable in how I conducted my practice. On the few occasions when I had to convince parents that surgery was not the best option for their child, I remember how hard it was to dispel their preconceived notions about the procedure, especially if they had the support of another physician or knew other children who had been successfully treated by surgery. Of course parents' intentions were good, but often they were quite insistent in their opinions. I had to explain how much easier it would have been for me to just go ahead and agree to tube insertion, as some doctors did, than to argue my case with them and risk losing a patient. My point is that when an individual's mind is made up about something, it is frequently a struggle to reconcile that conclusion with the facts.

It didn't occur to me that I was guilty of ignoring the facts when it came to other issues. I had been careful to use facts and the latest research in my practice. So it came as rather a surprise to me when I confronted facts about the death penalty that ran counter to the beliefs I had held for most of my life. I couldn't just dismiss them. I admit that I tried to find facts that would support my basic views. I found some, but they were easily refuted. Either data were missing or misstated to reach the desired conclusion or there was a lot of emotional argument that had no real foundation. As I read more, I realized the enormity of the consequence of this policy. We were literally killing people based on false assumptions. Once I recognized and admitted this, I had to let go of my old opinions and revamp my thinking on the issue.

Whatever our belief systems, we are totally convinced that they are correct and based on factual evidence. We wouldn't believe something if we thought it was untrue, so we continue to defend conclusions regardless of their basis. Most of us, and I was guilty of this, don't take the time to examine our views. It seems so simple, yet it is not. The issues get muddied over time and our views get clouded by our unacknowledged prejudices.

Realizing how sorely lacking in fact my belief about the death penalty had been was like a punch in the stomach. It wasn't easy to acknowledge that the foundation for my opinion had been so erroneous. The more I read, the more I realized how much like quicksand it was—once you accept false premises, they suck you in to arrive at the desired conclusion. I was fascinated with the subject not only because of the inherent life-and-death issues but also because of how I had subscribed to endorsing the policy. The subject of course brings up issues of injustice and inequality, also topics I had been wrestling with. I became so involved in the subject that I decided to do my master's thesis on it. I attacked the problem like a child in a toy store, reading everything and absorbing as much as I could. While my illness intervened from time to time, I had found my mission and would not be deterred.

I realize that although my evolution felt like a smooth and natural transition for me, it was not so easy for those around me. This wasn't the old Robbie that they knew. My newfound belief system bucked the mainstream of my own social circle. Prior to my own change in view, I hadn't known many people who were against the death penalty, or at least many who had been willing to admit it. Mine was a radical change that even those closest to me found it difficult to absorb. Not only was I adamant about my new view, I was anxious to share it with anyone who would listen. I had to go against the grain of family and friends who, sometimes half-jokingly, at least in the beginning, attributed my transformation to the drugs I was taking for my illness.

While in the master's program, I often tested out my new ideas, sometimes to clarify them for myself, other times to test the reaction of others. Since some of my research findings were contradictory of my own personal views, I had to struggle with reconciling them, particularly as they related to my thesis on capital punishment. But I had been willing to let fact win the battle and had changed my views accordingly. Could I expect that from others?

During this period, I would occasionally meet friends and colleagues on the golf course. Many of the friendships I had cultivated over my lifetime were cordial if not close and the golf course has always been an environment conducive to easy conversation. That was one of the things that attracted me to the game when I first started playing more than a dozen years ago. Besides catching up on the news of family and friends, we would often discuss politics and current issues. Of course my friends had been through all the ups and downs of my illness and career change and they were genuinely glad that I had found a new vocation; however, most hardly agreed with my mission statement.

Some of my friends were surprised at my new choice of study. It was hard for them to imagine themselves doing something similar. Nevertheless, most were quite supportive even if they took issue with my new views and didn't quite understand the change. I could usually count on a lively discussion. The golf course was a place where I could test some of my new ideas among friends, even if they disagreed with me.

I occasionally brought up the topic of capital punishment as it was a prime concern for me. Knowing my new student status, some would humor me and go along with the discussion. Others were genuinely interested in the debate. It was interesting being among professionals who had no real knowledge about the subject that I was now studying but were never short on opinions about it. As the "student" in the group, I was often given the "junior" status. It wasn't until later, when they realized how serious I was about my mission, that they began to treat the subject less frivolously. Sometimes I would get questions, usually related to something in the news, and a discussion would follow.

More often I was met with jabs like, "Oh, here he goes again—what gem are you going to enthrall us with today?" It was good-natured for the most part, and I think there often was a sincere curiosity about what it was like to go back to school after the passage of all those years. Some were eager to engage in conversation, much like a parent who enters into intellectual sparring with their college-student child; it is perceived of as fun and endearing, albeit a bit patronizing. Some just liked to jaw about anything. They enjoyed the camaraderie, whether on a golf course or in a restaurant. Others perhaps enjoyed an opportunity to reinforce their old views and prove to themselves how misguided "liberal" education really is.

Most of my friends were roughly my age and most were native Southerners. No matter what their education and current profession, their opinions had also been shaped by their experiences in the South of the 1960s and 1970s. Of course I understood all of this. It was only recently that I had made my own change. While my own changes had evolved over a much longer period, on the surface that was not apparent, especially to people who were not familiar with my more recent attempts to reach out to minority communities. It wasn't something I had talked about a lot in the past, and my own efforts to treat people more equally was done quietly without thought of or need for recognition. I was barely conscious of this change in myself, so how could others have known?

Most of what we hear in defense of capital punishment is that it deters crime. So as I set about my research, I read many of the studies on this point. Mind you, this was before I had made the u-turn in my thinking. I was merely trying to be diligent in my work and look at both sides of this particular argument. What I found was that there were no credible studies that linked reduced crime with an increase application of the death penalty. In fact, just the opposite seemed to be true—states that used capital punishment had more murders. That didn't seem logical, so I read further. In study after study across time and geography, the death penalty had no discernible effect on the homicide rate. The only studies that demonstrated a positive correlation were shown to be hopelessly flawed. I was dumbfounded. Although I was not at this point feeling particularly positive about capital punishment on moral grounds, I had been quite firm in my belief that the policy was a deterrent. Now I had to reassess my thinking. Was there any other choice? Could I simply ignore the facts? Not anymore.

On one particular spring day, I was out on the greens with my friend Joe, a retired accountant whom I considered rational and open-minded. I have known Joe for at least ten years. I had just been reading about the argument that capital punishment acts as a deterrent to crime, which it does not, and I related this fact to Joe. I was fascinated with what I found and thought for sure he would be, too. But Joe didn't quite believe that I had the facts right.

"You know you can derive many conclusions of a different nature from a study depending on your perspective. I think you may be reading liberal propaganda. What are they feeding you at BSC?" he asked jokingly. "I'm sure there are other studies that prove just the opposite. This just seems like another example of the liberals trying to push an agenda."

I assured him that this was not the case, that I had carefully combed the library, and there was just nothing that really supported the premise and plenty that proved the opposite.

"Well, as far as I'm concerned, we should have more executions," he replied. "I have never heard of any executed killer ever killing again. And it also serves as an example to others as to what will happen if you kill someone. In other words, it serves as a deterrent."

I agreed that it seemed like that should be the case but the data didn't support it. I explained that there are just no credible data that show the death penalty to be a deterrent. I cited Alabama as an example of how we had a high murder rate and more people on death row per capita than most other states.

"How do you explain that discrepancy?" I asked him.

"What about the lesson it provides?" Joe asked. "Statistics can't really measure that. The ultimate punishment is a scary thought. When people know that they will be punished for killing someone, of course they will be restrained by it. It's just that we can't measure this type of thing."

He had avoided my question, but I was getting better at defending my arguments. Since I had recently read so much and because I had actually had concurred with Joe's position not that long ago, it was easier for me to respond.

"You're right," I told him. "You can't prove a negative—about anything. I'm not fat because I don't eat fried foods. Can you prove that? Should we say that if fat people just stop eating fried foods they will lose weight and be thin?"

That argument stopped him, momentarily at least. But he still would not concede the point. The subject changed and we played a few more holes. Then I had another thought.

"What about some guy who's consumed with rage about something his wife has done? He pulls out his gun or knife and in a fit of anger, kills her. Do you think he has considered what state he's living in and whether or not there's a death penalty in place before he acts?"

"Probably not," Joe conceded, "but that's not very common and those aren't the people on death row."

"True," I told him. "Many of the people who commit that sort of crime get by with a lesser sentence. So do you think if the death penalty applied to them, they would stop in their tracks?" I didn't want to shift the argument by bringing up the racial disparity.

"Maybe," he said. I doubted his sincerity on this one, but I let it go.

"And a large portion of murders are committed under the influence of drugs or alcohol," I added. "Do you think someone who is drunk and/or high on drugs thinks about the law?"

"No, they probably don't even remember much of what they do," Joe replied.

"Exactly. So why should they get the death penalty?" I continued.

"Because people have to be held accountable for what they do," Joe said.

"Ah, but those are two different things. I'm not advocating no punishment for someone who murders. But the death penalty doesn't prevent the crime."

"Sure it does," he told me. "Dead is dead. Once a murderer is dead, he can't kill again," he argued.

"Well, that's true," I said, "but it's also true that if he's locked up he can't kill again, either. And isn't the result then the same? Why do we have to kill him?"

"Because it shows that we're serious about crime and that we don't take murder lightly," he replied with an edge of exasperation bordering on anger.

Joe couldn't buy the argument that the end result of death versus life imprisonment is the same. To him, capital punishment acted as an object lesson—right out there in the open for all to see what would happen should they dare to defy our laws—which brought us right back to the same place in proving the negative. It also circumvents any other rational arguments. If the death penalty really served as an object lesson, we'd have no more murders. And why are we more serious about some murders than others? Not every murderer gets a death sentence. But I knew that these were not questions that Joe could have answered. His argument was really an emotional one and he was starting to get emotional about it. There was no point in trying to push him further now. I understood that he felt more secure thinking that the death penalty was a safeguard because he believed it would deter people from harming others. No information I could give him was going to loosen up that belief for it was based on fear and the 'law and order' mentality that addressed it. I respected his view, though I no longer could agree with it. At least one of us felt consoled by the way the law operated.

I stand as an outsider in my new views and I can understand the discomfort my perspective brings to others. I can easily recall the distaste I had for the Northern invaders who came to force the issue of integration in the South. While I'm not forcing anyone, my fervor forces others to notice, as I am not shy about voicing my concerns. While I try to temper my views knowing that people don't like to be challenged, I am aware that if people become more knowledgeable about the facts, some will change their views. But I am sympathetic to those who still disagree; it wasn't that long ago that I was one of them and I was no more open to changing that view then than they are now.

Certainly my family continued to be supportive, even if they didn't agree with my new position. Some family members and friends were interested in the information and the logic behind my change of heart. They wanted to know more and I was always glad to share what I knew. This didn't necessarily change anyone's opinion; it merely helped people understand me better. They rightly perceived it as a reformation of my whole self and my shift on the death penalty as just one facet of the changes in my whole being.

There were inevitably some acquaintances who hadn't known my previous views. Now that I was less likely to keep my opinions and views to myself when the subject came up, I was quickly labeled a "liberal." Not that the label means anything, but in the South, it's a pejorative. On the other hand, there were some who said things like, "You are the first liberal that I really like!" or, "You know, you are a liberal, but a really nice guy." While I was flattered by their willingness to accept me in spite of my views and glad to know I had been heard, it changed nothing.

It's only in the last eight to nine years that I have begun this journey to seek truths about myself. The culture in which I grew up and thrived supported bigoted and false facts. If these false claims had no negative impact, if they had caused no harm, I could just ignore them and move on. But they do cause damage. They breed hatred and keep us separated from our fellow humans. Although the term "truthiness" wasn't in use in the culture in the South or elsewhere until recently, the concept was alive and well during my childhood and much beyond. It is a concept that I had to acknowledge late in life and hope that others will do the same.

Under the new sphere of principles by which I now attempt to live, I look back and feel embarrassment, and shame—ashamed of myself because my views were not consistent with the message of Jesus Christ, his moral law, and the Christian ethic. Therefore they were sinful. I say this about myself, not in judgment of others' attitudes or behaviors but as a facet of my own past that I have come to terms with. We all must develop and stand on our own principles. The ideal for everyone is "to love your neighbor as yourself." Believers will understand this as the "second greatest Commandment" issued by God through Jesus Christ in his teachings; nonbelievers may understand it as a version of the "Golden Rule." In either case, all religions embody the principle somewhere in their precepts; it is a moral and ethical stand that feels intuitive, regardless of belief system. We need to promote and respect our differences, and that includes differences in opinion.

I understand there are many who have views opposite mine on the issue of capital punishment, and they feel strongly about their opinions. Some may even feel they are sound in their reasoning and logic. Their opinions are no less important than mine. Where we differ, however, is in the facts upon which we have based our decision and the moral framework within which we feel bound.

While not one of my friends or family members rejected me based on my opposition to the death penalty, I did not always find myself in that zone of comfort that exists among those who hold the same views and values and nod knowingly in assent at each others' commentary. To my knowledge, I did not lose friends over my change but there may well have been some who avoided further contact and friendship because of the liberal label I now wore. That kind of thing happens and may be more prevalent in the South. Such things are not "within my sphere of influence."

I had spent most of my life trying hard to fit in and be accepted in the professional class to which I now belonged, so when moments of discomfort occurred, they were noticeable to me. That is not to say there were many of these. In the past, for the most part, I accepted the views learned in my family and peer group and had not seriously questioned my own ingrained attitudes until my illness. But I was no longer the same person. I was no longer a prisoner of my old need to be accepted by everyone nor was I threatened by someone who disagreed with me. Getting older has its benefits. Whether this freedom is because of age and maturity or the comfort I feel from the covenants that God provides for those who believe in him, or some combination, I can't know. I do know that I feel good walking down a path lit by the true light. I feel both empowered and humbled in my pursuit of this mission.

It's not that over the years I never had any disagreements with friends or that everyone in my social circle was always in perfect accord. Surely that's not the case. I have had ample, sometimes heated discussions about social issues including abortion, welfare, poverty, health care, etc. But the death penalty in Alabama is an issue that is larger than life; it has a political life of its own, much the way race did fifty years ago.

Change comes slowly, whether personal or political. And as was the case during the civil rights era, it takes time for the law and public opinion to mesh, and these kinds of big changes are never without dissension and struggle. Even when there is a groundswell of public opinion, people don't suddenly give up beliefs that they have held for years. I can attest to the slow pace of my own change before I was "born anew" and God's will became my own. It is a lifelong pursuit; nevertheless it is my intention.

I also recognize that my change was triggered by events and circumstances that are not necessarily shared by the average person. And, let's make no mistake about it: there is no groundswell of public opinion in support of abolition of the death penalty. There are small outcries that are getting louder, but they are mostly lost in the divisive politics of our time on national and state levels. Some make headlines for a short time, generally on a local level, and then they die a slightly slower death than their subject.

8

STACKED AGAINST BLACKS

In August 2006, an Alabama death row inmate lost his appeal for a stay of his execution. There were no big headlines. To most people, Darrell Grayson was at best a number, an overdue expiration date. For all but a small handful of people, whether Grayson was to live or die was of no consequence. Most are not interested in his story or in looking at what it says about us as a society and a culture that sanctions killing when it suits us. Here in Alabama, there is widespread support for the death penalty, although it does seem to be changing a little. Though people don't talk about the death penalty in racial terms, race is hard to ignore it as an overriding issue. No surprise, then, that Grayson was a black man. Race is the subtext of the crime of capital punishment.

What may come as a surprise is that the strongest support for abolition of the death penalty comes from the black communities where poverty and race merge. It is also in these more rural, western parts of the state that the official crime rate is somewhat higher than the rest of the state. Although blacks are more frequent victims of crime, they support abolishing the death penalty in far greater numbers than their white counterparts. They know firsthand the inequities of the criminal justice system and they understand that blacks are much more likely to receive harsher sentences, including the death penalty. It seems quite reasonable that the people who would most oppose the policy are those who are most likely to be affected by it. Blacks who oppose capital punishment don't need statistics to tell them how unfair the system can be, although one look at the official statistics shows that capital punishment is one of many societal injustices involving racial bias.

Support for the death penalty is strongest in the more conservative, white middle-class and wealthier segments of the population. Though Alabama is one of the poorest states in the nation, plenty of people are wealthy and, as is the case in most places, they tend to hold the most political power.

When I read the news story about Darrell Grayson, I was reminded of conversations I've had over the years with death penalty supporters. They don't see capital punishment as a racial issue; to them, race doesn't really enter into it. To them, it's about personal safety: Kill "them" so they can't kill again. The odds of being killed in an auto accident in Alabama are three times higher than the odds of being murdered, yet people continue to drive their cars without fear and for the most part without demanding safer vehicles.[30] With a few notable exceptions, there is little outcry for the imposition of the death penalty for people who kill someone while driving drunk. Yet drunk driving is surely a killer that knows no bounds and affects thousands of innocent people. Being killed by an automobile and being killed by a "low-life criminal" both have the same result. Why then do we perceive the latter as an imminent threat and the former as unlikely even though the reverse is true?

Logic is not part of the death penalty conversation because the death penalty isn't logical. Capital punishment is an emotional response with historical baggage. The topic is fraught with fear and a wish for control over one's destiny. It also appeals to our baser human instincts to exact vengeance on those whom we judge to have harmed us or whom we fear have the potential to do so. We pass judgment on the criminal, casting him as evil, as subhuman, as one society should exterminate so the rest of us can have peace of mind and feel safer. This is an illusion that creates a myth about personal safety. Criminals are but reminders of the imperfect world we live in and our own vulnerability and lack of control over our lives. The reality is that we live in an imperfect world among imperfect fellow humans, and we can never have perfect safety.

As for peace of mind, that particular serenity is in God's hands and, although the door is open to all, is reserved for believers. As humans, we are imperfect beings: we err, we seek forgiveness. We don't live perfect lives except perhaps as John Wesley believed, through "purity of heart." Though we may strive for perfection, we can never achieve it, for only God is perfect. We have little control over when we are born and how we will die.

Darrell Grayson's case shines a light on some of the reasons why rethinking the policy of capital punishment is needed. Grayson lost his last appeals and was executed in 2007. He had been denied the right to submit to DNA testing, which might have proved him innocent. Alabama Governor Bob Riley refused to issue a reprieve or intervene in any way, saying that "no new evidence has come to light that would warrant a reprieve or a commutation." If we actually took the time to scrutinize the other 201 inmates still on death row in Alabama,[31] we would find similar problems, all of which point out how misguided such a policy really is.

I have traveled in many different social circles during my life. Though I grew up in a white enclave, my family social status was only a notch above that of the blacks whose neighborhood bordered my own. Over the years I have come to know many of the minority families who were part of the Alabama Ear Institute outreach programs. As I became more aware of the disparities and the problems inherent in being a minority, I became more sensitive to racial bias and racial issues. And of course having a child of mixed race, who was on occasion the object of racial slurs, made me more sensitive to the issue. As I was increasingly aware of the problem, I earnestly tried to observe racial divides and help dispel stereotypes.

We live with many stereotypes. Mostly we don't notice them. Often we at least smile at a joke directed against some "other" group, thankful that we are not the ones being derided this time. I am often in groups where racially bigoted remarks and jokes are commonplace. Perhaps this is true of all social groups and it has always been the case. The object of the prejudice is irrelevant: it could be blacks, Hispanics, Chinese, Muslims, Jews, or any number of other ethnic minority or religious groups. It sometimes extends to people who are gay, obese, or handicapped or otherwise different. Some comedians make their careers on this type of demeaning humor, and I admit that I used to enjoy it. Conversations in which this kind of banter takes place no longer make me laugh. More often I am chagrined and sometimes even get angry.

"Well, it's just a joke," many will say. "Can't you take a joke?" Pose that question to the butt of the joke and you will not find the same sense of humor. It's not that I am above it all. I certainly have made mistakes and at one time willingly participated in such dialogues. I thought nothing of them at the time. My subsequent experience and perhaps maturation has left me with a desire to live in a way that would please God, and even abstract diminution of any of his "children" is an affront to all he represents and those represented by him. I have become sensitive in absentia because I have developed a strong feeling of empathy for those who can't always defend themselves. Facing mortality also shapes your sense of time. In my case, I have used that time to give thought to subjects that had eluded me in the past. We all need to spend more time in contemplation of who we are and what we value and how we represent ourselves to others.

We assume all inmates are guilty of some heinous crime, that they are bad people, that they are irredeemable, that they are not like us, that they are not deserving of humane treatment. I can attest from personal experience visiting prisoners who have been convicted of terrible crimes that this is simply not true. We are all sinners—it's just a matter of degree. In our own criminal justice system, the type of crime committed, the skin colors of both perpetrator and victim, and the perpetrator's socioeconomic class determine how the accused is treated from the minute of apprehension to the announcement of the verdict.

It is not condoning crime to insist that justice should be meted out equally. Our system is far from ideal and has a definite racial and economic bias. The person who steals one hundred dollars from a grocery store cash register is likely to pay a much higher price for the crime than the person who embezzles one million dollars.

Our prejudices automatically put a black face on the robber and a white face on the corporate embezzler. The robber is a lot more likely to be caught and convicted than the embezzler. Yet corporate crime is both more insidious and more pervasive. When tobacco companies colluded to addict people to their products, thousands of people died who might otherwise have lived much longer and healthier lives. Yet no tobacco company executives have received the death penalty or a life sentence or even gone to jail. Monetary damages have recently been overturned, once again making the efforts of the companies and those who run them "priceless."

We don't acknowledge that the punishment for crimes is rarely equivalent. The poor are far more likely than the well-off to be arrested if picked up, to be convicted if charged, and to receive prison time if convicted.[32] This disconnect in how we differentiate among criminals is called recruitment.[33] We differ in how we recruit murderers. Those from higher socioeconomic groups are called fraudulent, although they manipulated their defective and sometimes deadly products with all the cunning and secrecy of a premeditated murderer. The numbers who have suffered serious illnesses and/or death by the hand of this type of killer are staggering in proportion to the victims of what we think of as the common murderer. Yet we don't call for the death of the white-collar killers. Only common murderers are considered expendable; we encode the laws to make the distinctions, lending an air of legitimacy to our fear and disdain for those who fall into the wrong category.

The population of Alabama in 2006 was 26.3 percent black and 71.2 percent white.[34] Yet when I first visited a maximum-security state prison in August 2006, even though intellectually I already knew that incarceration rates were racially skewed, it still startled me how many more black faces I saw than white ones. But numbers by themselves don't tell the story.

The West Jefferson Correctional Facility is located in a remote area of the county in which I live and is "home" to roughly sixteen hundred inmates, including twenty-five on death row. I thought that if I was going to advocate for abolition of capital punishment, I should know just who I was defending. Having read so much of John Wesley in recent years, I felt inspired to help bring the message of Jesus Christ to those in prison, and many of these inmates were products of an unjust system. Though I am neither saint nor apostle, my acceptance of Christ and renunciation of my past has contributed to my sense of mission. As the Apostle Paul said: "I am grateful to Christ Jesus our Lord, who has strengthened me, because he judged me faithful and appointed me to his service . . . The saying is sure and worthy of full acceptance, that Christ Jesus came into the world to save sinners—of whom I am the foremost" (1 Timothy 12–15).

It was another awakening when I met several inmates who also had grown up in my hometown and the adjacent community, both now suburbs of Mobile, where the color lines have slowly followed the white flight away from the city. Of course I hadn't known any of these men. I had long ago left that neighborhood and during the time that I lived there, the lines of demarcation were clearly drawn. Even after integration in housing was accepted, those who followed in the neighborhood were not always aware of how the color lines simply moved.

I had decided to get involved in the prison ministry as part of my mission to contribute to righting the wrongs of capital punishment and to minister to those I felt were victims of injustice and/or unfortunate circumstances. "For I was thirsty and you gave me something to drink, I was a stranger and you welcomed me. I was naked and you gave me clothing, I was sick and you took care of me, I was in prison and you visited me," Jesus said (Matthew 25: 35–37). The strong basis of hometown commonality served as a building block for developing relationships with some of the inmates. I, too, felt at home! My familiarity with the prison population and the lens through which I viewed their circumstances because of own experiences and my study and research on capital punishment added to my identification with both the inmates and the environment. In a strange way, I had come full circle to the place I was meant to be and to serve. God's will? I think so. It certainly felt right.

I wondered after my exposure to the inmate population at this prison whether the racial mix was typical of that in other prisons in the state. So I checked the most recent data.

The numbers tell the story. For the period between October 1, 2006, and September 30, 2007, a total of 29,235 inmates passed through the Alabama corrections system. Of these, 17,354 (59.4 percent) were classified as African Americans, 44 were either "unknown" or classified as Asian or American Indian," and 11,837 (40.3 percent) were classified as white. Alabama does not use Hispanic as a separate category so there is no way of knowing how this skews the numbers, but it is clear that minority populations are incarcerated at much higher rates than whites.[35]

We should also note that these numbers represent only those in the state system. The numbers for federal prison facilities are not broken down by both race and by state, but the national numbers are only somewhat less disproportionate than the state numbers. We don't know if the figures for the federal facilities in Alabama would be closer to the national average or closer to the state numbers. In either case, they are very much disproportionate to the population; nationally, blacks represent just over 12 percent of the population.[36]

TOTAL INMATES BY RACE[37]

U.S. FEDERAL FACILITIES AS OF APRIL 2008:

White	114,657	(57.04 %)
Black	79,464	(39.5 %)
Native American	3,571	(1.8 %)
Asian	3,425	(1.7 %)

Further, the data from the Alabama Department of Corrections (see Appendix A) also shows a gross racial disproportion in sentencing. In fact, the longer the sentence, the more disproportionately distributed is the race of the inmates who have received the sentence. For some sentences, the ratio of black to white inmate is two to one or higher.

As of August 2007 half of all inmates executed in Alabama after 1976 have been blacks, which is almost double the proportion of blacks in the state population. If we look at the inmates currently on death row, it is equally startling: as of the end of May 2008, in Alabama, there were ninety-seven black inmates and 106 white inmates. There are another two inmates who are classified as "other," so they are minorities as well. Minorities don't account for almost 50 percent of the violent crime in the state. Bear in mind, blacks are only a little more than one-quarter of the state's population.

Another buried statistic is perhaps even more disturbing: 80 percent of those on death row in Alabama were convicted of murdering someone who is white even though more than 65 percent of the annual murders in the state involve black victims.[38] Furthermore, thirty-two of the thirty-eight people (84 percent) who have been executed in Alabama since 1976 were convicted of killing white people.[39] Surely if blacks were murdering whites in these proportions, we'd have a racial revolution on our hands. But the numbers show us why there is no such problem. Only 6 percent of the murders in the state were committed by black defendants whose victims were white. So how could it be that over 60 percent of the black inmates on death row involved a white victim? In more than half of the capital cases in this period (1976–2001), the jury was either all white or included one black juror even though the counties in which these cases were heard were 33 to 47 percent black.[40]

Unfortunately, this is not an anomaly; it is equally true on a national scale. Between 1976 and 1999, 51 to 56 percent of murder and non-homicide victims were white; but whites were the victims of 81 percent of the murders for which the defendant was executed in roughly the same years (1976–2002).[41]

DEFENDANTS EXECUTED IN THE U.S. SINCE 1976[42]

RACE	DEFENDANTS	% OF TOTAL
Black	353	34.0%
Hispanic	69	6.0%
White	595	57.1%
Other	24	2.3%

RACE OF VICTIMS* SINCE 1976[43]

RACE	VICTIMS	% OF TOTAL
Black	219	14%
Hispanic	72	4%
White	1234	80%
Other	32	109%

PERSONS EXECUTED FOR INTERRACIAL MURDERS IN THE U.S. SINCE 1976[44]

White Defendant / Black Victim	14
Black Defendant / White Victim	208

CURRENT U.S. DEATH ROW POPULATION[45]

RACE	INMATES	% OF TOTAL
Black	1,411	41.9%
Hispanic	354	10.5%
White	1,527	45.3%
Other	78	2.3%

The preceeding figures are bolstered by the statement issued in February 1990 called "Death Penalty Sentencing":

> In 82 percent of the studies [reviewed], race of the victim was found to influence the likelihood of being charged with capital murder or receiving the death penalty, i.e., those who murdered whites were found more likely to be sentenced to death than those who murdered blacks.

DARRELL GRAYSON IS BUT the latest victim of the injustice of our criminal system in Alabama. In 2007 in addition to Grayson, Alabama executed two other men. Grayson's case is quite typical of the statistics. In all three the defendant was black and the victim white. Race is certainly an issue, not just in Grayson's case, but his case will amply illustrate the problem.

Grayson was arrested and later convicted of murdering an elderly woman in 1980. He was given a life sentence and then the death penalty two years later. At the time of his arrest, Grayson was nineteen years old. He had no history of criminal activity—no accusations, no juvenile record, nothing; he had never been in trouble with the law before. This is not to say that he was living a typical middle-class life with few problems. His family was poor, he had dropped out of school at the age of fifteen, and he already had a significant alcohol and drug problem. While all of these variables have a high correlation with criminal activity, in and of themselves, we can't conclude that every person who shares these characteristics is a criminal or a potential criminal. Nor would Grayson's background absolve him from guilt if he were guilty.

When Grayson was arrested, the police who interrogated him and his co-defendant assumed his guilt. They told Grayson that his co-defendant had confessed that it was the two of them who had committed the rape/murder. Grayson at last agreed to this explanation since he had no recollection of the events of that fateful evening; he had been drinking and remembered nothing. Though he didn't think he could have done something so terrible, he did not remember it, so he naively assumed that it was possible. We all know that lots of things are possible. But isn't the criminal system supposed to be designed to protect the innocent? Isn't that what the American system of justice says—you are innocent until proved guilty beyond a reasonable doubt? Possible is not the same as beyond a reasonable doubt. Yet Grayson was convicted by an all-white jury purely on the basis of what was possible.

Like others who do not have the means to defend themselves, Grayson was given a court-appointed attorney. According to Alabama law at the time of Grayson's prosecution, court-appointed attorneys, even for cases in which the death penalty may be imposed, were permitted a fee not greater than one thousand dollars. Even twenty years ago, that sum was inadequate for defense of a petty crime, much less a murder case.

The expertise and competence of a defendant's representation is a telling measure of determining whether a defendant will receive the death penalty or be acquitted. U.S. Supreme Court Justice Ruth Bader Ginsburg said, "people who are well represented at trial do not get the death penalty . . . I have yet to see a death case among the dozens coming to the Supreme Court on eve-of-execution stay applications in which the defendant was well represented at trial."[46]

Grayson's appointed attorney asked his family for more money, which they didn't have; the attorney later stated that if this had been a civil case, he would have been sued for malpractice. He could safely say that since he surely knew that Grayson did not have the financial means to sue him in any court, criminal or civil. Along these lines, it's interesting to note the daunting hurdles to filing a malpractice suit against an attorney in a criminal case. In many states, the defendant first has to show exoneration in order to prove damages. This is a catch-22: exoneration is the result the criminal was seeking through the same attorney who lost the case; had the defendant been exonerated, there would be no need to sue. We also need to keep in mind that almost all capital defendants are indigents. And those few who have resources are not dependent on court-appointed attorneys.[47]

That Grayson's attorney was incompetent and no other legal assistance was provided were not considered mitigating factors and Grayson was convicted of capital murder. After many years of legal limbo, he got some additional legal help. His subsequent request to review DNA evidence, which might have exonerated him, was denied. Once the wheels of justice start turning, it is very difficult to change their direction. People in positions of power do not like to be called to the carpet. While they play out their political and social power scrimmages, real people are crushed. People like Darrell Grayson spend years living with the knowledge of their death sentence, knowing their day will come, knowing they have no control over their lives, and that nothing they can do will change that. Grayson was executed on July 26, 2007, after spending twenty-five years on death row. Society never learned whether he was guilty or innocent.

OFTEN, THE FACE ON the problem is black and that of the power structure is white; there is no big backlash. Add large voting blocs who believe that state-sanctioned killing is justified and it's easy to see why there is no up-roar. This is not to elicit sympathy for Grayson so much as to point out the disparity in how we deal with crime, particularly capital crime. While each case is unique, when taken as a whole, it is hard to avoid the conclusion that race is a contributing factor. By comparing Grayson to another case, the disparity becomes more obvious.

More than thirty years after the bombing of the Sixteenth Street Baptist Church in Birmingham in which four young girls were killed and more than twenty others seriously injured, some of the responsible parties were finally brought to justice. This high-profile case is instructive because it says as much about race relations and the fight for civil rights in the South in the 1960s as it does about capital punishment today. It also points to the progress we've made, though sometimes it's hard to call it that, and the struggle that remains before we can say there really is equality.

The bombing, which took place at the height of the civil rights movement in 1963, rocked the local community and sent tremors over the national news wires. Even hard-line segregationists had trouble rationalizing the murder of children inside their own house of worship. A month after the event, Robert Chambliss, a member of the KKK, was arrested and charged with the bombing. However, the evidence wasn't sufficient, at least as it was presented at the time, and the jury freed him on the murder charge. He was found guilty of possession of dynamite, paid a $100 fine, and received a six-month sentence, which was suspended.

It wasn't until Alabama elected Bill Baxley attorney general in 1971 that things started to turn around. Baxley investigated charges that the FBI had withheld evidence in the case. Though he wasn't able to obtain all the data, he was successful in reopening the case and prosecuting Chambliss. Chambliss was convicted in 1977 by an all-white jury and was given a life sentence. More recently, two other guilty parties in the case were finally rounded up and also convicted: Thomas Blanton and Bobby Frank Cherry. They too were sentenced to life without parole in 2001 and 2002, respectively.

Yes, the wheels of justice can be awfully slow, so shouldn't we be glad that eventually they turn in the right direction? I'd give a qualified yes to answer that question. But the fact remains that no one has ever clamored for imposing the death penalty on these convicted murderers. Let's be clear: I am opposed to death sentences for these men. But why is it okay, in the words of many supporters of the death penalty, to "waste taxpayer money on life imprisonment" for the Blantons and the Cherrys in our system, but not for the Graysons?

We need to distinguish between justice and revenge. Interestingly, the families of the 1963 bombing victims did not seem to be interested in revenge. They had already learned to forgive those who were responsible for killing their loved ones. They were satisfied that the perpetrators had been caught and brought to justice, even though it took forty years. To them, justice meant that the guilty parties were held accountable. A public trial that exposed and convicted them and imposed lifetime jail sentences was enough to give them closure.

Justice is a legal term that defines fairness and punishment for noncompliance of the law; there is no implication of revenge in the term. Revenge is emotional payback; it is a throwback to times of anarchy and lawlessness. We need to keep these two concepts separate because when they merge, it means the legal system is being controlled by instinct and mob rule rather than reason and even-handedness. Revenge is not and should not be what we mean by justice in a democratic institution ruled by law.

By the time the government successfully prosecuted Blanton and Cherry, there was no longer much sympathy for the violent racists of the 1960s; most people, even those unrelated to the victims, were glad that the KKK bombers finally were brought to justice. But it is instructive to point out that many of those who were satisfied with the sentencing of Chambliss, Blanton, and Cherry would be up in arms if Grayson had been given a similar life sentence. And this does not even factor in any of the doubt surrounding Grayson's guilt, which is much shakier than that of either Blanton or Cherry.

9

The Three R's—Redemption, Retribution, and Revenge

Karla Faye Tucker, the first female executed by the state of Texas since the Civil War, had a redemption as complete as her crime was gruesome. Despite pleas for her sentence to be commuted, she died with needles in her arms on a gurney in a Texas facility in 1998. Her case shows how profoundly politics affects capital punishment and how our deeply seated beliefs are played out in the political arena.

Even when someone is guilty of a heinous crime, God forgives them if they accept Christ and repent. Tucker spent fourteen years on death row and in that time she changed. I can't vouch for the authenticity of anyone's change other than my own, but from her statements, her interviews, and her writings, it seems clear that she was no longer the drug-mired woman of her past. If we don't believe we are capable of change, then we are all prisoners of our past sins, fated to live them out without forgiveness and redemption. Sin doesn't come in sizes. We sin, we ask God for forgiveness, and we take measures for redemption.

Tucker had become "fully rehabilitated [and] posed no future threat to society" her attorneys wrote in their petition to the court to request a clemency hearing. She had become "a socially safe and faith-conscious citizen." Tucker herself had appealed to the clemency board of the state and to then-Governor George W. Bush. She wrote, in part: "I have purposed to do right for the last fourteen years, not because I am in prison, but because my God demands this of me . . . I know right from wrong and I must do right . . . If you commute my sentence to life, I will continue for the rest of my life in this earth to reach out to others to make a positive difference in their lives."

Though some accused her of being an opportunist and dishonest in her conversion, evangelist Pat Robertson believed her redemption was real and spent five years trying to get her sentence commuted. In her defense he said: "I am one who has supported the death penalty for hardened criminals. But I do think that any justice system that is worthy of the name must have room for mercy . . . In the case of Karla Faye Tucker, she is not the same person who committed those heinous ax murders . . . She is totally transformed, and I think to execute her is more an act of vengeance than it is appropriate justice."

Despite appeals from Pat Robertson, the Pope, Newt Gingrich, and others from all sides of the political spectrum, Governor Bush coolly rejected the pleas. A year after her execution, Tucker Carlson interviewed Bush for *Talk Magazine*. Bush was then running for the White House. Given the reputation of the state of Texas as the "death state," Carlson asked Bush if he met with any of those who were requesting clemency for Tucker:

> Bush whips around and stares at me. "No, I didn't meet with any of them," he snaps, as though I've just asked the dumbest, most offensive question ever posed. "I didn't meet with Larry King either when he came down for it. I watched his interview with Tucker, though. He asked her real difficult questions like, 'What would you say to Governor Bush?'" "What was her answer?" I wonder. "'Please,'" Bush whimpers, his lips pursed in mock desperation, "'don't kill me.'" I must look shocked—ridiculing the pleas of a condemned prisoner who has since been executed seems odd and cruel—because he immediately stops smirking.[48]

Many were dismayed by Bush's response. Even conservative Republican Gary Bauer said: "I think it is nothing short of unbelievable that the governor of a major state running for president thought it was acceptable to mock a woman he decided to put to death." Bush denied that he had intended to make light of the issue.

Bush was the only one who legally could have influenced Tucker's sentence. Governors have the option of granting clemency to convicted criminals in their state. Clemency does not forgive the crime; it merely lifts some of the sanctions, not necessarily the whole punishment. Historically, clemency was designed to be an act of mercy. It is not widely used with the notable exception of Illinois Governor George Ryan who in 2003 granted clemency to all 167 inmates on death row when that state's handling of capital cases was shown to be utterly flawed after several condemned persons were subsequently proved innocent.

We have grown comfortable with the idea of social banishment and state-sanctioned killing. But the attitude of "burn 'em till their eyeballs pop out" and "lock 'em up and throw away the key" exemplifies a mean-spiritedness that I find both horrifying and sad. We forget that inmates are humans, and we remove some of our own dignity as we strip inmates of theirs. What happened to forgiveness and redemption in this process? Hearts that are full of hatred can't forgive; hatred is all-consuming. Accepting the good grace of Christ into your heart offers a cleansing of that negative spirit, a path to forgiveness and peace. This is important not just for the sinner but for everyone.

Some studies have shown a significant inverse relationship between the belief in the possibility of rehabilitation for criminals and support for the death penalty.[49] This makes sense logically: if you believe in the grace and mercy of Jesus Christ and universal redemption, capital punishment intervenes in a process that is up to God, not humans. One can't be for capital punishment in theory but not in practice just as one can't believe in redemption for some and not others. There are no exceptions to the power and possibility of God's grace; it is available to everyone who accepts his teachings.

However, Pat Robertson has continued his support for the death penalty. He says he was willing to make an exception for Tucker because he believed in her transformation. But he admitted that he could not reconcile this contradictory position. After all, how could Robertson or anyone know that a person on death row has not been or could not in the future be transformed? And why is Robertson the judge of who is transformed and who is not? President Bush disagreed about Tucker, but maybe he would find someone else worthy. In the end, it is only God who can be the judge. Once we end someone's life, we have snuffed out the possibility of redemption. If redemption is always possible, capital punishment flies in the face of belief in God as the eternal light and mercy and grace in the face of sin and evil. Of course there are some people who can't control their violent impulses and need to be kept apart from the community. That is why we have life imprisonment. We assume that those who sit on death row are dangerous and deserving of the ultimate punishment. Yet some who have been convicted have later been found innocent of their crimes and others have managed to make changes in their lives.

Each of us is capable of redemption. We must learn to accept God's grace and forgiveness, no matter what the sin. How quickly and effectively one manages redemption is between the individual and God. But capital punishment removes the possibility of remorse, repentance, and penance. Are we to judge one another by the worst acts of our lives or by the best we can be?

The redemptive power of Jesus and his message is clear. "For it is better to suffer for doing good, if suffering should be God's will, than to suffer for doing evil" (1 Peter 3:17). I have found great resonance in the ministry that serves various prisons in the state. As the Reverend Jacqueline Means, director of prison ministries for the Episcopal Church, has said, "When we kill somebody legally what we are saying is that God cannot change a person's life. And I don't believe in that. God can do what God wants to do. And even the worst person in the world doesn't deserve to be executed."[50]

IT'S IMPORTANT TO RECOGNIZE the high incidence of mental illness and limited intellectual abilities among the inmate population. According to a 2006 Justice Department Bureau of Justice Statistics study, more than half of all inmates have a mental health problem.[51] These inmates should be cared for and treated humanely, but few are likely to make changes in their lives. While God can forgive their sins, and we may do the same, that doesn't preclude our obligation to keep potentially dangerous people apart from the rest of society. But removing such people from society to ensure public safety and killing them are not the same thing. These people are incapable of understanding and controlling their actions. We cannot be a moral society and perform eugenics on the most vulnerable people. As Fyodor Dostoyevsky said, "The degree of civilization in a society can be judged by entering the prisons."[52] I have entered the prisons and indeed we have a long road to become civilized by that standard.

For those who made mistakes and have seen the error of their ways, have made changes in their lives, and are no longer the threat they once were, then putting them in a hopeless situation removes their dignity and humanity. Isn't hope what we all live for, in some form? We hope for a better life, however we define it. When stripped of hope, nothing matters and there is nothing to look forward to, nothing that has any meaning. This is a recipe for the kind of prison violence that we have come to think of as stereotypical and that becomes part of a cycle of devolving behavior—there is nothing to lose.

We have adopted an attitude that borders on magical thinking: while we remove hope from the lives of prisoners, we infuse our own lives with the false hope that the death penalty will eliminate crime and make us safe. Hope must be reserved for personal wishes and dreams, things that can improve our lives, things that lend optimism to the future. When we use false hope to build public policy or even critical judgment, it cheapens the concept because it adds an element of chance and of the unknown to something that is entirely concrete and knowable.

I have sometimes stood in contrast to other doctors who would recommend surgery in the "hope that it would help." I didn't think "hope" was a reasonable rationale for surgery when applying the "first, do no harm" axiom. Surgery was always the last resort, with patient safety as the priority. When I look at how we arrived at some of our public policies, hope has played a role. It has become a feel-good substitute for analysis and facts and it is misplaced in the context of capital punishment. Hope is not a reasonable rationale for the death penalty. We cannot "hope" that killing will make us safer. We must give "hope" to those who have lost their way, committed crimes, and have sinned, harming others in the process. We must "hope" for their redemption. We must "hope" that we can forgive them, as in the Lord's Prayer: "Forgive us our trespasses as we shall forgive those who trespass against us."

When I started to apply reason to my own opinions, I was hopeful that others would be able to find the same path. There are so many positive gains that can come from understanding the real issues and acting on reason rather than emotion.

IN ADDITION, THE DEATH penalty as our legal framework clearly doesn't accomplish the goal of preventing or decreasing crime. What it does is keep alive the desire for vengeance rather than change the focus to healing. Besides the corrosive effect of continuing the anger and hatred that is an integral part of the "lock 'em up" attitude, we must also consider that for each prisoner we kill, we destroy a family. While it is hard to imagine for those who are not exposed to families who have a loved one in prison, every prison sentence doled out to the convicted is also a sentence for a family. Because we perceive inmates as one-dimensional crime machines and define them by their crime, we forget that they have other facets to their lives. Their crime is no more the sum total of who they are than my disease is the sum total of who I am. The fact is that most prisoners are parents; more than 1.5 million children have a parent in prison.

I have seen inmates become better parents than they were prior to their imprisonment. When prisoners begin a sentence, they do not leave their family ties behind. These ties are generally one of the few positive factors in their lives worth building on both for the sake of helping the inmate change and for the sake of the family members who still care about and love the prisoner. As parents, prisoners can make meaningful contributions to their children's well-being. Plenty of children grow up in single-parent homes and doing so doesn't preclude influence from the absent parent. On the contrary, the absent parent is important to the well-being of the children. So why does the system rarely consider these factors?

As with the rest of the criminal justice system, there is a racial disparity here too: one in fourteen black children grow up with a parent in prison.

Based on current rates of first incarceration, an estimated 32 percent of black males will enter state or federal prison during their lifetimes, compared to 17 percent of Hispanic males and 5.9 percent of white males.[53]

There are few support programs for the families of prisoners. Frequently, the system places the inmate in a facility that is difficult and expensive for the family to reach, further breaking the familial bonds. When we send a criminal "away," the fallout is exponential. A prison sentence also represents a loss of financial and emotional support for other members of the family. The poor make up a large majority of the prison population; they have few resources and there are few government organizations available for assistance. In the process of exacting punishment on the offender, we also punish the family. The stigma that the children have to bear is formidable. It is hard to justify.

It is appropriate to remove from society individuals who have harmed others, for they have broken a social contract with the rest of society, especially if they still pose a threat. But we need to distinguish between warehousing people to punish them and creating a system that protects the public. We need to allow people the opportunity to change. We all make mistakes and in God's eyes, we all are redeemable; only God can judge us for eternity. Surely there must be a better way to hold people accountable for their actions and behavior, one that doesn't seek retribution as much as it does restitution.

Retribution is endless. Just as prison life breeds more crime, taking one life for another continues the cycle of hate and revenge. A ten-year-old whose father was executed tried to understand this concept and asked her mother, "They're going to kill him because he killed somebody, so when they kill him, who do we get to kill?"[54] A simple question, yet profound only in the way a child can sometimes be.

Victims of the system are not restricted to the executed criminal and his/her family, though the family is deeply affected. There is also the family of the victim of the crime to consider. The brother of the woman Karla Fay Tucker killed was at first outspoken in his desire to seek revenge and make sure Tucker got her "due." He was full of rage and hatred for the person who had killed someone he loved. Eventually, however, he recognized that these negative feelings had taken over his life. "I knew I had to do something with the hatred and the anger that was within me. It was consuming me," he said. Like many of those who grew up with and clung to their hatred toward blacks in earlier decades, he eventually learned to let go of his negative feelings. During that process, he found religion and absolution. Through faith he came to terms with the tragedy and forgave Tucker. "I learned that if I want to be forgiven, I must learn to forgive," he explained. Through God and his all-forgiving grace, both Tucker and her victim's family found redemption and peace of mind.

In contrast, the husband of Tucker's victim has never forgiven her. He cheered at her execution, saying, "What goes around comes around." He continued to accuse her of lying about her transformation. There are those who argue that people who commit heinous crimes should never be forgiven, regardless of their religious or other transformations. We often demand that the guilty show remorse; when they do, some ignore it anyway. If God forgives the remorseful, we are obliged to do the same.[55]

In a recent murder trial in Birmingham, the family requested that the defendant get life-without-parole rather than the death sentence. They were interviewed after the sentencing and said that there was no reason that two families had to be destroyed. The victim's family and that of the perpetrator embraced in tears after the trial.

A surprising number of families of crime victims agree with this sentiment. Their testimonies about letting go of the hatred show a renewed spirit and peace that those who continue to hold onto their anger never experience. As with other decisions we make, we can decide to make peace with our lives, pray for guidance and redemption, and move on or we can let the anger fester and drive our lives. It's a personal choice, and which path one takes underlies not only one's opinions about capital punishment but how one lives and interacts in an imperfect world.

If we believe in redemption, we know that remorse and rehabilitation are possible. When we invoke the death sentence, we are revoking that belief. We are in effect saying that this person is not redeemable. In God's eyes, this is simply never the case.

WHILE THERE ARE PEOPLE such as some mentally ill and mentally disabled persons for whom rehabilitation to the degree needed for reintegration with society is not possible, for the most part we do not think it is humane to kill them; the Supreme Court has taken this position.

The sick and the disabled have always been the "disposables" of society. From the days of Dorothea Dix to the present, we are reluctant to examine our policies when it comes to these segments of society. We too often lock them up and hope for the best. While there has been progress in the last century, there has also been frustration at a return to more rigid and inhumane policies. In our zeal to get tough on crime, the broad sweep has overshot the boundaries, reducing or eliminating many of the programs that offered education, job training, and drug treatment for those incarcerated. That is beginning to change again as a reaction to the overwhelming numbers of prisoners in our system and perhaps recognition that ultimately there will be few left to round up and send off.

It is interesting to recall that the British Empire used some of its colonies as a politically viable solution to prison overcrowding. Georgia was originally populated with people who were being held in British debtors' prison; Australia became the prison colony of choice after the American Revolution.[56]

It has been shown that support programs for families of the incarcerated have a positive effect on recidivism, yet there are not enough of them. The culture of prison tends to destroy families rather than help them. Often death row inmates are allowed no physical contact with visitors. A poignant description of these non-contact visits was penned by death row inmate Mumia Abu-Jamal, the former Black Panther, describing in his book *Live from Death Row*, a visit from his young daughter:

> She burst into the tiny visiting room, her brown eyes aglitter with happiness; stopped, stunned, staring at the glassy barrier between us; and burst into tears [. . .] as her petite fingers curled into tight fists, which banged and pummeled the Plexiglas barrier [. . .] Break it, break it, she screamed [. . .] why can't we kiss [. . .] why can't I hug him [. . .] sit in his lap [. . .] why not?"[57]

Karl Menninger, the renowned psychiatrist, thought that non-contact visits were "needlessly cruel" and "a violation of ordinary principles of humanity."[58] Besides the cruelty of this scene for the inmate, it is also destructive to the child. There are small and relatively inexpensive ways that we can help transform people who have made mistakes. Is it because the criminal justice system is overwhelmingly black and poor that we pay so little attention to its reform?

Retribution is an endless cycle of hatred that must be broken. We can't seem to build prisons fast enough to keep them from overflowing. In California, lawsuits are forcing the state to reduce the unsafe overcrowding that exists in their prison system. California has the second-largest prison system in the country, the worst overcrowding, and the highest recidivism rate. The state spends more money now on building prisons than it does on its own state universities. Governor Arnold Schwarzenegger has requested $6 billion in additional funds for new prison hospitals. That's in addition to the $1.4 billion already allocated by the legislature in 2008. These expenditures are in response to the legal challenges. While California has been in the news because of the legal challenges, it is hardly unique. Over a twenty-year period (1987–2007), state spending on corrections doubled but state spending on education increased by only 21 percent.[59]

A proposed federal court settlement for California offered in May 2008 could keep the state in compliance with the court mandate to alleviate the state's overcrowded prisons. Suggestions include early release for low-risk inmates, treatment programs, electronic monitoring, and job training and education programs, among others. None of these ideas are unique, untested, or novel. The real question is why it took so many years and wasted so much energy, time, and money in legal fees to conclude what we already knew.

In numerous studies, it has been shown that the recidivism rate is reduced enormously by education. In a 1997 report, Alabama showed a 35 percent recidivism rate, but a 1 percent recidivism rate for those inmates who completed college degrees while incarcerated.[60] So why do we defund prison educational programs and then show public outrage at those who continue to commit crimes?

By warehousing prisoners rather than trying to rehabilitate those who show the interest and capacity for change and by imposing long sentences even for lesser crimes, we have forced many young inmates to grow up with and grow used to the prison environment. It is not a natural state and it results in inmates who are no longer eager to leave prison. Years of prison life have left them without the basic life skills needed in a normative environment; certainly they have no job skills should they be lucky enough to get a job. They wind up feeling more secure inside, bad as it may be.

Many people behind bars could lead useful and productive lives if given the right assistance. But if after years of confinement we release prisoners by dropping them off at the nearest bus station with ten dollars and no place to live and no job, can we really expect a successful result? We cut prisoners off from their families; we restrict every movement they make; we give them nothing that they could use to try to improve their stock, and then we are surprised when they resort to crime again after they get out. Given the limitations of the environment, the scarcity of resources, the lack of skills, money, and support, why would this be surprising?

There's a normalization of prison life exemplified by those inside who are afraid of leaving; it's what they know, a way of life. And while we on the outside have grown used to the idea that having millions of our population locked up is the just the way it is, if we want low crime—or perhaps harmony—we have to pay to be our brothers' keepers. We pay the fees in economic costs but forget about the social and emotional costs.

10

FEAR AND LOATHING MEET

The greatest derangement of the mind is to believe in something because one wishes it to be so. — LOUIS PASTEUR

As I can attest from my own experience, racial prejudice takes a long time to change. It took years of slow recognition of the false attributes ascribed to blacks before I came face to face with my own prejudice and was able to start to change my behavior. The light of truth dispels fears and false reason. As Martin Luther King Jr. once said, "Darkness cannot drive out darkness; only light can do that. Hate cannot drive out hate; only love can do that." Change is not always easy, especially if we have grown up in an atmosphere of fear, distrust, and bigotry. But it is our duty to change the dynamics of hate, whatever the source.

Our reaction to people who are different is often fear disguised as the rationale we use to stigmatize others for those qualities that set them apart, whether it is mental or physical disability, addiction, race, a criminal record, or even illness. Succumbing to these fears breeds hatred and rejection. Once we overcome these fears, however, we are free of the negative feelings and we can find empathy and compassion for others, whatever their differences from ourselves.

One way to overcome these fears is through exposure to the "others." Studies clearly indicate that children with disabilities are more accepted and do better in school when they are in classes with students without disabilities. Importantly, the benefits are not confined to the disabled children; the other students in the class develop empathy and resourcefulness as they accept and interact with the disabled student. The disability starts to look "normal" as it becomes accepted by the other children and the focus moves onto qualities that are the same and positive rather than those that are different and perceived of as negative. I have experienced this firsthand through my involvement with deaf and hard of hearing children.

Similarly, as I was personally more exposed to people from other racial groups in an environment in which they were on equal footing with everyone else, over time their color faded. They were no longer different and the ugly stereotypes were lost in the bustle of our daily work. This was as true of people in my own family as it was of strangers I saw in town or said hello to in local stores or businesses.

The more regular contact we have with "others," the less we notice the differences and the less we continue to categorize them. As the last several decades have proved, people of different races can and do live in the same communities and get along. As they do, their fears of one another dissipate along with their preconceived ideas and stereotypes. It was not my grandparents who were fearful of the blacks who eventually became the majority in their neighborhood; it was the other members of the family who feared for my grandparents. The fears were unfounded, as it turned out, and while everyone was pleased as well as relieved, they were as likely to attribute the lack of trouble in the neighborhood to luck as they were to irrational fears. My grandparents were as safe as they had always been, and probably as safe as the whites who had fled to other neighborhoods.

When you grow up in an environment of prejudice, hatred, and false truths, it is not easy to make the transition to a fact-based view. I have clear recollections of family talk about the evils of mixing the races and the risks that would accompany such action.

My father was particularly vocal about blacks. "I know what they are like. I work with them and they work for me. Don't ever tell me they are equal!" he would impress upon us. These ideas were reinforced by my environment. As a boy I just listened and was frightened by the prospect of the terrible blight that would be engendered by any hint of integration. As a teen, however, I was sometimes tempted to take the opposite view for spite, even if I wasn't sure I disagreed. I would never have challenged my father, but I did lose respect for him, at least partly for his bigotry. I remember asking him if blacks' brains were really smaller than ours. I expected him to back down on that one—part of me was goading him on that question—but I had miscalculated. "Oh yes," he told me with absolute certainty and authority. "They have measured them." At the time, I couldn't have argued with him even if I had had data refuting his fallacy. Debating would have made no difference and would have enraged him all the more.

It took many years for me to recognize these as bogus claims. While I don't think my father ever recognized them, he did come to accept his granddaughter. As he got to know her, her skin tone faded into the background; she was not "other" anymore, and he loved her as much as he loved his other grandchildren. By tearing down the walls that separate us, the need for those hateful bogus facts dissipates. Though he never let go of the "facts," she simply didn't fit into that category. The more people we eventually move outside of that "other" category, the lower the walls become, allowing us to peer over the top and notice the similarities.

From the perspective of several decades after desegregation, it is easy to see how wrong-headed were the predictions of dire consequences of integration. But excising the old stereotypes and evaluating people for their character and not their color takes a conscious effort. These changes don't occur overnight, but they do occur and they make a difference. Sometimes we don't even notice them because they are so slow to evolve. The process often occurs in the background while the conscious mind is unaware. The lessons of childhood that are embedded in our unconscious rule more of our behavior than we often acknowledge.

Tom Cherry, son of Bobby Frank Cherry, one of the convicted bombers of the Sixteenth Street Baptist Church, surely grew up in an atmosphere of hatred and bigotry. But even he mellowed, despite his upbringing that included attending Klan rallies with his infamous father, and was able to apply some reason to the "facts" he was fed as a child.

> I remember when everyone was worried about Russia doing this and Cuba doing that and us all getting blown up and everyone in Alabama was worried about being integrated. It's a sad thing, isn't it?

After we went to school together, we found out there wasn't much difference in any of us. We were all struggling just as hard to buy groceries as they were. They was all wanting bicycles for Christmas just like we was.[61]

In the end, the truth is we all do want the same things. Sometimes politics gets in the way of seeing that truth and often our own views are shaped by the politics of our time. The entire South has changed a lot in the post-civil rights era, perhaps more so than other areas of the country where racial prejudice wasn't quite so inborn and acceptable. None of us are completely free of prejudice. Perhaps it's just human to fear what is unfamiliar and/or different and what we're not used to. Too often our differences become the foundations for our fears. So it was that I successfully hid my illness for a couple of years, fearing that I would be branded as unfit. Indeed, some differences are easier to hide than others. Race is not among them.

It also bears noting that when we succumb to our fears, we leave ourselves vulnerable to the rabble-rousing rhetoric that promises to remove the object of fear. It doesn't matter how outlandish the plan, it's what we want to hear to ally our fear, so we tacitly let go of reason and let these unfounded fears dominate. It's not a conscious effort. It is a natural instinct to rid ourselves of fear and a normal desire to feel secure. But demagoguery also allows us to hand over our reasoning powers to another human whose agenda may not be pure, and lets us put our trust in someone else's hands instead of using our own judgment and the guiding hands of God and his truth.

Like me, many people in the South and undoubtedly elsewhere cheered for George Wallace and Bull Connor and the other political players of the civil rights opposition. These "leaders" played on our ingrained fears of integration and of blacks, conjuring up all the bogus myths. They were going to "save us" from the horror of integration. What exactly those horrors were, we didn't know—they were never directly articulated, but surely they were terrible. So we followed along.

Without questioning either the basis for the fear or the segregationist policy, those of us who followed blindly never got to the more fundamental question. Surely we were all for supporting democratic ideals and principles, moral behavior and justice. But our fear atrophied our judgment and rational thought that would have questioned how it was that segregation and hatred of blacks passed as moral principles and justice didn't apply to blacks.

It is important to question public policy in a democratic system and examine how and what influences various policies. These were but some of the issues that were raised during my coursework at Birmingham-Southern College. As I look now at the variables that impact the policy of capital punishment and the criminal justice system, there seem to be distinct parallels.

Throughout U.S. history, public opinion has played a significant role in forming the criminal justice system. That states determine their own criminal code was inscribed in the Constitution. The fact that most criminal laws are state laws accounts for some of the regional differences in capital punishment. It also accounts for the differences in how criminals have been treated historically; the racial divide was always more visible in the South, where the remnants of slavery and resentment remained with less oversight. What happens when racial prejudice becomes the basis for public policy? All we need to do is look at the history of slavery and segregation in the South. So are we to allow the remnants of prejudice to be the guiding forces in shaping our policies? As Bill Moyers noted in *A Parable for Our Times*, "Drawing from the Hebrew prophets and the Book of Revelation, the abolitionists simply said this: 'the rule of law has become moral anarchy. God's light clarified that the rule of law had become moral anarchy.'"[62]

For me, God has clarified the moral bankruptcy that is capital punishment. That it is the law of the land right now does not make it more moral than segregation was in 1960 or slavery in 1860. In fact, the two are inextricably linked. If we could eliminate racial prejudice, what would our policy about capital punishment look like? As it turns out, it would be quite a different story.

Two researchers from the University of Maine have been studying the impact of racial prejudice on public policy for more than two decades. What they have found is consistent and troubling. In one survey, they polled whites about their attitudes toward blacks and had them rate the degree to which they thought blacks were "lazy, unintelligent, desirous of living off welfare, and unpatriotic." The survey also asked how they would feel about having black neighbors and how they would feel if a close relative married a black person.[63]

Steven Barkan and Steven Cohn, the researchers, then correlated the data from their surveys with surveys about support for the death penalty. The data showed a high degree of association between the two variables. The results demonstrated how much our policy of capital punishment is driven by white support that includes "antipathy to blacks and with racial stereotyping." Barkan and Cohn argue that basing criminal justice policy on public opinion, if that opinion is based even in part on racial prejudice, is anti-democratic and should not play a role in legal decisions.

Public opinion polls have come to play an increasingly large role in public policy. We hear politicians cite polls every day and of course politicians are particularly tuned in to those who keep them in power. Most of the time, it is not only those who vote but also the financial contributors who have the greatest influence. This small closed circle keeps minority voices from having equal impact. The Gallup Poll taken in 2007 shows what has been historically the case: white support of the death penalty exceeds that of black support by 73 percent to 40 percent. This poll also included Hispanics who are about evenly divided on the issue: 48 percent support the death penalty while 49 percent oppose it. It is in the white community that support has been consistent and strong.[64]

Given this data, it is not surprising that political advocacy for continuing the death penalty is still loud and clear. On the other hand, polls show that only 1 percent of U.S. police chiefs believe that the death penalty deters crime; yet that poll has had little effect on public policy. This attitude was confirmed to me in several conversations I've had with local law enforcement officials—from a police chief to a county sheriff to a warden at a state death row facility—all of whom expressed opposition to the death penalty, mostly on grounds that it had no deterrent effect. One was rather sanguine in thinking that perhaps if the system was more efficient and the penalty could be swift and certain, it might be of benefit.

The troublesome issue is how the death penalty supporters arrive at their views. A long-term study at Columbia University examined death penalty cases over a twenty-three-year period and found a 68 percent prejudicial error rate. Looking at cases that were appealed, almost seven out of every ten capital cases were found by the courts to contain serious, reversible errors.[65] The researchers also expressed great concern that the courts were not reversing these decisions.

In part two of the same study, the researchers looked at why the error rate might be so high. They concluded, "We find that the conditions evidently pressuring counties and states to overuse the death penalty and thus increase the risk of unreliability and error include race, politics and poorly performing law enforcement systems."[66]

Further, the study found the more whites perceived that they were at risk of being victimized by crime and the greater the proportion of black population in a state, the higher the error rate. The Columbia researchers suggested that

> When whites and other influential citizens feel threatened by homicide, they put pressure on officials to punish as many criminals as severely as possible, with the result that mistakes are made, and a lot of people are initially sentenced to death who are later found to have committed a lesser crime, or no crime at all. The more African Americans there are in a state, the more likely it is that serious mistakes will be made in death penalty trials. This could be because of fears of crime driven by racial stereotypes and economic factors. It is disturbing that race plays a role in the outcome of death penalty cases, whatever the reasons.[67]

While I understand the angst of the South and the vestiges of hatred that remain from earlier, sordid parts of my own history and that of the state where I grew up, the insidious hatred is hardly confined to the South. It was not that long ago that William Bennett, former Education Secretary in the Reagan administration and Drug Czar in the administration of President George H. W. Bush, said, without a trace of remorse, "You could abort every black baby in this country, and your crime rate would go down."[68]

The remark was made in the context of a discussion on the crime rate, a statistic often used to rationalize and perpetuate the stereotype that blacks are "prone to crime." The fact that proportionally, blacks are arrested, convicted, and sentenced at higher rates than whites was totally ignored. A 2005 report on racial disparity in sentencing found that even controlling for severity of offense and prior criminal record, white males between the ages of eighteen and twenty-nine were 38 percent less likely to be sentenced to prison than their black male counterparts. In addition, unemployed blacks were incarcerated at five times the rate as employed whites.[69] These are intelligent people making, at best, uniformed claims and, at worst, pure racial remarks based on false premises.

Regardless of the context, Bennett tried to backpedal by attributing the concept to a recent economic analysis made by Steven Levitt in the book he co-authored, *Freakonomics*. But Leavitt did not actually make that claim. Levitt never mentioned race; his claim was based on economics.

To make matters worse, Britt Hume, Fox News commentator, further perpetuated the fallacy, asking on his news show, "What was false? Well, as a matter of fact, is it not a fact that the per-capita crime rate among blacks is higher than whites? What is false here?"[70] What was false was the conflation of crime with blacks. The racial disparity in all facets of the criminal justice system combines to skew the results of any raw statistics. In fact, Levitt specifically said he wouldn't use crime rates in his analysis because "the crime data by race is generally not deemed reliable." Millions of people watch Hume's show. Undoubtedly many will continue to believe his false analysis.

More than fifty years after the civil rights movement, national commentators and people in positions of national leadership are still defending racist remarks and acting self-righteous in their defense. This perpetuation of false information is merely a continuation of the antiquated stereotypes of black inferiority that were part of my childhood environment. Neither Bennett nor Hume (or probably any of the others who were quick to defend him), grew up in the South. The South is not alone in its collective guilt.[71]

11

POLLS VS. POLS

The public is starting to shift its view on capital punishment. For the first time, a significant number (48 percent) of those polled in 2000 say they would favor a sentence of life without parole instead of the death penalty. It's a trend to watch, but not one you would know about from listening to the political rhetoric, at least not in Alabama. The Supreme Court's removal of the lethal injection moratorium may reverse the trend, but it's too early to tell what the longer-term effect will be. The Court's decision left plenty of room for further litigation, though it seems clear that the Court still reflects the majority—mostly white—support for capital punishment.

With DNA evidence more readily available and so many condemned prisoners being found innocent because of it, more people are questioning their support for the death penalty. But their discomfort about the policy of capital punishment is often related to errors in the criminal justice system, not with the policy itself. People neglect to acknowledge that it's not only error in DNA evidence that makes for an unjust system. Even in the best of circumstances, some errors are inevitable. Our system is created and developed by humans and carried out by humans; there will always be some error, no matter how careful we try to be.

Bryan Stevenson of the Equal Justice Initiative explained the problem of fallibility: "To carry out capital punishment, we would have to have a perfect system of justice so that no errors would occur nor innocent people executed; but there is no way to have that."[72]

In addition, public doubts, no matter how pervasive, do not automatically translate into a clear call for rescinding the policy. Given the fear factor, the power structure, and the vestiges of racism and bigotry, overall policy change does not seem imminent. We must also remember that the judges in capital cases are mostly whites and are as likely as the rest of the majority to harbor the same fears and specious (though probably unconscious) racial bigotry. Sentencing judges may base their decisions on their own perceived stereotypes and latent prejudice that includes the same misinformation I once held about racial "facts."[73]

While we acknowledge that our judicial system is less than perfect, we continue to allow it to take human life even when errors become public. Through use of DNA evidence, more than two hundred prisoners in the U.S. have been exonerated since 1989. In 2006, the Innocence Project, a nonprofit group that works to overturn erroneous convictions, found that false evidence had convicted one man who had already been executed and another who was on death row. In the latter case, the man was exonerated and released from prison after seventeen years; in the former, of course, it was too late.[74]

Indeed, Texas leads not only in its race to the death chambers but also in its vigorous prosecution of capital cases that deftly try to subvert Supreme Court rulings. In an effort to get ahead of the Supreme Court ruling on lethal injection, the Texas court "closed the courthouse at its regular time of five p.m. and turned back an attempt to file appeal papers a few minutes later," according to a complaint in a wrongful-death suit filed in federal court.[75] Later that evening, Texas had the distinction of executing the last inmate to die before the Supreme Court issued its moratorium.

In a study conducted by Richard Moran, a professor of sociology and criminology at Mount Holyoke College in Massachusetts, it was found that "many wrongful convictions result from official malicious behavior, prosecutors, policemen, witnesses or even jurors and judges could themselves face jail time for breaking the law in obtaining an unlawful conviction."[76]

Will those politicians who are now staunch supporters of capital punishment someday rescind their statements and declare they were only doing what the people wanted, as eventually happened with segregation? That claim can still be made in the shadows of today's divided poll numbers, though what is buried underneath the public façade is shameful.

If the majority of support for the death penalty comes from racially based foundations, shouldn't we remove these variables from the judicial decision-making process? Alabama is not alone in the racial disparity of how it deals with crime and punishment. In California, less than 27 percent of the prison population was white as of June 2007, while 38.6 percent was Hispanic, and 28.8 percent was black.

We should note that the number on death row is only a small percentage of those charged with homicide. The arrest rate is significantly higher for blacks than for whites, as is the conviction rate. This supports the premise that the criminal justice system is more bent on eliminating the "fear factor" from the equation than on administering justice. And politicians are the first to pander to the public and take credit for changing the crime rate. The fact is that whites are more likely to make bail and be acquitted. Long after slavery and segregation, the system still contains an inherent bias toward whites.

Most often when we follow politicians and others who should know better, we do so based on an emotional response. We respond to information we are given without thought and form opinions without bothering to use our God-given intelligence; this is an affront to God. Galileo himself struggled with this age-old problem: "I do not feel obliged to believe that the same God that has endowed us with the sense, reason, and intellect has intended us to forgo their use." The strength that can be found by turning to God can allay our fears and make peace with them. With God representing our "core values," we can turn toward ourselves and the power of our own thoughts to discern truth from fiction and right from wrong. God can help us make moral choices and keep us on the path of righteousness, but if we place our own powers of reason in the hands of another human, we have abrogated our responsibility as citizens and as God's children.

OUR FEAR GROWS ALONG with the unprecedented rise in the incarcerated population that began in the U.S. in the 1970s. According to a 2008 report from the Pew Center on the States, our prison and jail population has exceeded 2.3 million people, and our correctional population (including

those on probation and parole) is over seven million.[77] This is historically unprecedented. The U.S. incarceration rate is 750 per 100,000—the
highest ever recorded and higher than any other country in the world, far
surpassing countries like China and Russia. Is there less crime in the U.S.
than elsewhere? No, we're about in the middle, but certainly not lower than
anywhere else in the world. Increasing incarceration has not brought us the
safety promised by those who advocate such policy.

Growth in our prison populations nationwide has been steady, regardless
of whether the crime rate has gone up or down. Along with this increase has
been a steady but exponential increase in the rate of incarceration among
blacks, disproportionate to the rest of the population. And as the Hispanic
population has grown, so have their numbers among the incarcerated. We
have succeeded in warehousing a large portion of our population at great
cost, but we have not succeeded in feeling less fearful. We install fancy locks
on our doors in our homes and cars, we build housing with security fences
and guards at the gates, we put cameras in banks and stores, and we use all
the high-tech gear we can afford. Has it made us less fearful? I don't think
so. If anything, it has given us a false sense of security and inured us from
the realities of living in a world that is full of human frailty. The more we
spend, the higher the walls, the more we separate ourselves from the "others,"
the more fearful we become of those who are more and more unfamiliar
and different. The cycle of fear serves politicians and security companies,
but not ordinary people. "The cave you fear to enter holds the treasure you
seek," said Joseph Campbell.

The United States now incarcerates its citizens at a rate five to eight
times that of most industrialized nations, yet we still have a higher rate of
violent crime than in those nations. Although there may be less nonviolent
crime in other industrialized nations, it is not five to eight times less. Do we
really want to continue to add to our prison population at the current rate
of greater than 3 percent per year? While there is some movement toward
providing rehabilitation options for certain prisoners, the louder political
voice interprets such ideas as "soft on crime." The way we treat prison and
prisoners in general removes all human dignity and sends the message that
change is not possible. I know that is not the case.

One of the inmates I have been working with in the prison ministry program has gone from being a bitter and hardened victim who always blamed the system for his problems to a bright and cheerful man who is beginning to drink from the half-full glass rather than the one that is half-empty. In this process, he has taken responsibility for himself, making sure his personal hygiene is impeccable and making genuine attempts to expand his knowledge. It is gratifying to see these changes but disheartening to know that there are thousands of others who get none of the help or support that could make such a difference.

While there are multiple reasons for the explosion in our prison population, racial inequality needs further public scrutiny. Our get-tough-on-crime policy has made the problem worse. The media too often negatively portrays light sentencing with little attention to the real issues and circumstances.

From my own personal prison visits and from looking at the statistics, it is obvious that the criminal justice system is overwhelmingly against the black and poor. At the end of 2006, about 1 of every 33 black men was incarcerated. The rate for white men was 1 in 205, but for Hispanic men, it was 1 in 79, still less than half the rate of black men.[78] We can't remove race from the equation. Is this why we tolerate the treatment we accord to prisoners?

THE TREND FOR DEATH row inmates shows the opposite of the trend for general incarceration; for the past five years, there has been a decrease in the number of inmates on death row and in the number of people issued a death sentence. Much of this change is attributable to the imposition of more life-without-parole sentences, the use of DNA evidence that disproves a guilty verdict, and/or stays of execution granted by some states (e.g., Governor Ryan in Illinois). Are juries more reluctant than judges to impose the death penalty now?

In some cases, yes; but this switch is a mixed blessing. These life-term inmates become invisible within the prison system. While there are a few resources and organizations that can be called upon for legal aid to inmates on death row, there just aren't enough pro bono lawyers for those who serving life sentences without possibility of parole. Some of these inmates inevitably lose all hope. They languish in an environment with few options to better themselves. Some manage anyway, but that does not remove the obstacles that are in the way.

According to EJI, Alabama remains one of the few states without a statewide public defender system. Increased hostility towards the plight of the poor threatens to undermine the equal administration of justice. Thousands of prisoners in Alabama have been sentenced to life without parole and other excessive punishments for nonviolent offenses. According to Leigh Eaton at EJI, one of their clients was an Alabama prisoner who had been sentenced to life imprisonment without parole for stealing a bicycle. Through their efforts, he has subsequently been paroled.

In the last decade, both the federal and state governments have drastically cut programs that contributed toward rehabilitation of prisoners: education, libraries, counseling. They were often considered to be "pandering" to criminals and not punitive; whatever funds suggested for allocation were painted as too costly. According to an October 5, 2005, *New York Times* article, "In interviews, lifers said they tried to resign themselves to spending down their days entirely behind bars. But the prison programs that once kept them busy in an effort at training and rehabilitation have largely been dismantled, replaced by television and boredom."[79] The trend continues unabated, especially at a time when the states are strapped for funds and the federal government is operating in the red.

If an inmate is given no tools to help him or her make changes in his or her life, how can we expect a change in behavior and attitude? We too readily treat prisoners like penned animals and forget their human spiritual needs. Fortunately, nonprofit and other mission-oriented religious groups help to fill the void through their volunteerism. Redemption is possible and even likely given the opportunity. Study of recidivism rates support this. We should be encouraged that someone as affected by the hatred and hard living that was surely part of Tom Cherry's childhood was able to make the transition from hatred to understanding. If he has been able to see the error of his thinking, can't we assume that there are others who are currently behind bars that can do the same, and perhaps already have done so? Why do we assume that "bad" people can never change? God is forgiving, no matter what the sin. Can we read Frank Smith's words and still have doubt that this man is no longer a threat to society?

The realities of incarceration and prison conditions refute the prevalent pubic attitudes about the "cushy" environment that our tax dollars support for inmates and "criminal elements." I can safely say that those who so label the ambiance of prison have never set foot near one. "Cushy" is not a word I would use to describe that environment.

One evening not long ago, I was at a local fund raiser and I ran into a man who had been in my public policy master's program at Birmingham-Southern College.

He had been in law enforcement at the time, and if my memory was correct, he was in favor of the death penalty although I know that many police officers actually oppose capital punishment. But that was several years ago and we hadn't seen each other since. He remembered that I had been ill and asked about my health and what I was doing. In all my research on death penalty issues I had been particularly surprised by the attitudes of law enforcement officials, who consistently opposed the death penalty because they thought it was an ineffective deterrent to crime.[80] It was one of the things that made me look more closely at the deterrence argument when doing my research in school.

I started to tell Jack some of my experiences with prisoners, which I thought he'd be interested in given his profession. So I was quite startled when he said, "Oh, yeah, give 'em a cushy room with TV and the like. That's hardly punishment."

It was clear from his opening salvo that he favored retribution, not rehabilitation or redemption.

"So how would you treat those in prison?" I asked.

"Well, I sure wouldn't let them sit around and watch TV all day," he said.

"Well, how should they spend their time? Do you think they should be able to get some job training or education?" I continued. I wasn't trying to challenge him but to understand his view. I wondered if he had an alternative idea that made sense.

"They should have to work, just like the rest of us," he said. "Only they shouldn't be paid, and they should do the jobs no one else wants to do, like digging ditches or busting rocks," he replied

"Like the old chain gangs?" I asked.

"Well, yeah, now that you mention it. What was wrong with those? They did some useful work for the state and it kept them busy. Why do we have to coddle these guys? After all, I have to pay for my kids to go to college. Why should some junkie get it for free?"

Now we were in a different territory. Were we talking about drug problems and their related crimes, or hardened criminals and slave labor versus restitution? All these issues conflated in the brief exchange. There were so many questions and statements of fact that might have easily shaken his arguments. But before I had a chance to address them, we were interrupted and the subject changed.

I thought about Jack and our conversation on my way home that evening. He had read the materials and heard the facts and yet was not persuaded. Unfortunately, emotion is a big deterrent to rational thought, one that is built into our system of "justice."

How do we address the criminals in our midst? In the imperfect world, there will always be some lawbreakers, and there will always be conflict and misunderstanding among people, and probably some degree of prejudice. Is it the role of government to intervene and help people to recognize their differences and dispel hatred? If we want to live in a just society, or at least aspire to it, then I think the answer is yes. Our government has to provide some basic rules of conduct. While the government can't eradicate prejudice by mandating civil behavior—conduct that is moral because it demands that all people be treated equally under the law—it can become the guide for such behavior. And that is all it can do. The rest is up to the people, to recognize their failings and try to overcome their pre-programmed prejudices. In practice, isn't this what occurred in the civil rights movement? Though it took a strong public display and several years of effort just to get the government to enact the legislation that mandated the changes, once the laws were in place, the federal government was able to enforce the laws and make sure that the states followed suit. Obviously, this is not a complete solution; there is still plenty of prejudice to go around. But democracy is fraught with problems and conflicts. Had the changes in the law not come from the federal government, would the South still be segregated?

It is the role of the government to keep its people safe but that safety should not be based on fear-mongering and pandering to racist instincts. We need to understand how linked our criminal system is to racial inequity and strife. Given that we now have the largest prison population in the world, one that has increased 500 percent in the last two decades, withdrawing the very programs that offer inmates a way to make positive changes in their lives is counterproductive; many of these programs were shown to reduce recidivism. Some reform organizations advocate for change and are making some inroads in establishing alternatives to harsh sentences, especially for low-level crimes, and for instituting rehabilitation and training programs, including drug rehabilitation. But they are still too few and far between.

FROM FEAR SPRINGS THE unfounded "fact" that the death penalty deters crime. This argument simply doesn't stand up. Fact: States that have or have had death penalty statutes do not have lower crime rates than states that do not. Fact: Crime rates have no positive correlation with the death penalty (in some cases the opposite is true). Fact: Most law enforcement officials concur that the death penalty does nothing to deter crime.

Deterrence always sounds good; it's a good sales pitch. Who doesn't want to be safe and live in an environment where no criminals lurk in the background? The reasoning is that if we lock up and kill the "bad guys," they are off the streets and no longer can harm anyone. The death of convicted murderers therefore, ensures that further crime is deterred. Although this is the logic most cited by those in support of capital punishment, there are several problems with it.

For one, those who so argue fail to distinguish between deterrence and incapacitation. They are not the same though they are often conflated. Of course once a criminal offender is removed from society, that criminal is incapacitated and no longer a threat to society at large. However, this part of the argument affects only the possible future activity of that person and no one else. It also assumes that the offender would murder again given the opportunity—that recidivism is a large part of the murder rate. According to the U.S. Department of Justice, only 1.2 percent of those who served time for homicide are arrested for a new homicide within three years of release.[81]

Even extending that statistic beyond three years, the number of murder recidivists is small—large enough to warrant caution in deciding who gets released but not large enough to be a rationale for the death penalty. In addition, keeping a convicted murderer in prison has the same incapacitating effect. The rate of escapes from high-security facilities is nil.

Deterrence is actually a different argument that rests on an entirely different rationale than that of incapacitation, though it is no more persuasive. In this line of thinking, the death penalty becomes an object lesson for anyone who would contemplate such egregious behavior. Deterrence proponents posit that having a death penalty in place assures that a potential murderer will think twice before acting. This assumes that the crime was planned in the first place, which rules out at least half of all murders. A large portion (40 to 45 percent) of murders are crimes of passion, i.e., murders committed in the heat of anger and rage, or committed while in a state of substance-induced lack of consciousness. Another large portion of convicted murderers are mentally ill and/or mentally incompetent and therefore do not have the ability to carry out such reasoning. The death penalty has no effect on the behavior of potential murderers in these groups. Former Los Angeles Police Chief Willie L. Williams explained that capital punishment "in and of itself, is [not] a deterrent to crime because most people do not think about the death penalty before they commit a violent or capital crime."[82]

For murderers not in the above groups, death penalty proponents have set forth another set of arguments, usually bandied about in more academic or intellectual circles. The argument posits that deterrence is effective if and only if three basic conditions are met: punishment must be severe, swift, and certain. While the death penalty is always severe, the fact that within our legal system it is never either certain or swift only bolsters this particular deterrence claim because its defenders can always say that the conditions weren't met and that's why the death penalty isn't working.

Beside the fact that this is arguing from a negative and illogical, the evidence doesn't support the premise, either. In earlier decades when the death penalty was carried out shortly after commission of the crime, the murder rates did not go down. As an object lesson, executions had no effect. And even if our system today were considerably better at the immediate apprehension and arrest and then the prompt trial and punishment of those who have violated criminal laws, the odds of being caught and convicted are still rather low overall. This is not a defect in our criminal code so much as a need for more police and better training of those already in the system. Even after apprehension of a murder suspect, less than a third are involved in capital crime prosecutions, and of these, only about a third result in a death sentence. Reviewing U.S. Bureau of Justice statistics, Richard Dieter at DPIC found that we had roughly 16,000 murders a year in recent years and sentenced 125 people per year to death. We executed not even half of those. Thus, less than 1 percent of murderers are ever executed. How could there be a deterrent effect?

Contrary to populist rhetoric, our laws do not capriciously favor criminals over victims. Our laws were designed by our founders to protect human rights and avoid the excesses of earlier governments who could (and did) arbitrarily arrest and punish whomever they wanted, whenever they wanted, whether perceived enemies of the state or lowly paupers who may or may not have been guilty of anything more than being impoverished. The innocent-until-proved-guilty foundation of our criminal code is a safeguard for everyone against authoritarian governments.

We live in a real world that is run by humans and our system is not perfect. Our Bill of Rights has served as a model for equality and justice worldwide since its inception. Could our legal system be improved? Of course. Fixing the imperfections in the system is highly preferable to changes to the very foundations of our system, which would risk dismantling democracy as we know it. In addition, bypassing the legal protections afforded the accused does nothing to reduce crime. It merely weakens our overall system of human rights and undermines our foundations. It does not serve our long-term interests.

Readily available statistics and comprehensive studies easily refute each of the deterrence arguments. This data also show how these conditions are so rarely met as to reduce the argument to its theoretical roots. When all is said and done, those who support capital punishment would do so regardless of its deterrent effect or lack thereof. In its essence the death penalty is retribution—legal murder for those who "deserve to die" for their crimes. All the arguments for the death penalty, all the discussion on variants on the law that "if only" we could enact them would deter crime and give us a safer world are based on hope and fear—unfounded fear of crimes not yet committed and hope that removing some of the safeguards protecting the innocent will let us more successfully prosecute crime so that we can live in a crime-free environment. Those who won't admit the vengeance inherent in the death penalty need only to look at the lack of broad protest over the administration of medical treatment to a dying man so that he would be healthy enough to qualify for execution. Dying of natural causes was not acceptable.

As we know, there is no such thing as a perfect world here on earth. Perfection exists only in heaven. As humans who are subject to error in judgment and behavior, all we can do is try to help each other when we have lost our moral standing before God.

Hope that new laws favoring the victims of crime will change the crime rate and reduce exposure to crime is no substitute for rational thinking or understanding of our democratic foundations. Certainly we should be sensitive to anyone who has been victimized by crime, but that does not preclude ensuring that the accused maintain their standing as innocent until proved guilty. All too often our rush to convict someone—anyone—to satisfy our need for vengeance bypasses our safeguards and increases errors in conviction.

12

Moral Relativity, or the Morals of Relatives

Our lives begin to end the day we become silent about things that matter.
— Martin Luther King Jr.

As humans, we need to be more open to the possibilities of redemption and more accepting of ourselves as imperfect beings. We also need to look at the larger picture of crime and acknowledge the discrimination and inequitable application of our legal system. Crime statistics do not tend to include white-collar crime and yet these crimes are more insidious; they affect people in less obvious ways and are often harder to prosecute.

The repercussions of white-collar crime are widely felt and more rarely prosecuted, Enron being the exception and the object lesson. It seems more likely that others who might think about following the Enron model will find alternative ways to avoid being caught rather than change their behavior. White-collar defendants who are convicted are more frequently granted permission to stay out of prison pending appeals than those convicted of violent offenses. Sometimes, but not always, this makes sense. Often the reality has more to do with the defendant's ability to make bail than with whether or not the convicted defendant is likely to resume criminal activity during the appeal process.

Greed is not going away any time soon; it has been a part of the human condition forever. This is acknowledged indirectly by the lack of public outcry for legislation concerning corporate crime, in contrast to that which is often proposed for other crimes. Hope is not applied to white-collar crime in the same way it is too often applied to other kinds of criminal offenses.

Those who support the idea that capital punishment deters crime are generally not of the same mind about white-collar crime. Often laws designed to deter white-collar crime get watered down in the legislative process, eliminating those portions of the statute that would hold the corporation and its executives accountable. Perhaps this is merely a function of the complexity of the laws. Laws governing corporate crime and financial fraud tend to be hard to follow whereas laws governing street crime are generally easier to understand or at least easier to communicate in sound bites that will play to voters watching the news. Perhaps even more telling are the politicians who both craft the laws and benefit from their implementation, whether directly or indirectly.

In earlier eras, the death penalty often was applied to crimes other than murder. Today there are only six states in which rape of a child, even if it doesn't result in death, can be prosecuted as a capital case. A recent case in Louisiana will inevitably wind its way to the Supreme Court, which will have to rule on whether or not crimes that do not involve the death of the victim meet the standard for capital punishment. Unsurprisingly, the man on trial in Louisiana is black and claims his innocence. He may or may not be innocent, but his race is not in dispute. Between the years of 1930 and 1964, fourteen rapists were executed in Louisiana; all were black.[83] There have never been any laws that were written to punish offenders of white-collar crime to the same extent. This may be a function of race and class, or at least morality applied differently where race and class are part of the equation. The Supreme Court has since ruled on this matter, and on June 25, 2008, rejected the death penalty for child rape. According to the *New York Times*, it is noteworthy that although there was a sharp division between the justices on this case, it could be an example of the narrowing application of the death penalty.

Morality, or perhaps immorality, shouldn't be quite so slippery, particularly as it has been applied to issues that involve race. Slavery was a terrible blight on humankind, yet it was not considered so utterly immoral two hundred years ago. Slavery has been with us since before the time of Christ and Biblical commentary on the practice can be found as early as Genesis 39 and Deuteronomy 15:12–18. Jesus speaks of slaves; they were part of the social structure in the time of the New Testament. But he also explains that the master is no greater than his slave, for all are equal in the eyes of God. And Jesus tells us that slaves/prisoners should be treated fairly. "Truly I tell you, just as you did not do it to one of the least of these, you did not do it to me. And these will go away into eternal punishment, but the righteous into eternal life" (Matthew 25:31–45). In this passage, Jesus is speaking of the equality of service toward the poorest, in spirit and flesh, and those who are defenseless. It's hard to keep in perspective that it was a mere 150 years ago that the Civil War marked the end of the brutal practice of slavery in the U.S. But did this really lead to emancipation?

Underlying the concept of slavery is the idea of a natural racial order that means some people are destined to live within the confines of others, that the others control and direct the lives of those so confined and reap the benefits. It is part of a larger power structure, affording those held in bondage none of the rights and freedoms of those holding the strings. As in any unequal relationship, those in power have to exert their control by force or at least the threat of force. Part of that equation is in the punishment that is inherent in this master/servant contract. While it is true that some slaves in the U.S. were well-treated, it is also true that many were not, and, of course, the slaves had no say in the system.

Also, being well-treated and being free are not the same things. Slaves were property and were treated as such. Some people respect their property and take care of it better than others. People of course have different reactions to property loss, and the variables are mostly dependent on the nature of the property and the degree of financial hardship represented by the loss. But in the end, loss of property is not the equivalent of loss of human life, and the loss of slaves—whether due to death or runaway activity—was considered an economic loss. To add insult to injury, if a slave tried to escape, it was indeed considered a personal affront to the owner and the owner had to tolerate not just the economic loss but also the opprobrium that came with it. Thus punishment for escape attempts was severe and often served as an object lesson for other slaves. A slave executed for his "crimes" also brought compensation to the owner from the government, one hundred dollars if the slave was considered a "good" one—an early example of restitution for property loss.

In addition, a dead slave served no economic purpose, so it was often better to use the threat of punishment as the bigger stick. Corporal punishment was common and could be applied to both adults and children as the owner saw fit. Disobedience was not tolerated and how such behavior was dealt with was not questioned, either socially or legally. However, slaves continued to disobey and run away; people of all races still murder one another. In fact, murder has been a part of human history across cultures since time immemorial. The only thing that has changed is how we view punishing those who commit such acts.

From our early existence as Americans, lynching was part of the way we dealt with those who we thought needed subjugation. Lynching generally refers to an illegal killing by a mob (defined as three or more people) that claims to serve justice. Though the practice of slavery was confined to the South, in newly settled lands the law was a distant theory and rough justice was often the rule. As expansionism crept westward, the "white man's burden" included Native Americans, Mexicans, and Chinese as well as blacks, among ethnic "others"—all were expendable. The first lynch mobs were paramilitary style groups formed as "Indian fighters" but their victims included whatever ethnic "others" were in the way.

The mini-societies that dotted the landscape of eighteenth and nineteenth century America took care of their own, and laws, if they were actually broken, were rarely enforced, particularly if the victim was black, or at least non-white. Vigilantism was not confined to the South, but the peculiar institution of slavery was, and lynch mobs there focused their wrath on slaves or freed slaves and other blacks who roamed the post-Civil War South. It is not that the South had a monopoly on cruel punishment; it may have been cruel but it was hardly unusual.

At that time, infliction of death as a punishment for crime was not a new concept in this country. Even in colonial days, it was part of our heritage from the English system of law. People were routinely jailed for what we might consider petty crimes today—for example, for unpaid debts—and death by hanging was not an uncommon punishment for some crimes. The crimes included murder and treason, but people were also hanged for stealing, rape, arson, blasphemy, and even horse-theft. In the pre-Civil War period, Americans in the North and South accepted hanging as a fact of life. It wasn't until much later in our history that hanging was slowly replaced by what were thought of as more humane methods of killing. What was really more humane, however, was removing the act itself from public visibility, the public display having been part of the object lesson. The last public hanging was in 1936 but the method itself was last used in January 1996 in Delaware.[84] Although Delaware dismantled its gallows in 2003, condemned inmates are still offered a choice of hanging or lethal injection in Washington and New Hampshire (though New Hampshire hasn't executed anyone since 1939).

In pre-Civil War America, lynching did not have specific racial connotations. It was part of the vigilantism that passed for law and order on a local level. Lynching was directed against different groups in different parts of the country. Hangings were the most common ultimate punishment and were displayed as object lessons in which the public was encouraged to participate. Indeed, these events frequently served as entertainment. As Peter Rachleff, history professor at Macalester College in St. Paul, Minnesota, described in a report from a conference on lynching held at Emory University in October 2002, "Photographs of lynching 'parties' reveal that members of the mob or audience often posed with the corpses of their victims, in a sort of trophy shot akin to those of successful hunters and fishermen."[85]

Often, lynching photographs reinforced the myth of white innocence and black guilt by juxtaposing the photographs of the hanging with photographs of the white victims of the black alleged criminals. Vigilantism also infused the "group think" of the time: blacks were to be feared and everyone was safer with the dead man hanging from a tree. And besides, he (or, rarely, she) didn't deserve to live. No doubt it felt safe to be on the "right" side of rough justice, but it was a false sense of security. It did, however, serve to keep the people in fear not because of the object lesson portrayed, but by fostering a sense of danger posed by anyone who was black. This fear was all the more encouraged by the mob mentality perpetuated at the lynchings that also served to further empower the politicos who maintained control.

Because lynching was not unique to the South, and because slaveowners were loathe to have their valuable property destroyed, it was not until after Emancipation that the term began to take on specifically racial overtones. Once federal protections for freed slaves was withdrawn with the ending of Reconstruction, mob violence was increasingly directed at blacks. Lynching became a way to perpetuate control over the newly freed population. The resentment toward federal authority was strong and an attitude of entitlement coupled with a belief in the overall inferiority of blacks prevailed. Although the violence inflicted on blacks and their exclusion from the rights of citizenry had become patently illegal, violations were rarely prosecuted. As before, Southerners could take the law into their own hands with impunity.

Laws weren't enforced equally and the local governments looked the other way. Mob violence against blacks increased, peaking in the 1890s. Between Emancipation and the Great Depression, nearly three thousand blacks were lynched in the South.[86] And these numbers are surely low, for many lynchings were not reported and records were not kept uniformly. The grim statistics only tell part of the story not just in pure numbers but also in the brutality and the hatred embedded in the practice.

For sure, slavery is an ugly part of our heritage. Yet it would be a mistake to look at human behavior outside of the context of history and culture. Human violence is a complicated web that takes place in many contexts: owners/slaves, wardens/prisoners, men/women, murderers/victims, parents/children, etc. Each relationship is complex and includes both offender and victim. Racial violence is no different and must be seen within its historical and cultural roots. This doesn't excuse the behavior; the human record of violence is replete with a history of hatred bred by unsubstantiated fear. It is time to reexamine this.

On a personal level I began to reexamine these issues; as my health was failing, I felt the need to look at other failings as well. My religious evolution compelled me to face my own issues of bigotry and racial prejudice. In seeking God's truth I found new ways to ponder these issues and found the issue of capital punishment to be another step on the new path set out for me through God's blessing. In this process I have been liberated of the fears once within me. Starting with the fear of rejection and expanding to fear of the unknown and including fear of exposing my inadequacies, I was often reluctant to participate in conversations in which I might be exposed. I can honestly say that for most of my life, I carried around a feeling of oppression. Perhaps these feelings eventually allowed me to identify with the plight of blacks, although I never experienced actual oppression. But my feelings were real and because of my feelings of inadequacy and insecurity, I built walls around myself and lived within them, avoiding unpredictable situations (strangers, social strata perceived to be above my own, educational strata above my own, etc.).

In spite of my education and professional achievements, I perceived many people to be superior to me in some way, whether personally, financially, or educationally. Although the walls separating me from others were self-imposed and those separating blacks and whites were imposed by the white power structure, my walls allowed me a small taste of the experience. I understand that projected feelings are hardly a substitute for real victimization and oppression. Nevertheless, I believe that experience sensitized me to the plight of those who are really oppressed.

I was able to rise above my feelings of insecurity and inadequacy through seeking holiness and I have become whole through my newly formed relationship with God. With the freedom, empowerment, and passion that only God can give, I have developed the respect and self-love that is essential to harmonious relationships and understanding of others. Freedom from my perceived ineptitudes liberated me to pursue what I came to understand as spiritually and morally "right." I now not only express outrage and upset at "what is" but I feel free to speak out as to what ought to be. Silence is no longer my friend and refuge.

Although humans are neither perfect nor all-knowing, and are certainly not all-powerful, we are led by a God who is. I know that in my own conversion, I have come to understand the true message of Christianity in the purest sense of faith in God and Christ as the embodiment of pure love and the virtues that emulate from that love: kindness, forgiveness, and the free will to act on what is morally right. Love is also a call to action, a call to serve your neighbor. I am humbled in the face of God, governed by my human limitations as well as by my own powers and abilities. We are obligated to use our powers to do good. I believe that all things that are good come from God, and anything that is not good does not come from God. Because of God and through him, I have been blessed with strength and abilities. To you, "O God of my ancestors, I give thanks and praise, for you have given me wisdom and power . . . " (Daniel 2:20–21, 23).

Feelings of insecurity and inadequacy are not often based on reality; rather they are self-perceptions that are based on many factors from parental messages to childhood environment to social exposure, among others. My exceptional school record and subsequent successful professional life had little to do with my feelings. Though I'm sure I appeared to others as secure, smart, and savvy—the paradigm of success—the inner feelings took a long time to catch up to the outer façade. But it took my own death threat and a newfound trust in God to come to terms with my feelings and recognize my place in the world. There is no pecking order among humans in God's universe; although different, we are equal before God. I am not less than the professor who instructs my class or better than the woman who cleans the bathroom in the school. We have different skills and different contributions to make to build a better world. Now that I have the presence of mind to actually experience the peace of mind that accompanies that understanding, I have no doubts about the equality that exists among us, no matter the color of our skin or ethnic origin. It's a good feeling—one that I can only hope others will experience as profoundly as I have.

I grew up in a household that was many times violent, with a father who prided himself on discipline in an era in which fathers were the disciplinarians and mothers the homemakers and peacemakers. That the discipline too often erupted in violence served mostly to create fear and anxiety. Most of my father's wrath took place after my mother's death from cancer, but there was some even prior to that traumatic event. During such times in my earlier years, my sister and I would go to my maternal grandparents' home for a while—usually hours rather than days—until the situation had calmed. My father's behavior was quietly accepted as if it were a permanent condition that just had to be tolerated. It was explained and described as a need to "settle down," the same kind of language used to calm animals as they are being patted, or on children being admonished when they get too wild. What he had to "settle down" from was never clear. I never remember him expressing remorse; I just remember that he always eventually "settled down." And so his violence was condoned by those who could have perhaps stopped it. It was personal rough justice, punishment for some crime for which guilt was assumed. The punisher always assumes that what is being doled out is deserved, or "just deserts" as it is called. It was and is still the way many parents handle their children. It was just the way it was, much as it was in the larger picture that upheld segregation and slavery before it. The societal lynching is now played out in officially sanctioned killing, and cruelty continues to be dispensed to those we, as a society, want to punish.

Though I am certain that my father loved us, and I respected his hard work that allowed us to have things many others did not, his cruelty often masked that emotion. Was this his way of mirroring the behavior he learned as a child? It was. He was no stranger to either insults or assaults on those he loved; yet I don't doubt that he would have defended us from the same behavior from others. Perhaps it was his way of "toughening" up his son. His methods were that of a bully but he was still my father and I could not defend myself easily, even when I might have physically been able to do so. Instinctively, I would assume fetal position to protect myself from further kicks and punches, as well as the verbal insults that accompanied them. The pain was not just physical, but psychic as well; his assaults left me feeling sick inside and out. I occasionally ran away from home as a teen, sometimes taking refuge at my grandparents', other times at the home of a friend.

Luckily, I was eventually able to remove myself permanently from that environment, but the contradiction in his behavior was confusing. It wasn't until much later in my life (in fact, quite recently, and much after his death) that I was able to forgive him. This was perhaps my most difficult accomplishment. I had deep-seated scars and emotions and I was unable to let go of them. Even after accepting God into my life, feelings of hatred persisted; I blamed my father for my own shortcomings and feelings of inadequacy and insecurity in addition of the list of his transgressions as a parent. I came to realize, however, that he acted on the model of discipline that he had learned as a child, never questioning the basis for his own actions or beliefs. It was said, and I am now still sometimes reminded, that he was a typical "Baldwin," alluding to perhaps a genetic predisposition or at least a temperament that had violent inclinations.

The man who was willing to beat me to teach me a lesson was also willing to work two jobs to make sure I got through college to become the doctor he wanted me to be. Was that for him or me? I think it was both, and while I might have chosen a different path at that age, I have never regretted it. He was determined to provide for his family and our education and was resourceful in doing so. I remember how he would collect pecans from his mother's trees, and then from those of other neighbors, to buy and sell on the weekends; operate Christmas tree stands during the holiday season; and borrow his mother's truck, rigged with horizontal spigots, to oil the dirt roads in our neighborhood in an effort to keep the awful dust down, earning two dollars per house in the process. In most of these endeavors, he would demand my help. In addition, I had to spend many a weekend cleaning brick from old buildings that were being torn down. He would sell the cleaned, used brick and other salvageable items, eventually earning enough to buy an eighteen-wheeler cab, which he then hired someone to drive.

While he certainly was entrepreneurial, though I didn't recognize it as such at the time, he was also as resolute in his pursuit of these activities as in his iron-fist rule at home. Although he still went to church and subscribed to the principles of Christianity, he certainly did not live by them.

As a strict disciplinarian, my father also insisted that I play sports. Though I always liked them, as I reached my teens I wanted to sit out an upcoming high school football season, but was not allowed to do so. He would tell me it "was good for me" and I had no choice. I believe he thought of sports as a way of building muscle and a macho image, both important to him and therefore important for me. On the other hand, participating in sports teams helped to keep me occupied after my mother died, though I'm not sure that it had anything to do with his reasoning. Looking back, I appreciate the good that came of it.

I also came to understand that his assaults, whether on me or my mother, were his way of maintaining control over his family; control brings with it a certain kind of order and security. While it caused me great insecurity as a child, it served to cover his own insecurity and fears—fears that he couldn't measure up, that he couldn't rise above his own family background; that his children wouldn't turn out to be the stars of the play he wanted to script for them. Order and rigid structure bring some security to the insecure. I saw that in myself in my own adulthood.

Often we hate that which we fear, and in our own insecurity we fear that others will rise above and surpass us, leaving us in the dust. We fear what's missing as seen in the mirror of our own lives, whether it is status, material goods, jobs, or other ways in which we measure ourselves. We ignore the biblical mandate: "Do not covet your neighbor's house . . . or anything that belongs to your neighbor" (Exodus 20:17). This attitude extends to include not just those who have more, but also those who think differently, hold different views, or live by different values

As an adult, I can reflect on my childhood experiences and see the strong link they have to my adult feelings of inadequacy and insecurity. My intent is not to malign or offend anyone by my recollections that include dark secrets held for many years. I have moved beyond these feelings and pray that any references to this period in my life will be understood as part of a process, and ask for forgiveness, both among the living and the dead, for any perceived offense. Some people may be blessed with a devoted family who offer examples of love and respect and a genetic makeup that provides innate abilities and talent, good health, and a sunny disposition, but most are not so blessed. To varying degrees, we learn to accommodate and overcome the hand we are dealt. Some have to struggle harder than others.

I have seen many examples in which persistence in the face of hardship, be it physical or emotional, leads people finally to their true destination in life, to be all they wanted to be or could be. I have witnessed the power of God to transform others and to liberate them into the new life in Christ. In fact, I have not only seen it in many others, I bear personal witness to the infinite possibilities of the transforming power of God's love. Because I have experienced it, I know it has happened and therefore is possible.

While I cannot compare my father's abuse to lynching, it was how he saw his role as disciplinarian and punisher that connects them. Lynching was the punishment du jour for the blacks who were "out of line." The crime did not have to have been proved; the mere accusation could result in lynching. Lynching didn't end in this country until after the issue of due process was enforced by federal mandate, by which time the death penalty had become its legal successor. Michael Pfiefer, in his book, *Rough Justice: Lynching and American Society, 1874–1947*, argues that the death penalty became "an efficient, technocratic, and highly racialized mechanism of retributive justice."[87]

It doesn't take a great leap of faith to connect the dots that go from slavery to reconstruction to lynching to capital punishment. In the pre-civil rights era, perfunctory trials in the South led the accused to the gallows; they didn't have to be legal convictions. We may not like what we see, but it is incumbent on us to look anyway. When lynching was moved to the courtroom, the results were often the same. The audience that was once entertained by the spectacle of mob-led hangings moved to the courtroom where the drama played out under the guise of local justice with the imprimatur of elected or appointed officials and local magistrates ready to contain any outbreaks. Some of those trials mocked the concept of justice, but blacks got a trial, and wasn't that the point? That they ended the same way—with official hangings instead of lynchings, and later the electric chair or gas chamber—wasn't seen as problematic. People could feel satisfied that they were doing the right thing by letting the law intervene. They didn't understand what the problem was and when the accusation of racial disparity and unfairness persisted, they blamed it on Northern interference and the "agendas" of outsiders, liberal or otherwise. While that part of our history in the South is past, there are still remnants.

Just as we still have traces of prejudice in our souls, the concept of retribution for capital crimes remains embodied in both our laws and our spirit. It's not that other parts of the country, including the North, are absolved of their own prejudices; there are many and we mistakenly think that slavery and prejudice didn't exist in the North. It did. But the abolition movement came from the North and was strong there, and won out over the long term. By 1804, all the Northern states had either ended slavery or established timetables to do so. By 1807, England outlawed the slave trade and in 1833 abolished slavery altogether. The economic repercussions were felt throughout the United States, especially in the South where the practice was an integral part of both the culture and the economy.

As slavery moved toward its end, its underlying prejudices did not; they were manifested differently in different parts of the country and they played out differently over the course of the next century. But the movement to compel civil rights for blacks was greatly aided by Northerners whose experience at a distance made them suspect to those in the South who lived with their own reality of racial issues and had more invested and then lost in the institution of slavery.

As we look at the criminal justice system we see that trials for murder can be as perfunctory today as they were years ago in the old stereotypical Southern courtroom. The November 2, 2006, *New York Times* reported on a capital trial in Kentucky in which the defendant's court-appointed attorney didn't even know his client's real name until after his case was later appealed.[88] Essentially, we go through the motions to give the indigent a "fair" trial, appoint attorneys to defend them, and look the other way at gross incompetence. That most of the victims of this practice are black doesn't seem to bother those who have the power to correct the system. Though the effects of the civil rights movement can be felt in many areas of social and political discourse, the criminal justice system has been the least affected—perhaps by design, or at least by benign neglect.

Lynching conjures up a different image from that of a legal execution. The latter carries an official stamp that removes us from complicity by injecting layers between us and those who do the dirty work of execution and actually see how gruesome it is. Yet both practices result in death and both are punishments for a crime, or an alleged crime.

Recent research has borne out what seems like an obvious parallel between lynching and the death penalty. The states that have used the death penalty the most are also the states that have a distinctly higher history of lynching.[89] As lynching declined, court-ordered executions began to replace them. As one of the authors of the study explained, "Lynching seems to matter and is relevant to our understanding of contemporary lethal violence" in the South.

In a 2005 study, researchers Mesner, Baller, and Zevenbergen examined the county data on vigilante lynchings between 1882 and 1930 in Alabama, Arkansas, Florida, Georgia, Kentucky, Louisiana, Mississippi, North Carolina, South Carolina, and Tennessee, and compared it to homicide data from 1986 to 1995, courtesy of the FBI and National Center for Health Statistics. The data showed a positive correlation between counties with the highest homicide rates and counties with the most lynchings; counties with fewer lynchings had fewer murders.

Even though the statistics were controlled for population, poverty, education levels, age of population, unemployment, and single-parent households, it must be noted that because records of lynching were never official, there are discrepancies in the data, including that upon which this 2005 study was based. Sources used to gather this data (see Appendix B) concerning the total number of lynchings by county and state had to rely on personal accounts, which were then verified by other sources. The likelihood is that the number of lynchings reported in the study is greatly understated.[90]

Lynchings took place across the continent, though the states of the Old Confederacy had by far the highest incidence of lynching, followed by some of the border states and western territories where the law was local.[91] Though violence against blacks was begun during slavery, it slowly morphed into a system of police brutality as Jim Crow laws sanctioned segregation as well as a culture of racial hatred. In many of the lynching photos that record this sorry period of our history, police officials can be seen along with the rest of the audience. The tacit acceptance and the implicit nod to local authorities continued until it met formal resistance in the civil rights era.

In another recent study, research showed that the number of death sentences was higher in states with a history of lynching. This correlation applied to all criminals, regardless of race. However, the case was particularly strong when extracting the data for death sentences for black defendants. The authors hypothesized that death sentences in these states grew as the states' population of blacks increased. The researchers believe that the trend suggests that "current racial threat and past vigilantism largely directed against newly freed slaves jointly contribute to current lethal but legal reactions to racial threat."[92]

I BELIEVE THAT CRIME deserves punishment, and I can sympathize with those who want to punish criminals, especially criminals who have brought harm to one's loved ones. I remember wanting to punish the "commie" Northerners who were interfering with my Southern comfort and they hadn't done anything to me personally. They just made me angry—angry at their attitude as well as their ability to inflict what I saw as harm. The irrational but strong feelings I had of hatred and anger are useful maps of the human, emotional response that people harbor toward the "others" in our midst, particularly if those "others" have brought harm to us or our loved ones or are seen as a threat because they are perceived to be able to do so.

I can now recognize the role of hatred and anger toward my father, which was rooted in his ability to inflict harm on me—and my mother, who I wanted to protect and couldn't—and identify the desire to avenge his behavior, though I would never have acted on it. Being uncomfortable with such feelings may have been a factor in alienating myself from him. Perhaps the fact that his hatred was often directed at "others"—outside forces that he could not control—helped me to also identify with the recipients of his wrath; I certainly was one of them, at least on occasion.

It is easy to blame our own failings on the "other" and then direct our anger and hostility there. Isn't the origin of hatred simply fear—fear of loss of control, of losing what we have, of being less than? All the hatred and bigotry directed at blacks was to "keep the niggers in their place," that is, make sure they can't take your place, whether in a job or social status or other. So long as they remained unequal "in their place," "they" were not a threat and "we" whites remained in control.

When we put ourselves in God's hands our own need for control is given to him. That doesn't mean that we do nothing and attribute everything that happens to God's will, however. Some things are in the range of human control: how we handle our anger, how we respond to the anger of others, how we treat others, how we choose to live. We can't control the color of the skin we are born with or when we are born and when we die.

We must give up thinking that we need to control other people and focus on controlling ourselves. We can't always control our feelings, but we can control how we act, and whether we react with anger and whether we act on bigotry and stereotypes. While none of us alone can control the government and the law, we do have a say as citizens in a democracy and each of us has a responsibility to consider how we contribute, by activism or default, to what happens in our name.

As a Southerner looking at our mottled history, I question the role of my own family whose roots lie deep in the Southern culture that supported this type of un-Christian behavior. Some who participated in mob violence were surely my ancestors and if they didn't directly participate, they condoned and encouraged it. How can people who are basically good and kind harbor such hatred?

I can remember walking home from church in the early dark of night with my mother, sister, and a few other relatives. The road we were walking on separated the black section from the white section of Toulminville at the time. We could see a bright glow as we approached the burning cross on the lawn of one the houses. It was quite large; from a child's perspective it looked to be thirty feet high, though in reality it was probably no more than eight feet tall. It was engulfed in flames and emitted a strong light as well as the distinct smell of fire in the crisp evening air. As we got closer, I could see in the windows of the house the faces of several black people who were watching it burn, but few others were to be seen. I could also feel the heat from the fire of the cross. I was probably seven or eight years old, and the very sight of it frightened me. I could hear an eerie quiet through the flames. I asked my mother why the cross was burning. I knew instinctively to keep my voice low; fear was in the air and in my vocal cords, which would have prevented me from speaking up even if I had known what to say. As we continued on home, she gently explained that this was the way the Klan tried to scare people when they didn't like what they were doing, especially black people. I didn't find that immediately comforting and I was worried that they might come after us, but she assured me that they did not come after "people like us" and that we were safe.

The image of the burning cross made an impression I couldn't quite shake. I was not totally convinced that such a frightening thing could not happen to "people like us." For many weeks afterward, I would peer out our front window at night, particularly if I heard a noise or a loud voice, to see if there was a cross burning in front of our house. The message to me as a child was clear: Obedience to authority was mandatory. Don't ask questions, just live by the rules and you'll be fine.

Most Southern white people did just that: they lived quiet lives and didn't make waves, whether or not they agreed with the practices of the Klan. Mostly they did agree that the "niggers had to be kept in their place." Klan culture came to dominate the South and grew stronger as its opposition grew. Opposition came mostly from the North and the resentment spilled over throughout. It was easy to rouse the troops with cries of Northern interference (again!). It's hard to know if people were more fearful of the outside interference—promoted as "Northern commies out to take over the country"—or of the Klan itself. Too few Southerners dared to ask the question, at least in the earlier days of the civil rights movement. I know for myself, though I intellectually didn't condone the Klan, I did fear their wrath. But in truth I also was afraid of the communists that we were told were about to land on our shores and bomb us in our own home towns. The air raid drills instilled fear and obedience in one fell swoop. We assumed that those who would protect us—teachers, local police and government officials—must know what's best. As children, we have to be able to trust those in charge. As adults we should not be so easily given to thoughtless obedience based on irrational fear.

I have to ask myself why it is that we are willing to give up our God-given reasoning abilities when confronted with conflict. God gives us the gift of reason and the freedom to use it and it is he to whom we all must answer. But somehow we forget this when we look at issues of race and power.

Instead of embracing our human capacity to reason and to live justly, we cling to false ideas, hatred, and anger. We are rejecting the moral principles laid down in the Bible, for it is there that we can find the basis for what is right, just, and fair. Whether we use as a yardstick for morality something as simple as the Golden Rule or as complicated as Kant's Categorical Imperative or the theology of St. Paul, often considered to be the foundation of

Christianity and responsible for its spread, the message of these principles can be summed up as "love your neighbor as yourself." Adhering to this precept does not require belief in God; it requires only a belief in moral living and fair treatment of others, often to the point of sacrificing what is in one's own perceived self-interest. While I have found answers to moral questions and great comfort and peace from the Bible, and I find it to be my own moral guide to what's right, just, and fair, I know that others may use other resources to reach the same conclusions on moral issues.

Regardless of what message in the Bible they used to defend their actions, or on whose moral authority, the Klan and the "rough justice" concept were still active in the South until the last recorded lynching in 1981. That incident in Mobile, Alabama, was a KKK chapter's response when a jury failed to convict a black man for the murder of a white man. Bennie Hays, the leader of that small, local KKK group, told his fellow Klansmen, "If a black man can get away with killing a white man, we ought to be able to get away with killing a black man." Later, his son and other Klansmen chose a random black victim to murder as a symbolic protest. Their intended object lesson cost an innocent young man his life. Ironically, it was the persistence and confidence of the victim's mother that finally brought an end to that particular Klan group, through a civil suit on behalf of her murdered son. Beulah Mae Donald called on national civil rights leaders on her deceased son's behalf to find justice. Were it not for her activism and the legal support she received from national groups, the Klan might still be a larger part of the Southern backwaters. We'll never know.

As I have argued earlier, I don't think even Henry Hays's execution for the murder of Mrs. Donald's son, Michael, served any purpose but that of revenge. The murderers were brought to justice. Klansman James Knowles testified against fellow Klansman Henry Hays and received a life sentence instead of the death penalty. It is worth noting that in the case of Darrell Grayson, the man who confessed and fingered Grayson was not offered a lesser sentence. Interestingly, Knowles expressed remorse but Hays continued to claim his innocence even though he is reported to have confessed to a member of the clergy before his execution.[93]

The culture that once supported and then tolerated the routine murder of blacks as object lessons is no longer routinely condoned. But that hasn't stopped people from being blinded by their latent prejudices and fears. During the last few years, the Alabama media has begun to change its tune: *The Birmingham News* and the *Huntsville Times* now support the abolition of capital punishment in Alabama. This is a huge change. If the local media is a reflection of the local community, this represents perhaps the biggest shift in opinion we have ever seen on this issue. These news outlets, among others, had led the pack with pro-death penalty attitudes until recently.

As those who investigate the issue begin to educate themselves about the facts, they have become more vocal about the inequity of the system. People are becoming more uncomfortable with the idea of innocent people being put to death, and with the advent of DNA testing, errors become more indisputable. Regardless of which facts are used to support a change, the slow leak is beginning to deflate the illogical arguments for capital punishment. As people start to question the "facts," attitudes start to change.

This small but discernible shift in Alabama, I think, reflects the national trend. Even recent editorials in local newspapers have been increasingly sympathetic to abolition of the death penalty. Whether this is a trend or a phase, only time will tell. The old joke is that people in Alabama like to say "Thank God for Mississippi." If not for Mississippi, Alabama would rank last in many measurements of state services. If one can consider death row a service, I suppose we exceed that of our neighbor where there are only a third as many inmates on death row. Mississippi has about half of the population of Alabama. Indeed, as of 2000, the most recent U.S. census, Mississippi's total population was 2.8 million people (2,844,658) and Alabama's was approximately 4.4 million (4,447,100). Also, Alabama's execution rate is almost three times higher—.076/10,000 in Alabama, to Mississippi's .027/10,000.[94]

People naturally like to be right and want to be on the right side of any given issue. As more credible information surfaces and leads to uncertainty, the doors open for further thought. My conversations with people lead me to believe that at this point in the slow evolution toward abolition of capital punishment, people don't necessarily think the death penalty is wrong so much as they are less sure that is it right. It is a mere fissure in the thinking about the issue. The more credible the source of the facts and the more often the facts are repeated, the greater traction they have and the greater the support for the conclusion.

It is clear that the debate on the issue has changed. Leaders of the abolition movement no longer cite race as the major factor in their argument, or that the "sanctity of life" is the basic issue, or even that the death penalty represents "cruel and unusual punishment." They now talk more about "due process," and "equal protection." By shifting the language used, abolitionists can refer to themselves as legal conservatives interested in defense of the law itself. It is a much more comfortable position because it reduces the moral issues to legal ones. But I firmly believe that racism is the nexus of the argument and that all other inadequacies in the system follow from that basic theorem.

Certainly if there were widespread support for abandoning capital punishment, the laws in every state would be changing radically; but they are not—at least not yet. But there is a shimmer of light under that barn door and people are beginning to examine the issue.

The way a prominent member of our Supreme Court stated it rings true. Justice William Brennan, writing in the Georgia case of *McCleskey v. Kemp* (481 U.S. 279,312), said:

> It is tempting to pretend that minorities on death row share a fate in no way connected to our own, that our treatment of them sounds no echoes beyond the chambers in which they die. Such an illusion is ultimately corrosive, for the reverberations of injustice are not so easily confined. 'The destinies of the two races in this country are indissolubly linked together' (560 Harland, J. dissenting), and the way in which we choose those who will die reveals the depth of moral commitment among the living.[95]

13

The Evolution of Myths

My own transition in racial matters was a slow evolution, softened over time by exposure to minorities I worked in the health care field in my early days of medical training and residency. While I never developed any close interracial friendships at the time, the open environment naturally replaced stereotypes with multi-dimensional people and peeled away some of my misguided concepts. Actually, I felt relieved. Some of those old myths had been mysterious and somewhat disconcerting, even for an adult. I was pleasantly surprised to find that "there wasn't much difference in none of us," in Tom Cherry's words. I buried the old hand-me-down myths as I developed genuine respect for people based on their abilities and their personalities. Skin color became irrelevant. I enjoyed their company, not because of or in spite of skin color, but because of the individual person.

These small but discernible shifts contributed to my acceptance of blacks on a personal level, but it wasn't until I actually spent time studying the data and reading about race in relationship to the death penalty that I experienced a "eureka" moment. I then had to reevaluate the perception common in some circles that blacks are more prone to crime when I was confronted with statistics like these: 455 men were executed for rape between 1930 and 1976; 90 percent, or 405, were black.[96]

It didn't take much in the Jim Crow era for a black man to be arrested and convicted of rape; all that was generally required was a white woman's accusation. I had to ask myself if 90 percent of the rapes in this country could have been committed by blacks. In doing some soul searching, I had to recognize the stereotypes that I had grown up with: blacks had particularly strong sexual tendencies, their African origins placing them just a few generations from wild men from the jungles, in need of taming; black men lusted after white women. I knew these stereotypes to be false and pernicious but during the 1930–1976 period of those statistics, they were still fairly widely held beliefs, at least in the South. Could this stereotyping account for those numbers? The short answer is yes.

Sexual paranoia was pervasive in the context of the myths and nowhere was chauvinism more pervasive than in the so-called gentlemanly South. Women were in need of protection from the "wild black savages" who were unleashed after emancipation. No one said exactly that, of course, but it was clear in the underlying attitude and in the media of the day—the early movie classic, *Birth of a Nation*, for instance—and it was broadly held to be true. It was a "fact" that was used to pronounce lynching as a rational response to the alleged crime. So if the public perceived white women to be at risk of rape by black men, it would come as no surprise that so many of the defendants in such cases were black; nor would it have upset the sensibility of the public at that time that these defendants would be executed for their crime, regardless of the numbers. The "black savages" had to be "kept in their place."

On balance, it is also important to note that state-sanctioned violence was not confined to the South; it was merely applied to a different population. In the nineteenth century and the early years of the twentieth century, whether by war or lynching, the removal of Native Americans who were seen as threats to Manifest Destiny was carried out with impunity. As the Native American population shrank from American assaults, there became less need for rough justice against them.

In the South, the black population continued to increase both through natural reproduction and importation of more slaves. The economics of the pre–Civil War South depended on slavery. After the Civil War, the slaves were free but Southerners were not free of their resentment or of the hostility toward those who destroyed their livelihood. Decades later, the myths of the "black savages" were still prevalent. "The mob stands today as the most potent bulwark between the women of the South and such a carnival of crime as would infuriate the world and precipitate the annihilation of the Negro race," warned John Temple Graves, editor of the *Atlanta Constitution*.[97]

The myth that white women were at risk of rape by black men had wide acceptance among whites in the early part of the twentieth century. In the South, lynching was a common response to this belief. Lest we think that the underlying concept was at such odds elsewhere, an editorial in the *New York Herald* noted that "[T]he difference between bad citizens who believe in lynch law, and good citizens who abhor lynch law, is largely in the fact that the good citizens live where their wives and daughters are perfectly safe."[98] The fear of rape perpetrated by the KKK, which was on the rise during that same period, also played on the fear of miscegenation—outlawed at the time in thirty states including all of the South. The dominant world view was still that of white supremacy; it was a view less relevant where blacks were a minor portion of the population and lynchings there were less prevalent.

While the KKK served to strengthen the myths and keep white social order, some social scientists of the period adopted eugenics as a foundation for racial superiority and a defense against "mixed breeding." The confluence of these ideas served to raise the level of fear of rape. The most offensive and unthinkable scenario was one in which there was consensual sex between a white woman and a black man. Such an act was deemed totally unacceptable, so much so that it was all too often used as a pretext for preemptive punishment. The Scottsboro Boys is a case in point.

The Scottsboro case centered around nine young blacks accused of raping two white women. That the nine were not adults, that they had little if any legal counsel, that they were convicted by an all-white jury, and that one of the "victims" later recanted her testimony did not dissuade the prosecution or the populist following that cheered their conviction. An arm of the communist party came to the legal defense of the boys, thus providing fodder for the later accusation of communist infiltration of the civil rights movement. When the U.S. Supreme Court ultimately overturned the death penalty sentences in the case and ordered new trials, the decision was largely seen as a repudiation of states' rights, adding fuel to the fire of the old argument over state versus federal power.

Lynching was accepted because it kept the "black man in his place." Is it also the underlying reason that a majority still accept the death penalty when the statistics clearly demonstrate its racist underpinnings? The following quotation is taken from a newspaper article in the *Washington Times* in 1900 and gives some sense as to the gruesome nature of these lynchings which so often become public spectacles:

Columbia, S. C., Feb. 17—Will Burts, a negro, nineteen years old, was lynched this morning in Aiken county. Three days ago he attempted to outrage Mrs. C. L. Weeks and failed.

A crowd of 250 tracked the negro fifty miles across last evening led by a farmer, who received $100 from the posse. The party returned to Greenwood, and at daylight this morning the lynching occurred. Some wished to hold the man till tonight and make a public demonstration of it, but this was outvoted. A clothesline was obtained, one end swung over an oak limb, and the other fastened to Burts' neck. He was then ordered to climb the tree and get out on the limb. This the negro did without hesitation. He was then shot from the limb. The rope broke, and, as Burts was not dead, he was again hoisted up and then shot to pieces.[99]

Significantly, whites who lynched blacks were seldom prosecuted and even when prosecutions occurred and convictions resulted, capital punishment was rarely invoked. A rare exception was in the Michael Donald case in Mobile, Alabama, in the 1980s, mentioned in the previous chapter. Henry Hays's eventual execution in 1997 was the first time a white man had been executed for a crime against an African American since 1913.[100]

It is important to take a macro view of the evolution of racism and its relationship to the death penalty. This historical context forces us to change the gestalt when examining our current policies and views. By 1930, the start date of these statistics, lynching was on the decline but the law allowed the death penalty to be imposed in rape cases. After the 1977 Supreme Court ruling in *Coker v. Georgia*, the death penalty was ruled out as a possible punishment for rape and the number of overall executions declined. Since most people no longer hold primitive views about blacks, it is time to reevaluate our criminal justice system within this framework. How many other wrongful rape convictions in that same period did not result in the death penalty and are thus not included in the statistics we've been discussing?

Only a handful of states still allow the death penalty to be applied to a crime other than murder. With the exception of Montana, they are all in the South (Texas, Oklahoma, South Carolina, and Louisiana), and with the exception of Louisiana, all apply only to repeat offenders. Patrick Kennedy was convicted of raping an eight-year-old; he is a first-time offender and has continued to profess his innocence. Kennedy and one other convicted rapist, who has a history of mental illness, are the only people sitting on death row anywhere for a crime that does not involve murder. The courts in Louisiana have upheld the state law that makes rape of a child a capital crime. In January 2008, the Supreme Court agreed to hear *Kennedy v. Louisiana*; the case was heard on May 16, and on June 8, the Supreme Court ruled in favor of the defendant, thus disallowing the use of the death penalty in cases of rape. Perhaps this decision will speak to the larger issue of applying capital punishment to a wider range of non-homicidal crimes.

It should also be noted that it wasn't until very recently that the Supreme Court barred the death penalty for juveniles (*Roper v. Simmons*, 2005). Prior to this ruling, fifteen- and sixteen-year-olds were tried as adults in most states. The decision overturned the death penalty for juveniles in the nineteen states that still allowed capital sentences for sixteen- to eighteen-year-olds, Alabama among them. In the six years prior to the ruling, twenty-two juveniles were executed; a majority were blacks. How far have we really evolved?

While we would now consider the rate of prosecution of blacks for rape cited between 1930 and 1976 to be alarming, at the time it served to allay white fears of blacks. The logic was that if they're being prosecuted and executed, it makes whites safer—the same bogus deterrence argument that is still used, now with somewhat less skewed statistics. In both instances, the underlying fear of crime, and in particular, crime by blacks, is met by a disproportionate anger based on the myth of the "black criminal tendency." The disproportion of the anger seems like a vestige of the outrage that generations ago was more openly expressed at the audacity of a black committing *any* crime against a white. Black criminal offenders were considered impudent and were not to be tolerated, regardless of the triviality of the crime.

So it was that the myths continued to get passed down, all over the country, but they were more intransigent in the South where the stakes were higher. It was only after the civil rights movement that these stereotypes began to be discharged, but not without a struggle. As I reexamined my own myths and my own struggle with erasing them from my unconscious, I had to look at the underlying assumption that blacks were particularly prone to violence. We are all predisposed to such thoughts—conscious or not. How we perceive situations and then react in them is determined by many factors as we size up the people involved. Variables include age, sex, appearance, speech patterns, and, of course race, among others. But if race were such a determining factor in the commission of crime, wouldn't there be multiple studies looking to understand how and why? My research began in earnest. As Mark Twain once said, "It ain't what you don't know that gets you into trouble. It's what you know for sure that just ain't so."

As I THREW MYSELF into answering the question, I learned that there have been many researchers and academics who have done extensive examination of the racial disparity shown in crime statistics. While the numbers of blacks charged and convicted of crimes are higher than those for other racial groups, most studies indicate that blacks are no more prone to violence than anyone else. Violence is associated with poverty, environment, and family dynamics; race in and of itself doesn't seem to be a factor.

Harvard sociology professor Robert J. Sampson has studied the determinants of crime and concluded that environmental factors (marital status of the parents, immigrant generation and socioeconomic composition of the neighborhood) account for more than 60 percent of the gap in crime rates between racial groups. Sampson found that perceptions were also a relevant factor: the greater the proportion of minorities in the neighborhood, the greater the perception that there were problems with crime. "There's a cultural stereotype [not only among whites] that violence and disorder is associated with minority groups," Sampson explained. "People are acting on beliefs that reinforce the patterns that exist."[101] Assessing real differences in rates of violence among racial groups is complicated by this perceptual bias. In multiple studies that I looked at, I realized that the numbers aren't quite that simple.

Looking further at the rate of rape, the same data indicate even more bias: of those executed, more blacks were juveniles and more blacks were sent to their death without any further judicial review of their case. After the *Coker v. Georgia* decision, twenty inmates were removed from death row, seventeen of whom were black.[102]

The imbalance in the number of arrests and convictions between blacks and other minorities and that of whites is not, as many would like us to believe, because blacks are more prone to crime. Blacks are sentenced more often and more severely for the same or similar crimes as those committed by whites.[103] In one study, it was found that "the concentration of poverty increases both black and white homicide rather equally."[104]

One of the courses I took during my studies at BSC was statistics. For that class, I wrote a paper on racial profiling in which I attempted to address the question of how the vestiges of prejudice are played out in modern Birmingham. I did a rather complicated statistical analysis of the issue, the results of which clearly indicated that racial profiling is alive and well in Birmingham. While this will not come as a big surprise to blacks in the community, several of the surveys I reviewed showed the disconnect between what whites thought and said about race and what their black counterparts thought and said about it—a result later confirmed by the Sampson studies. The data show that blacks continue to feel the effects of racism and racial profiling in many facets of their lives. One particular study, the Birmingham Pledge Survey, analyzed how people react to racial issues and how they themselves define it. The survey revealed statistically significant differences between the perceptions of blacks and whites. Blacks recognized that race is a problem; whites in the survey either failed to recognize it, or ignored it, thereby excusing themselves from more meaningful dialogue and any action directed at eliminating it.

Before writing this paper, I would not have predicted the facts I subsequently found during my research, although I had started to become more aware of existing racial disparity in general. By this time in my life, I had already made some rather large steps toward changing my attitudes and prejudices toward blacks. But the depth of the differences gnawed at me. The more I read, the more I recognized my own attitudes and the project took on a rather personal nature as an ugly question reared its head: Is there any latent racism still lying deep within my own self? This required some particularly in-depth analysis as I attempted to unbury any latent prejudice in myself; it was there. Although much of it had been dispelled over the years, there were still some ugly and bogus concepts that lay at the heart of some of my thinking. The hard part was bringing them to the surface. Once I rejected the facts as I had known them, I was able to understand some of the attitudes that I had held on to. It was not an easy catharsis; but I knew that if I was in search of truth, they could no longer be a part of my being. Being aware of it allows me the privilege of stopping it in its tracks and I can laugh at some of the more ridiculous falsehoods in my own thinking as well as in that of others.

As my own life became more rooted to religious principles and morality driven by my reading of the Bible, I gained moral clarity, and, yes, shame at the bogus and hateful beliefs I once held. There simply is no place for any prejudice against anyone if indeed you adhere to the principles taught and lived out by Christ. Contrary to the trend of our post-modern society, I believe that shame does still matter. It also explains why I am perplexed at some very intelligent people who still use truthiness—the term popularized by comedian Stephen Colbert to mean gut beliefs unsupported by facts or research—to defend what they think or say about the death penalty.

Racism lingers not just in Alabama, but in the nation as a whole. However, it is not generally blatant; latent, or modern, racism lurks beneath the surface and is thus more insidious and, in its own way, more lethal because it is buried. Since whites do not fully recognize their own deep-seated prejudice, they have a polite excuse for not addressing it. The racism that I evaluated in my analysis touched all aspects of society: education, social issues, business, housing, and crime. Given that this is not something I alone discovered—many academics and civic organizations in Alabama and across the country have reached the same conclusions—we have to assume that the disparity seen in the justice system today is a reflection of the racism that still exists in more subtle forms than that which existed openly in the pre-civil rights era.

While I often hear people remark that they have black friends who are "just like family," this part of the family somehow isn't invited to the Easter buffets or Christmas dinners at the local country clubs or finer restaurants. While efforts to "take care of them" may be genuine and even generous, it begs the question. Those who are "just like family" are not equals economically or socially and being in a position to be charitable demonstrates that inequality. Among people who are financially comfortable, it is not difficult to give materially. What is difficult is to work toward and support leveling the playing field, for that might mean giving up the handicap. I know I was guilty of this kind of thinking and I now recognize how I got satisfaction from my charitable overtures—they made me feel good about myself. My actions did help people on an individual level, but on a more global scale they did nothing to change the system that sustains racial prejudice and discrimination. The problem must be attacked on both fronts. Charitable giving is important, but not without more charitable thinking that includes an attempt to give people genuinely equal opportunities.

It is no longer politically correct or acceptable to overtly express racist views; in fact, it is often thought of as boorish. So instead of expressing bias, people consciously express support for equality while perhaps unconsciously act in ways that reveal subtle but real prejudice. Although racism may not be obvious in our words and public persona, it is more apparent in our deeds. This becomes more obvious from looking at the statistics of our criminal system in terms of who is arrested, who is convicted, and who is sentenced to death rather than to life without parole. Unfortunately, race is more statistically relevant than the actual guilt or innocence of any particular individual. When we focus on an individual case, it is easy to overlook the larger picture.

To change something, one has to recognize and acknowledge that there is a problem, and this in itself is a problem. The Birmingham Survey showed that while whites don't see race and racial profiling as a problem, blacks do. Across the board in every facet of life, a majority of blacks perceive racial prejudice while a majority of whites don't think that race relations are a big problem. Considering the long history of racism in this country and in Alabama, in particular, changing it will be and has been an evolving process. But first, one must recognize that the problem exists. Of course we see the surface behavior—from racial slurs to exclusion from the country club. But what about when bias is not so obvious?

While I had become more cognizant of racial prejudice since my age of "enlightenment" in early 2000, discovering how large a role it played in the criminal system still came as a shock. Even after I was well into my master's thesis preparation and preparing for my eventual graduation in May 2003, I was struck by a headline in the January 8, 2003, *New York Times*: "Death Penalty Found More Likely If the Victim Is White." For some of my research, I had found the *Times* to be a reliable source. My old prejudices to the contrary, it did not turn out to have a wildly liberal slant on this issue. I wasn't actually surprised by the idea that the odds were stacked against blacks. My research had revealed that discrimination was widespread in our criminal justice system, particularly in the administration of capital punishment. But I had not considered race of the victim as a major issue in how punishment was doled out.

The article discussed a study commissioned by the state of Maryland. In brief, the study found that prosecutors seek the death penalty much more frequently if the victim is white and the perpetrator is black. When the defendant is brought to trial, race doesn't seem to have much of an effect on the process of determining guilt. The races of the victim and the defendant seem only to be an issue when it comes to sentencing. The newspaper article forced me to factor in this issue in my thesis. I read further and discovered other studies in other states and around the country that had reached the same conclusion.

During this process, I was frequently so aghast at the "new" facts that I was eager to share the information with those around me. While I'm sure that it was sometimes aggravating to my family and friends, at first it surprised me that others didn't react with similar outrage. In fact, most of my closest family members strongly support the death penalty; they are also deeply religious. I understood that no one else had the same experience and no one else had done the same research. But I did talk to other people about the issue, and many of these people had extensive knowledge about the criminal justice system and the death penalty; some were even experts. And like Jack, who had been in the BSC program with me, they refused to let reason rule.

As determined as my father had been to change his station in life, I was convinced that if people had the correct information, they too would change their opinion on this issue. I was wrong on that front, too. Although most of the time, my friends and family would listen to me expound on the unfairness of the system, more often than not they would shrug and continue to believe what they had always believed. I learned quickly that not everyone shared my enthusiasm for the subject.

On occasion, however, I was able to engage family and/or friends in a lively discussion and I looked forward to such talks. After all, this closed circle created a safe environment; even if we disagreed, we all knew it would not get ugly. However, I didn't always confine my quest to close friends and family. By now, I had gained more confidence in my own belief system and its inherent morality; I was trying to live under God's law, which included using my God-given abilities to reason. I no longer felt insecure or intimidated so I naturally pushed ahead with no thoughts or worries about being wrong or inferior in some unspoken way. This in itself was a great blessing and relief and I owe my thanks to God and the message and example of his perfect son for helping me take this path. It has led to the healing of and sustenance for my body and the purification of my mind and a feeling of serenity.

One afternoon shortly after reading the *New York Times* article, I attended a professional medical conference and ran into a colleague I hadn't seen in a couple of years. Henry and I had known each other briefly during our residency, but he doesn't live in the Birmingham area. He knew that I had retired from practice and asked after my health and current activities, and I gave him a brief summary of my new "career." Based on past conversations we'd had and the fact that he was a Southerner by birth, I assumed Henry's views would be similar to my old attitudes toward capital punishment, though it wasn't a subject we had actually ever discussed.

Henry does a lot of research in his field, so I began telling him how my research turned up evidence that was counter to what I had expected. He seemed quite interested. We briefly discussed the difficulty of research that doesn't conform to your assumptions. It happens across all disciplines and it is a caveat that researchers are trained to deal with so as not to bias a study. Then I told him about the *New York Times* article. I wasn't quite prepared for his response.

"I avoid the *Times* like the plague," he said without hesitation.

I paused, slightly surprised at the vehemence of his statement, though the statement itself is the prevailing wisdom in the South. I didn't want to turn the conversation into a defense of the *Times*. "Well, the article is actually just a report about a study commissioned by the state of Maryland," I said, trying to bring us back to the original topic. "The study found that blacks that kill whites in their state are much more likely to face the death penalty than blacks who kill blacks or whites who kill blacks. Now is that not a shame!"

"Well, these kinds of studies are often misleading, you know," Henry said. "I don't believe that is the case. You know, you can derive many conclusions of a different nature from a study depending on your perspective. This just seems like another example of the liberals trying to push an agenda."

I had known Henry over the years to be an extremely intelligent, generous, and thoughtful man. I had never asked him about his views about either race or crime, but I had no reason to think that his attitudes were significantly different from most others who grew up in the post-war South and lived through the civil rights movement. But I also knew that in the last decade he had been active in providing medical services to the poor and making financial contributions to several charitable foundations. He had also given his expertise to developing a system of providing prenatal care to those not able to afford it, which included mostly minority patients. But I wanted to tread lightly.

"As a matter of fact, I was surprised by the research, too," I explained. "In truth, I was quite skeptical when I first started getting interested in the subject, so I did additional research. But all the statistics add up to the same conclusion: blacks who kill whites are much more likely to face the death penalty than blacks who kill blacks or whites who kill blacks."

"Well, I would have to look at what other factors were in play with those statistics," he replied with just a tad of annoyance, still sure in his knowledge.

"This data has been confirmed by numerous other studies," I explained, trying to reinforce the science rather than focus on the conclusions. "What other factors are you referring to?" I asked. "I don't know what other data would be relevant," I told him. "If you just look at the raw criminal justice statistics, the data on the subject confirms beyond a doubt that gross discrimination exists in the selection of who will die for killing and who will live. The bias is clear."

"Well, I don't know that," he said matter-of-factly, apparently in an attempt to punch holes in the data I referred to, although he had no evidence to support that position. In effect, Henry was questioning not just the data, but my reporting of it via the *Times*, or my ability to correctly interpret it, though I'm sure he did not intend to be dismissive of me.

Henry was always a quick thinker. Even in our early days at the hospital, he liked to challenge the residents and make us think about how and why we formed a patient's diagnosis. Similarly, by taking that same tactic, I had not consciously set out to embarrass him or put him on the defensive. As well, he wouldn't want to think that he could hold such obviously unfair and unjust views. His self-image and belief system could remain intact.

So I asked him directly, "Henry, what are your feelings about blacks in general?"

As was the case for most of the white people questioned in the Birmingham Survey, Henry does not think of himself as prejudiced, nor does he believe there's a race problem. He believes that blacks should be treated fairly. As was true of those surveyed, he also believes that blacks are treated fairly. So in his mind, the studies I referred to couldn't possibly be correct. Furthermore, if he entertained the possibility that there is such gross inequality, he would also at least have to allow the possibility that the death penalty is being wrongly administered.

Henry's arguments were not calculated; rather, his responses reflected the habits of those who use such arguments to defend their positions when there is no factual basis for them or they don't like the facts being put forth. The way Henry positioned his argument was quite typical of other white professional men in Alabama with whom I have had discussions about these issues. It is a tactic people (myself included) frequently use when they feel their belief system is being threatened. Defending a belief system that is deeply held is natural and seems effortless because it is so ingrained. He did not have to pause to think about it; he already knew what was at the core of his beliefs: murderers should get what they deserve.

"For the sake of argument, will you assume that these facts are indeed facts, and tell me what you think about the situation?" I asked him, trying hard to be reasonable and to bring him along with me.

"There's just too many ways that these kinds of things can be manipulated," he told me. "I look at murderers as a cancer in our society. No different from a cancer in your body. Just like you do with a cancer—remove it, kill it with x-rays or chemotherapy. I think you should remove this societal cancer."

Now I knew where he stood. "Well, back to the original question," I said. "What is your feeling about the discrimination that exists among blacks and whites, and along the same line, black, poor, or Hispanic discrimination in our justice system? Don't you think that it is hard to call it 'justice' if the process itself is discriminatory against minority groups?"

"But those groups of people commit more murders than whites and that probably accounts for why more blacks are put to death," he replied.

"Wait a minute now," I said with a smile. I wanted to keep this friendly and light although I knew he was misusing the facts. His line of thought is one of the underlying assumptions that feed latent racism. I pointed out the problem with his "facts."

By this time, Henry probably knew he was on shaky ground since I had been studying the subject and could provide evidence for the data. He couldn't argue the data since he knew his argument was without merit. Again, he moved the argument off subject. "But you also have to look at the heinous nature of some murders, like brutal rape, mutilation, child predators, and the like," he responded, "and those groups may participate in more of those type murders than the others."

"Yes, some murders are particularly heinous," I agreed with him, trying to soften the dialogue. "But the racial disparity is caused in most cases by the prosecutors and who they decide should be charged under capital-case guidelines, like for crimes associated with rape, child killing, etc.," I explained. "Look, again, at the numbers. Is it justice or not?" I asked.

"I think we have to do the best we can to protect our society against those that will not abide by the standards set for us, and particularly those who would kill. Those that kill deserve to be killed, and to me that is justice," he answered, ending the conversation and resuming talk of the seminars at the conference.

My short conversation with Henry illustrates once again that the "eye-for-an eye" form of justice prevails. Racial inequity is not an issue so long as we are safe from "those groups" of criminals, whoever "they" may be, and so long as "they" is not "us." Much as I tried, I could not get Henry to even consider that race was part of the issue. He could not concede that the justice he assumes in this equation doesn't apply equally to blacks and whites. Much like those questioned in the Birmingham Survey, if he doesn't perceive that there is a problem, there isn't one. If the problem doesn't exist, he doesn't have to address it. Nor did it occur to him that the "standards" he held up as setting the bar for everyone were not universally applied, particularly when used to try a murder case. It is still the white power structure that not only sets the standards used in our legal system but also decides who meets them. Those who think they are color-blind often do not see the red flags of racial prejudice.

When thinking about it later, I also realized that vengeance and fear were both subtexts in our conversation, though neither was acknowledged. The way Henry framed his argument was purely unconscious, but it illustrated the divide between blacks and whites. "Those groups" lumps all blacks into one big pile of "bad people." This type of language would never be used to characterized people in this kind of argument if we were talking about other societal groups who are white. It indicates how wide the gulf is; we are still framing the issues as "us and them." Henry had no evidence to support his premise that "they" commit more heinous crimes; that convenient "fact" simply serves to buttress his argument: If "those groups" commit more heinous crimes, then they deserve to be killed, even if it is disproportionate.

I know Henry to be an upright citizen and a compassionate man, like many others who hold very similar views. It is an attitude that is as firmly entrenched in mainstream Southern thinking as segregation was fifty years ago. In defending capital punishment, the underlying racism is ignored, though it is an important variable. In Henry's view, the argument of "just deserts"—murderers deserve to die for their crime—is the equivalent of justice. The basis for this assertion rests on two premises. The Biblical component of eye-for-an-eye morality is derived from Deuteronomy 19:21: "Life for life, eye for eye, tooth for tooth, hand for hand, foot for foot." Using this rationale for morality, every crime would need to have a punishment that is the equivalent of the crime. On the surface, it sounds good because it lends the weight of religion to the moral argument and makes us feel less helpless in the face of a crime by putting some moral balance back into the equation. *Lex talionis* (Latin for "law of retaliation"), originally derived from the Code of Hammurabi and reflected in the Old Testament (Exodus 21:23–27), however, was actually also a doctrine of restraint. It served to make sure that the punishment for a crime did not exceed the level of the criminal act itself, that it fit the crime. One might say that it was "due process" before its time. In practice, there are several problems with this thinking.

We must keep the Holy Scriptures in their religious context and understand that they are subject to wide interpretation as well as modern sensibilities. The Old Testament also advises death for various other offenses including adultery, disrespecting parents, working on the Sabbath (remember they tried to kill Jesus for healing a man on the Sabbath), and profaning the Lord's name. While we certainly can and should have God as our conscience and act in according to God's will, we must also use our intelligence to interpret Biblical text as it applies to contemporary life. There are many conflicting stories in the Bible, depending on which version, which chapters one reads, and who is doing the interpreting. We must recognize that although the Bible is God's word, it is God's word as transmitted though inspired revelation via humans over the ages and thus is open to varied interpretations, depending on the culture, traditions, and context of the times. We must bring to bear the strength of moral courage to understand those universals that are inscribed for humankind in the Ten Commandments.

In addition, eye-for-an-eye morality as played out in our criminal system entails trying to match the punishment to fit the crime. Thus, justice is to be meted out according to the severity of the crime; those who kill deserve the ultimate punishment in the form of their own death. If we are to take this reasoning to its logical conclusion, however, every crime would have to result in killing anyone who commits a murder and take equivalent revenge for every criminal act in a never-ending cycle of vengeance. We cannot rape the rapists as punishment or sodomize the sodomists any more than we would stone our children for disrespecting us.

We have evolved from the ancient days when blood feuds provoked generations of hatred and bloodshed, from the ancient Greeks to *Romeo and Juliet*, culminating in present-day sectarian violence in the Middle East and gang warfare right at home, which as a society we denounce. Such an environment is not the one we have envisioned as formed from the democratic principles of our evolving civilization. We want to be moral and just, fair and humane. In doing so we must reject a policy that is none of these.

The eye-for-an-eye premise necessitates a policy that would mandate the death penalty for certain crimes. In practical application, there are many problems with attempting to exact rigid life and death decisions on human behavior, which is complex, unpredictable and tremendously variable. In the absence of equal application of the death penalty for the same crimes, the ruling becomes arbitrary and therefore discriminatory—a notion confirmed by the Supreme Court in the 1972 *Furman v. Georgia* decision. In light of that influential ruling, our system of capital punishment now requires a judge and/or jury (depending on the state) to determine whether the death penalty is imposed. In another ruling in 1976, the Supreme Court decided against mandatory imposition of the death penalty (*Woodson v. North Carolina*; *Roberts v. Louisiana*). This reinforced the concept of discretion in rulings by either judge or jury or both.

In my conversation with Henry, I might have predicted his response to capital punishment, given the nature of the subject and his background. I presumed, however, that his views about race had softened a bit over the years. I also thought that evidence-based facts would appeal to him and that I might be able to get him to rethink the issue of capital punishment by pointing out the racial disparity in these facts, which would also appeal to his sense of fairness. I hadn't predicted the extent to which he would defend the underlying racism.

Like many if not most other capital punishment supporters, Henry's "just deserts" defense totally disregards the fact of unequal treatment and quickly devolves to the core of his rationale for the death penalty: murderers get what they deserve. Like many others who hold the same beliefs, Henry's reaction is emotional, not reasoned. It reminded me how difficult the journey from emotion to reason is in all of us. We act on emotions everyday, without consciously knowing what is driving our response. In most cases, these actions are inconsequential, from buying a cereal because of the packaging to returning a smile from a stranger. On the death penalty, however, our unconscious emotional reactions have serious repercussions. For this reason, dissecting the rationales and beliefs we hold about capital punishment, including its inherent racism, whether latent or overt, is central to any discussion of the issue. The big question remains, "Do you have the heart, mind, and courage to do it?"

14

CRUCIFIXION AND
CAPITAL PUNISHMENT

Some argue that Christian morality demands the death penalty, but I find the reasoning for this position a bit dishonest. The portions of Biblical text typically used to defend capital punishment are found in the Old Testament. These scriptures have no greater moral authority than those in the New Testament and many, in fact, are not applicable to a modern society and in themselves are contradictory. Death penalty advocates who quote the Old Testament ignore other scriptures that are obviously inappropriate in today's environment and evolved standards of decency. For example, one of the verses sometimes cited in this context is from Genesis 9:6: "Whoever sheds the blood of a human, by a human shall that person's blood be shed: for in his own image God made humankind." But such advocates often conveniently forget Jeremiah 31:31–34: "I will make a new covenant with the house of Israel and the house of Judah. It will not be like the covenant that I made with their ancestors when I took them by the hand to bring them out of the land of Egypt . . . for I will forgive their inequity, and remember their sin no more."

Although the Bible had varied contributors, its texts were not written in isolation of one another and the context of their times. If we extract excerpts, we lose the more profound message. For the full message of the Bible, the Old Testament must be viewed along with the events of the life of Christ and the text and spirit of the New Testament in which those events are described. God gave Moses the law, but Jesus brought mercy and forgiveness.

To ignore the latter is like using Article I, Section II of the Constitution— "[apportionment] shall be determined by adding to the whole number of free persons, including those bound to service for a term of years, and excluding Indians not taxed, three fifths of all other persons"—to argue the legality and perhaps even the morality of slavery. While the New Testament did not rescind portions of the Old Testament, it did build on the story of humankind and add to our understanding, evolving in a similar way to the Constitution. Certainly Biblical texts in the Old Testament mention slavery, but those who argue for capital punishment would not condone slavery today. Both practices are immoral and should be in the same category of anachronisms that no longer serve us in modern times.

More importantly, though also often overlooked, the teachings of Christ as evidenced in the various texts of the New Testament are generally consistent and in keeping with the precept of "thou shalt not kill." Capital punishment is premeditated murder by the state, and it runs counter to all that is forbidden by scripture. As Christians, this precept is as relevant to our lives as it was during the time of Christ and it spans cultures and time.

Christ also defended the neediest among us and it is the members of this group who are most often sentenced to death. The vast majority of those who have been executed as well as those now on death row represent those members of society who have the least in terms of material goods and comforts, have the fewest connections to the community, and in general have the least to lose by resorting to crime. They are often racial minorities, mentally ill, or mentally retarded (or some combination of these conditions); more often than not they are poor and lack the resources to hire their own attorneys and ensure an adequate defense. Many are minors, or were at the time of their arrest. These are the most vulnerable among us—the very people Christ preached about helping. It seems disingenuous for people to go to church and pray to Jesus on Sunday and then on Monday advocate the execution of those Jesus tells us need our forgiveness and help. How can we call ourselves Christians—empowered by Christ's crucifixion and guided by its lessons to follow his teachings—and then demand that the most vulnerable segment of our population, those who Jesus would minister to, should be executed in a modern-day simulation of his death?

I still recall vividly the burning cross displayed as a symbol of the power of mob rule in the South of my youth. For me, its symbolism has been conveniently transferred to the inside of the death chamber, where the inmate who has been given his last supper and the opportunity to say his last words, lies splayed out on a gurney, hands and feet bound by leather straps rather than nails, in a horizontal rather than a vertical cross position. Though the inmate's death takes less time to arrive and is less painful than crucifixion, the end result is the same.

The limited but carefully chosen witnesses who are permitted to view an inmate's final moments are often ill prepared for what they see. "You think of dying as something personal, and it was just a really horrible, public and invasive way to die. I would not want to see that again," said one witness to an execution in December 2006. Many are driven to tears; some get sick to their stomachs. Yet, a few are driven by the eye-for-an-eye thinking and are unfazed by the spectacle: "I think they need to feel some kind of pain. I know it's horrible to say, but they did horrible things to people," another witness remarked.[105]

IF WE LOOK AT the lessons of the Crucifixion, I think it is hard not to conclude that capital punishment is immoral and counter to the teachings of Jesus. Whatever our faith, the story of Christ's execution and its parallels with capital punishment today are instructive. My own reading of Biblical texts and my deep faith in God have led me to what I believe to be rational and reasoned views, guided by the historical facts. Though I certainly believe in both the message and the truth of Jesus Christ as the son of God, even if one does not subscribe to this particular aspect of the history of Jesus, we do know that he was executed. Whichever of the Gospels we read that tell us of his words and the events surrounding his last days, the bare facts of the condemnation for his deeds and his execution are indisputable.

Some of what we know about those fateful days before his execution is from historical documents and some is from Biblical accounts. Scholarly research sheds some light on the most likely scenarios, but each who has faith in the message of Jesus as the anointed son of God must make his or her own judgments. Regardless of which readings are used to tell the story, there are some threads that run through all of the sources.

My own experience with faith and redemption has opened my mind to the texts of the Gospels and the truth of his word. I know this is but one version of a chain of historical events, but it is the version that makes sense to me and the one that gives me faith and comfort. The point here is not to debate early Christian history; I'll leave that to the scholars. Our current view of capital punishment, however, is derivative of many of the same responses to differences of opinion, cultural divides, and clashes of power.

There is no singular message from Jesus in the Gospels. However, there is a large body of parables and precepts that can guide moral behavior and lead to understanding, humility, and compassion and love of fellow humans. From treating the sick to forgiving the sinners, those messages include universal calls for love of humanity and care for those among us who are least able. "The rich and the poor have this in common: the Lord is the maker of them all" (Proverbs 22:2) and "be kind to one another, tenderhearted, forgiving one another, as God in Christ has forgiven you" (Ephesians 4:32).

Because Christ's crucifixion is central to all of Christianity, it is useful to review the circumstances and examine the legal issues we can glean from historical as well as Biblical accounts. It is worth recalling that in Biblical times, religion and politics were one. When Jesus went to Jerusalem, he was already despised by some who thought his preaching and his claim to be the son of God were blasphemous. Jesus knew that he might face an angry mob in Jerusalem, but he was determined to follow his call to celebrate the Passover festival. He also wanted to bring his message of the Kingdom of God to more people, and he knew that the festival would attract large crowds who would hear him.

Since the Roman invasion of Palestine, King Herod had rebuilt the Temple in Jerusalem. It was considered a symbol of Roman power as well as a holy place of worship and the center of religious life for the Jews of the day. It also served as a central bank for collecting taxes and tithes—a practice regarded as defilement by both the Jews and Jesus. It is also important to remember the symbolic importance of Passover for Jesus. Passover is the festival that celebrates the escape of the Jews from enslavement in Egypt and from the Angel of Death. Given the teachings of Jesus and his disciples, the festival celebration can be seen as a symbol of at least one prong of his message in advocating for the oppressed, and the importance of Jesus in making the trip to Jerusalem can have political, moral, and/or religious meaning.

During this particular time it would have been important to Jesus to make his message clear to the Romans by commemorating freedom even though the Jews were once again being oppressed, this time by the Romans. Jesus had thus stirred conflicts both among the Romans who held the power and among the group of Jews who disbelieved in his pronouncement as the true Messiah. He anticipated a reaction but was undeterred. "While Jesus was going up to Jerusalem, he took the twelve disciples aside by themselves, and said to them on the way, 'See, we are going up to Jerusalem, and the Son of Man will be handed over to the chief priests and scribes, and they will condemn him to death'" (Matthew 20:17–19).

The accounts of the events surrounding the crucifixion vary depending on which texts are read. The following is my view but I offer it in an attempt to show the similarities between the fate and message of Jesus and present-day capital punishment policy and its consequences. If we take a step back into history and review the legal procedures used to defend the Crucifixion as offered in the Gospels, the parallels are striking.

Christ entered the Temple and was offended by the money changers who were set up in the temple. "My house shall be called a house of prayer, but you have made it a den of robbers" (Matthew 21:13). Christ may have known that his words would provoke the reaction that it did. "When Jesus had finished saying all these things, he said to his disciples, 'You know that after two days the Passover is coming, and the Son of Man will be handed over to be crucified'" (Matthew 26:1–5). So as not to stir further public unrest, Christ was arrested in the middle of the night by the high priest Caiaphas and other Temple police. The Gospels offer us somewhat different accounts of the trial itself, but all agree that it was Pilate, the Roman prelate, who ordered the execution and Judas, one of Jesus's own apostles, who betrayed his identity to the Roman officials.

After Christ was taken into custody, he was questioned. "Then the high priest questioned Jesus about his disciples and about his teaching. Jesus answered, 'I have spoken openly to the world; I have always taught in synagogues and in the temple, where all the Jews come together. I have said nothing in secret. Why do you ask me? Ask those who heard what I said to them; they know what I said'" (John 18:19–24). We don't really know what actual charges may have been leveled from a historical perspective, but from the Gospels, we could conclude that the charges were blasphemy (claiming to be the son of God) and threatening to destroy government property (the Temple at Jerusalem).[106] "As Jesus came out of the temple and was going away, his disciples came to point out to him the buildings of the temple. Then he asked them, 'You see all these, do you not? Truly I tell you, not one stone will be left here upon another; all will be thrown down'" (Matthew 24:1–2).

Those of us who take it on faith that Jesus was the Messiah of course know of his innocence; he had spoken the truth and had not destroyed anything. Yet in his trial, Caiaphas questioned Christ and brought in witnesses who testified that Christ planned to destroy the Temple and then rebuild it. "The high priest stood up and said, 'Have you no answer? What is it that they testify against you?' But Jesus was silent. Then the high priest said to him, 'I put you under oath before the living God, tell us if you are the Messiah, the Son of God.' Jesus said to him, 'You have said so . . .' Then the high priest tore his clothes and said, 'He has blasphemed! Why do we still need witnesses? You have now heard his blasphemy'" (Matthew 26:62–68). Though the testimony against him was conflicting, he was declared guilty. We should take note that Christ did not call any of his own witnesses; nor did he have anyone representing him.

Bearing false witness is a precept that goes back to the Old Testament and is forbidden by the Ten Commandments. We need to acknowledge the imperfections in our current criminal system. This doesn't preclude the importance of the system and its other strengths. Some errors are inadvertent and minor while others may be calculated; all have serious consequences. Recent studies have found that perhaps thousands of people have been wrongly convicted of crimes just in the last decade. These errors were largely caused by eyewitness misidentification, police perjury, and coerced false confessions. With better legal counsel, some of those errors might have been avoided.[107]

There may be no Biblical precedent for the right to counsel, but there is a Constitutional one codified in the Sixth Amendment ("the accused shall enjoy the right to have the assistance of counsel for his defense"). Most of those on death row must use public defenders and are usually offered the least able among attorneys. Numerous examples of shoddy representation can be found from attorneys who fall asleep or are inebriated during the proceedings, to attorneys who have no background in criminal law. With proper counsel, some of these defendants might not be sentenced to death; others might be exonerated altogether.

While the right to legal counsel was upheld by the landmark Supreme Court case, *Gideon v. Wainwright* (1963), the unspoken problem is in paying for it. More than forty years later, a defense system for the indigent remains vastly unfunded. Those left to fend for themselves represent about 75 percent of felony case defendants. Once again, the "commoners" stand alone.[108]

So Christ was alone in defending himself. Whether he could have brought in others in his defense is speculation. His death sentence was pronounced but Jewish law forbade capital punishment, so the verdict had to be appealed to a higher authority, in this case to Pilate. "Then they took Jesus from Caiaphas to Pilate's headquarters . . . So Pilate went out to them and said, "What accusation do you bring against this man?" They answered, "If this man were not a criminal, we would not have handed him over to you." Pilate said to them, "Take him yourselves and judge him according to your law." The Jews replied, "We are not permitted to put anyone to death" (John 18:28–19:1). Pilate would be the judge, though he had a terrible reputation for inflicting harsh punishments. At first Pilate defended Christ, but when mob rule grew, he bowed to the pressure. Mob rule has its origins in the Gospels and just as in the story of Barabbas in the book of John, in which Pilate acceded to the populist view, Pilate asked him, "Do you want me to release for you the King of the Jews?" They [the mob] shouted in reply, "Not this man, but Barabbas!" Barabbas was a bandit and some thought he was a murderer. Pilate had the power to release him from prison, as it was the custom to release one prisoner during Passover, and did so. Then he took Jesus and had him flogged (John 18:28–19:1). Pilate asked them [the mob], "Shall I crucify your King?" The chief priests answered, "We have no king but the emperor." Then he handed him over to them to be crucified" (John 19).

ALTHOUGH THE LAWS UNDER Roman rule and Jewish tradition were primitive by today's standards, many of the concepts form the basis of our own laws. At least there was a trial, though primitive by modern standards perhaps, and a sham in terms of justice, both then and now. Surely it was one-sided—the deck was stacked, the verdict assured before the trial began. Two millenniums later, it's hard not to bemoan a lack of progress in our own standards of decency and justice.

It is difficult to review the crucifixion and its injustice and reconcile it with imposing a similar fate on someone two thousand years later. Hanging from a cross must be one of the most excruciating ways to die, but others of the time were not much more humane. However, crucifixion was the method considered the most humiliating—it was a public display and object lesson; it was also the method used on slaves and other non-Roman citizens considered "commoners." We need to remember that Jesus belonged to this class.[109]

In our modern quest to ease our collective conscience we have tried to make intentional killing easier to look at and think about, though the message is the same and the result is still death.

It is important to recognize the parallels in Christ's execution and today's system of capital punishment, and God's purpose in designating Jesus as his son sent to transmit his message. I don't draw comparisons between Jesus and murderers—surely they are not in the same realm. Jesus as the son of God died for our sins, knowing it was his fate. I don't believe any of those now awaiting their fate on death rows are messiahs, though some may be innocent, as indicated by the large numbers of inmates who have been released after new DNA evidence proved their verdicts wrong. According to the Death Penalty Information Center, 130 people on death row have been exonerated since 1973, for reasons ranging from DNA evidence to misidentification by witnesses, faulty legal representation, false confessions, among others.[110] Nonetheless, it is our sin of capital punishment that people are dying for. Some convicts also may have remained silent in response to their accusers, and they too are being used as object lessons for others who might be accused of crimes.

How many of those on death row have repented to no avail? How many have been convicted on the testimony of a witness turning state's evidence? With conflicting and flimsy evidence? How many innocent persons have been executed? How many have been convicted on the basis of the mob of public opinion whose politics influenced a judge? On the basis of a judge's decision to overrule the jury? Or with a corrupt judge presiding? How many have been convicted without competent legal counsel? How many witnesses have been paid to testify at trial, refuting other witnesses, against defendants who wind up on death row? How many defendants are arrested in the middle of the night to avoid publicity and ensure an easier arrest?

These questions have unknown answers, but they do have resonance in the context of the death penalty case that changed the world. In each of these questions, there is a footprint of Jesus—we have trod these paths before. Now we need to find an alternative to the road to perdition.

Christ's teachings are clear about redemption and forgiveness; Jesus forgave his own executioners and asked that the public do the same. "Father, forgive them; for they know not what they do" (Luke 23:34). Jesus's sermons are replete with examples of doing good, of service to mankind, humility before God, and forgiveness of those who have sinned. "Therefore, I tell you, her sins, which were many, have been forgiven; hence she has shown great love. But the one to whom little is forgiven, loves little" (Luke 7:47). Included in Christ's message is the need for repentance, as first reported by John the Baptist in his announcement of Jesus as the Messiah, and in subsequent pronouncements by Jesus to his disciples: "repentance and forgiveness of sins is to be proclaimed in his name to all nations, beginning from Jerusalem" (Luke 24: 47).

It's hard to read the New Testament without finding examples of forgiveness and redemption, but we have yet to put this part of the teaching of Jesus into practice in any uniform or codified way when it comes to criminal justice, especially if we are asked to forgive the most depraved or hapless "others" in our midst. We would much rather lock them up and forget that they exist. If the message of Jesus is to love and heal, what is our message when we forget instead of forgive?

It was striking to notice the response of the Amish after several of their children were gunned down in cold blood in the fall of 2006. It's hard to imagine a more brutal and senseless crime. In the tradition of forgiveness and redemption, however, the families supported one another and reached out to the family of the perpetrator. One of the Amish men was quoted as saying, "We're very concerned that no message of revenge gets out. We believe in forgiveness." As another man from the community explained, "They don't want to be trapped by bitterness." It is natural to feel anger, even rage when someone we love is murdered, and in that rage is buried a desire for justice. But justice is not the same as revenge.

Surely that message is in keeping with the teachings of Jesus, but contrast that kind of attitude with some of the remarks made after the trial of Andrea Yates: "It sickens me that a rule of law exists thats leave [sic] her without accountability. It makes me ill that someone can methodically plan out the murder of five innocent children in a way that promotes the most pain, agony, cruelty and suffering upon those children and then winds up in a country club environment." Or the comment on an internet post on the death penalty: "Kill all of them, it's God's job to sort them out."[111]

Those who advocate using the death penalty seem to forget that Jesus preached not only forgiveness of sin, but also the danger of damnation. "Come to terms quickly with your accuser while you are on the way to court with him, or your accuser may hand you over to the judge, and the judge to the guard, and you will be thrown into prison" (Matthew 5:21–25). The rule of the mob and those who express such views do so in opposition to Christian principles. We still have vestiges of mob mentality buried in the death penalty. I believe that those who express such hatred are not at peace. When we are unwilling to forgive, it keeps us chained to negative emotions that infuse our being, affecting everything we do. Jesus teaches the principles of kindness and forgiveness, for it is in these actions that there is salvation. "Blessed are the merciful, for they will receive mercy; (Matthew 5:7) Blessed are the meek, for they will inherit the earth" (Matthew 5:5). St. Paul also taught, "do not let the sun go down on your anger" (Ephesians 4:26).

Though people often expect that they will feel relieved at the execution of the murderer of someone they loved—that their personal pain will die with the executed, this is rarely the case. "I saw Floyd Medlock die, and I can tell you this: Nobody gets closure by witnessing somebody else murdered. Forgiveness is the only thing that allows you to go on," explained Johnnie Cabrera Carter, whose seven-year-old granddaughter was raped and murdered by Medlock in 1990.[112] And there was Sandy Miller, whose expectation that the death of her son's murderer, serial killer William Bonin, would bring an end to her rage, was not realized. Miller finally talked to Bonin's biographer; her anger started to dissipate when she began to understand some of Bonin's background. "As a boy, [Bonin] had been raped and put in an orphanage— not that he didn't deserve what he got, but maybe he wouldn't have gotten to the point he did if the system had helped him," she said.[113]

MILLER'S COMMENT REMINDED ME of a recent conversation I had with an old acquaintance. I have known Ralph for a number of years, having served with him on a local corporate board, and we run into one another every once in a while at local business events. We don't really socialize together, so we tend to talk about business and finances. We had both attended a business meeting and were chatting in the parking lot afterwards, mostly about the tax raise the governor was requesting and the budget problems. Though I still think of myself as a fiscal conservative, our conversation made me rethink the label somewhat. Of course no one wants to pay more taxes, but Ralph's complaint included the "enormous" sums spent on prisons and criminals, and how wasteful he thought it was. At the time, he didn't know about my more recent interest in and connection to local prisons. I asked him how he would fix the broken system. (Alabama has had court orders mandating solutions to its prison overcrowding, forcing the expenditure of additional money to relieve the problem.)

Ralph thought about it briefly, then replied, "Well, I'll tell you one thing. Keeping some of those people alive on death row for years doesn't help anyone, and it's expensive. Now there's a place where we could save a lot of money!"

"So you don't think prisoners should get life sentences?" I asked, stating the obvious.

"What purpose do they serve?" he asked. "What good is there to keep them alive when they are killers and have violated another human being's right to live?"

I hadn't anticipated the direction of this conversation so I wasn't sure of where to try to take it. "I guess you think the death penalty is a good policy, then," I said, trying to feel him out further without being rude.

"Sure," he answered. "Why do we need killers in our midst? If they've killed someone, we don't need to waste the public's money by just keeping them in prison forever on end."

"Well, you know," I said, "it actually costs more to prosecute the death penalty than it does to keep someone in prison for a lifetime."

"Must be those 'hotels' they house them in," he laughed. "Or the high-priced lawyers they get. I resent my taxes paying for that. Lawyers can be expensive, you know." Actually, I did know. Ralph had been involved in several lawsuits in business matters. I didn't know the details or the outcome, but I was sure he had run up a sizeable legal tab.

"Well, it's like that with legal fees, as you know," I told him. "You have to pay them up front. With a life sentence, it's more like a mortgage. It's spread out over an average of forty or more years." I wanted to add, but didn't, that the state-supplied lawyers were not paid anywhere near what his lawyers cost. But I had learned to keep some of my fervor to myself when the situation called for it. My analogy caught him slightly off-guard and he paused before responding.

"That's an interesting way to think about it," he admitted.

Then I told Ralph about some of the work I had been doing. "Actually, we have the worst of both worlds with the death penalty," I explained. "We spend a lot of money on extra trials and legal procedures that take a long time—years usually. So we pay to house the inmate during that time and beyond if we don't execute him. I think it would be better if we abolished the death penalty and helped some of these people to be productive and useful. Never mind the murderers, our prisons are full of people who could be in programs that would help prevent their return to prison. Those programs are much more effective than jail time."

"Why, Robbie," Ralph grinned. "You're really a sheep in wolf's clothing.

I didn't know you had become such a liberal! It's a good thing I already like you."

We both chuckled, said our good-byes, and went on our separate ways.

On the way home, I thought about the overcrowded prisons that have been big problems in this state for many years and the attempts to remedy the situation by farming out inmates to other states. There is now a movement to develop community corrections programs, mostly in response to the runaway costs of incarceration and noncompliance issues in the state. It costs the state $39.46 a day to house a prisoner and $12.97 a day for a prisoner to be placed in an alternative program.[114]

It's a shame that abolishing the death penalty has not been considered as an option for budgetary cuts given that its cost drains the judicial system and the money could be much better spent elsewhere. California has the largest death row population and spends more than any other state on the death penalty. It is estimated that California spends over $117 million per year to prosecute approximately twenty death penalty cases, at least $22 million more than the state would spend to prosecute the same defendants seeking a life sentence. Each execution in California costs more than $1.1 million more in taxpayer dollars than a non-capital murder trial.[115] In Kansas, capital cases cost 70 percent more than comparable non-capital cases, including the costs of incarceration.[116] In April 2008, New Mexico dropped pursuit of two death penalty cases and instead will prosecute them as non-capital cases because of lack of funding for the defendants' legal fees. The move to abandon capital charges because of their cost is unprecedented.[117] Most states are currently facing renewed fiscal problems; whether others choose to make cuts by excising the costly process of capital punishment remains to be seen.

Alabama has a poor record when it comes to prison reform and criminal justice. In the last twenty-five years, the overall population of the state grew less than 20 percent, but the prison population in the state quadrupled. We neither deterred crime (the state was below the national rate of crime reduction in that period) nor saved money.[118]

The overcrowding continues despite efforts to curb it. The system is in serious need of overhaul and rethinking. Though I may be labeled "liberal" in this quest, or "soft on crime"—perhaps they are considered the same—I don't like crime any more than anyone else. I have seen up close and personally the pain and distress it brings not just to the victims of crime but to the offenders and those who get caught up in the system. Those whose jobs are part of the process of execution also suffer from long-term effects similar to post-traumatic stress disorder. Because executions are so grim, most states that allow capital punishment offer counseling to all execution witnesses (except those related to the condemned). In this day of tight budgets, that this type of program has been spared speaks for itself.

In his book, *Public Justice, Private Mercy; A Governor's Education on Death Row*, former California governor Edmund G. "Pat" Brown reflected on the use of the death penalty during his governorship. Over his eight-year tenure, he oversaw the death sentences of fifty-nine convicts—thirty-six were executed and twenty-three were granted clemency. He wrote: "I am eighty-three years old as I write these words . . . And looking back over their names and files now, despite the horrible crimes and the catalog of human weakness they comprise, I realize that each decision took something out of me that nothing—not family or work or hope for the future—has ever been able to replace."[119]

While I realize that being sympathetic toward people who have harmed others doesn't make me popular, I believe in the redemption and message of salvation through Christ. Repentance is a necessary part of forgiveness in the return to God, but it is a two-way process: the guilty party must repent and we must learn to forgive and return to "the way of the Lord." As Peter said in Acts 2:38: "Repent, and be baptized every one of you in the name of Jesus Christ so that your sins may be forgiven; and you will receive the gift of the Holy Spirit." While rage and hurt are natural feelings when someone is murdered, revenge is not part of the teachings and spirit of Christ.

15

REHABILITATION VS. PUNISHMENT

As a nation, we still haven't quite come to terms with the purpose of prisons. Is the function of a prison to punish the offenders and reinforce the power of the state in controlling those who don't conform to the mainstream, or is it to rehabilitate people who have broken laws? Because we are of mixed mind about this question, the conflict presented by the competing views creates tension and public polarization. The public is never presented with the question stripped bare of its wolf's clothing; we are fed platitudes and conclusions often rooted in opinions rather than facts, designed to elicit fear rather than provoke thought and understanding of the issue. Penal reform remains untried and/or underfunded, lacking the drive of political will.

No society, from the early Greeks to present Western cultures, has had definitive answers to the questions of handling those who do not conform to social norms. Prisons as the means of punishment were largely unknown before the American Revolution. Prior to that time prisons were traditionally used to house those waiting for a trial; for those found guilty, punishment was largely corporal, but those with the financial means could often pay a fine instead.[120] Capital crimes were reserved for the most egregious offenses, and flogging and public torture were common. The pillory served to embarrass the offender and act as an object lesson for anyone else who might similarly offend the pubic sensibility.

While colonial law was mostly modeled on the mother country, many colonists were critical of capital punishment and some of the other severe punishments in practice in Great Britain, for example, debtor prisons. The American Revolution, as a rejection of the colonial system of justice, also brought with it a reform movement. Leading the way was Dr. Benjamin Rush, a surgeon from Pennsylvania and signatory to the Declaration of Independence. Rush strongly opposed the death penalty and advocated developing "houses of repentance" as an option for punishment of criminals. In 1792 he wrote in an inspiring pamphlet, *Considerations on the Injustice and Impolicy of Punishing Murder by Death*:

> An execution in a republic is like a human sacrifice in religion. It is an offering to monarchy, and to that malignant being, who has been styled a murderer from the beginning, and who delights equally in murder, whether it be perpetrated by the cold, but vindictive arm of the law, or by the angry hand of private revenge.

Rush's influence was formidable. Even prior to publication of his pamphlet, in their quest to distinguish themselves from the black marks of autocracy, the fledgling colonial governments began to eliminate the death penalty at least for some crimes (Pennsylvania, 1786; New York, New Jersey, Virginia, 1796). By 1820 all the states had either abolished it or limited its application to only the worst crimes.[121]

As support for capital punishment waned, a replacement was needed to deal with lawbreakers and imprisonment became the punishment of choice. Implicit in the concept of incarceration was both the need for separation of criminals from the rest of the population and also the idea of penitence (thus the word penitentiary).[122] The Quakers of Pennsylvania were early, vocal opponents of capital punishment and led a successful push for an alternative. The Walnut Street Prison in Philadelphia became the first in America to carry out punishment in lieu of execution and to separate violent from nonviolent offenders.[123] The idea was that if prisoners were kept separated from one another, they could reflect on their crimes and repent for their sins, after which they would be able to be returned to society. As Paul the Apostle preached, "that they should repent and turn to God, and do deeds consistent with repentance" (Acts 26:20). The goal was rehabilitation, not lifelong incarceration.

By the early nineteenth century, a fledging prison system was developing along with the thriving new country. The Enlightenment also contained the idea of prison reform and in 1831 the French government sent Alexis de Tocqueville and Gustave de Beaumont to North America to study the U.S. prison system in the fledgling democracy.[124]

Accustomed to the aristocratic society of France and the upheaval of the French Revolution, de Tocqueville saw the United States as a classless and equal society (at least outside of the South). In his seminal work, *Democracy in America* (1840), de Tocqueville expressed his admiration for the equality and sovereignty he observed in the American people. He believed these traits were the foundations for democracy and the reason the United States enjoyed its success. This concept formed the framework for de Tocqueville's ideas about crime and punishment.

De Tocqueville argued that lack of equality in a society leads to poverty and to criminality, which he defined as "deviant" behavior that thus was a consequence of social conditions. After returning to France, de Tocqueville and de Beaumont wrote *On the Penitentiary System in the United States and its Application in France* (1833), documenting their visits to American prisons and their thoughts and conclusions based on this experience. Though this book was largely overshadowed by de Tocqueville's later book, its ideas were taken seriously and many attempts at prison reforms can be traced to it.

De Tocqueville believed the function of a prison was to reform deviants/ offenders, which could be accomplished by rehabilitation rather than harsh punishment. "It is well known that most individuals on whom the criminal law inflicts punishment have been unfortunate before they become guilty," de Tocqueville wrote. He thought such policy was in the public interest because rehabilitation would bring productive citizens back into society.

De Tocqueville detailed how reform was to be accomplished; social equality and the opportunity to improve one's station in life remained at the foundation. He advocated a penitentiary system in which the inmates were separated from one another and left in solitude at night in order to reflect on their crimes and repent. During the day, they would work. He believed that was the path to successful rehabilitation. But De Tocqueville opposed absolute solitude, noting that "it does not reform, it kills."[125] The idea was to give the prisoners skills and something productive to do with their time during the day and time alone to reflect on the error of their ways at night. The objective of incarceration was not punitive and our early prisons were developed along these lines; this was also the system that became a model for European prisons.

De Tocqueville's strong belief in rehabilitation, along with his central themes of equality and opportunity, explains his shock at the prisons of the South and the institution of slavery. "In locking up the criminals nobody thinks of rendering them better, but only taming their malice; they are put in chains like ferocious beasts; and instead of being corrected, they are rendered brutal."[126]

Even during the early periods in our history, the prison population in all states was disproportionately represented by blacks, but the South was by far the greater culprit. In New York state, for example, 1814 records indicate that 29 percent of the inmates (144 out of 494) were black. De Tocqueville remarked in his book, "In general, it has been observed that in those states in which there exists one Negro to thirty whites, the prisons contain one Negro to four white persons." In the pre-Civil War South most prisoners were white; runaway slaves could be imprisoned, but often their owners meted out their own corporal punishment. However, in the post-Civil War South, more than 75 percent of the inmates were black.[127]

Although the early goal for prisons was the improvement and even the perfection of society through the rehabilitation and reform of its "deviants," it was not long before prisons once again resembled the dungeons of our European predecessors. The evolving penal system eventually included the worst of both worlds: solitary confinement and chain gangs of leased labor to private enterprise. Used widely in the South, chain gangs were a throwback to the system of indentured servants and an attempt to ensure that blacks "stayed in their place." While inhumane prisons could be seen all over the country, they were more numerous in the Southern states where the post-Civil war labor market had been disrupted by the liberation of slaves. Post-war Black Codes also meant that blacks were more frequently arrested and imprisoned for minor violations of the law and then forced into chain gangs to repay their debts, once again supplying cheap labor.

The cycle continued with periods of deteriorating prison conditions followed by new reform movements. By the late nineteenth century, reform for the first time included the separation of juveniles from adult offenders.[128] But adult offenders of both minor and severe crimes, as well as the mentally retarded and mentally ill, were all housed in the same facilities. Gradually, behaviors such as marital infidelity and blasphemy were decriminalized.

Reform movements in the early part of the twentieth century were somewhat successful in calling attention to the abhorrent conditions of the prisons and made some inroads in moving the mentally ill to other facilities. While this didn't always guarantee better treatment, it served to separate, physically and conceptually, the mentally ill from the rest of the prison population. This was a new enlightenment of sorts, during which time there was some recognition that not all criminals were cut from the same cloth; some were more culpable than others. We began to recognize the role played by a person's mental capacity in the commission of crime. The growing acceptance of psychology as a bona fide discipline in the twentieth century ultimately brought with it recognition of mental illness as a subset of disease. Together, these factors contributed to the overall understanding of the human condition and helped usher in a change in attitude in which the mentally ill were no longer automatically viewed as criminally culpable and were prosecuted accordingly.

Of course the system wasn't perfect—there were (and are) still many injustices including abysmal conditions in mental institutions that precipitated a later call for reform. The very thing that had stimulated de Tocqueville's assessment of America and declared its success as a democracy was being questioned. The civil rights movement that began as a demand for the civil rights of blacks broadened its reach, making room for other groups of people to be included in the quest for equality. In 1963, President John F. Kennedy called on Congress to reduce the number of people housed in mental institutions and create programs to "restore and revitalize their lives through better heath programs and strengthened educational and rehabilitation services."[129] His request demonstrated an implicit understanding of both prongs of reform: the ability of people to change and be reformed and the need for reform in those institutions that were needed to help them in the process.

That same year, Congress passed legislation called the Mental Retardation Facilities and Community Health Centers Construction Act to build public and private nonprofit community mental health centers, paving the way for treatment and/or education for the disabled rather than relegation to custodial institutions that simply housed them. The category of "disabled" widened to include large and disparate populations. The original legislation ushered in big changes. Implicit in them was the perception that individuals with proper guidance—education, medical treatment, supervision—could change and become productive members of society. "Boot camps" and "reform schools" were modeled on this concept. This effort led to a large number of people being institutionalized. Some received good care and were able to go on to lead productive lives; others were simply warehoused and removed from the streets, further hiding the problem. In time, these institutions were criticized for rewarding criminals, and the cycle continued.

As the population of the mental institutions declined, the population of our jails and prisons soared. In 1955, the proportion of the population housed in mental health hospitals was 339 per 100,000; in 2001, the proportion was 21 per 100,000, a number that continues to be on the decline.[130] The deinstitutionalization of public mental health hospitals that started in the 1960s began a process of turning our jails and prisons into warehouses for a large portion of our population that even today we don't care to acknowledge. "Over the past forty years, the United States dismantled a colossal mental health complex and rebuilt—bed-by-bed—an enormous prison," explains Bernard Harcourt, University of Chicago law and criminology professor.[131] Unfortunately, the "deinstitutionalization" was not always accompanied by the programs necessary to lend support to those released. As politicians bickered over the cost and the nuts and bolts of various programs, many people who were not equipped to live independently were released; with no safety nets in place, many wound up living on the streets and getting in trouble with the law.

Rehabilitation as a concept has come under attack from both political fronts. Some on the right charge such programs as being "soft on crime" and call for more punitive measures; some on the left charge that some programs are coercive and a move toward authoritarianism. With an exploding prison population, more thought is being given to community programs to help alleviate the overcrowding. These programs range from transition facilities and services, job training, and drug rehabilitation.

One of the newer models for reform of the criminal justice system is restorative justice, whereby victims and perpetrators are brought together to make amends. It is a system in which the offender can actually repent and the victim or his family has the opportunity to forgive. There are many programs under the restorative justice umbrella, with quite a bit of variance among them, but most largely remove the government from the equation relegating a larger share of the responsibility to the community to determine the appropriate response to each case. These programs have shown enormous success in reducing recidivism and helping people become responsible, contributing members of society. One program in Virginia showed only an 8 percent recidivism rate. Others vary, but all are more successful than the general warehousing and laissez faire policies of many prison systems.

Restorative justice is also a more humane treatment in that it includes the opportunity for an exchange of respect. It attacks the problem at its roots, giving help to those who need it. New Orleans prosecutor and public defender Eric E. Malveau, who has seen a large increase in crime since Hurricane Katrina, explained: "You can put a cop on every corner, and you will not stop the murders. As long as you have a large population that is uneducated and has no job and no hope, what else is there to do but sell drugs? Until you fix that, it's hard to see the problems getting much better."[132] The inclusion of love, humility, and kindness that Jesus tells us is necessary for redemption is part of many of the restorative justice programs. As Jesus said in Matthew 11:29, "Take my yoke upon you, and learn from me; for I am gentle and humble in heart, and you will find rest for your souls."

When we show people respect and remove the poverty of low expectations, they are more likely to rise to the task. Restorative justice programs are relatively new and there are not enough of them to have a major impact on the overall system, but they do offer hope where there was none as well as a new way to address a broken system.

LIKE OTHER ISSUES RELATED to our criminal system, race is also a factor when we examine the intersection of mental health, mental development, and criminal justice. Although the proportion of major mental disorders found in the U.S. population—e.g., schizophrenia, bipolar disorder, depression, and panic disorder—is similar for racial and ethnic minorities and for whites, studies have found that blacks are more than four times as likely as whites to be diagnosed as schizophrenic, and Hispanics are more than three times as likely to be labeled with this diagnosis as whites.[133] The disparity is not in the number of people afflicted with these disorders; it is in the diagnosis. No other variables have been able to explain the disparity in the numbers of those diagnosed with these problems.[134]

In specific subgroups, like inmate populations or the homeless, we find higher rates of mental illness within ethnic groups. In these subgroups, minorities are overrepresented, although they are underserved.[135] They tend to have less access to mental health services and therefore are less likely to get the health care they need. In addition, when they do get treatment, it is often of lower quality than that received by non-minority patients.[136]

These facts make it clear that there is also a racial problem within the system. The mentally ill have a diminished capacity of clear thought processes, which ultimately the Supreme Court found should protect them from execution if convicted of a capital crime. However, a recent case shows the blatant inequity that runs through the system.

Guy Tobias LeGrande was accused of murder in North Carolina in 1996. He was permitted to represent himself even though he claimed he was getting signals from Oprah Winfrey and Dan Rather and he insisted on wearing a Superman T-shirt at the trial. A pre-trial examination of LeGrande by a psychiatrist at a state mental facility assessed him as having "hypomanic traits." All other medical records clearly indicated his history of mental illness and severe mental incompetence. He was prescribed antipsychotic medication, but refused to take it. Yet, the trial was allowed to proceed and he was convicted. LeGrande is black; his jury was all-white.

LeGrande's prosecutor wore a noose-shaped pin throughout the trial, to "boost morale"; he had a tradition of giving the pins out as rewards for attorneys in his office who won capital cases.

Even more unsettling is that LeGrande was not the sole player in this crime. Both of the other men who were involved are white. One, Tommy Munford, hired LeGrande to kill his wife so he could collect the insurance; the other, a friend of Munford's, supplied the gun. Munford received a deal in exchange for his testimony against LeGrande; he will be eligible for parole. The other was never even charged. LeGrande was scheduled for execution in December 2006 but has received a stay while he gets further medical evaluation.[137]

That LeGrande pulled the trigger is not in dispute; that he knew what he was doing is.

The National Mental Health Association has estimated that from 5 to 10 percent of those on death row have a serious mental illness.[138] The federal Bureau of Justice estimated in a September 2006 report that more than half of all inmates had mental health problems.[139] The latter report is based on inmates' reports of their symptoms, not an official diagnosis, but an earlier report by the same agency said that more than 10 percent of prisoners had serious mental illnesses and just under 10 percent were taking psychotropic drugs. This number has certainly increased since the general use of such medications has increased in the years since that report. Although we don't have accurate figures, we do know that it is a pervasive problem.[140]

We have no historical statistics for mental illness in the inmate population, but in recent years, some states have noticed a significant increase in the number of inmates who have been officially diagnosed with serious mental illnesses. Mental illness and mental retardation are not conditions that are automatically tested in the criminal justice system. If an inmate has delusions or outbursts of violence, the condition is mostly ignored or punished unless legal counsel demands testing or medical treatment. Those inmates who are most likely to be afflicted with the mental health problems that interfere with normal functioning are least likely to get the help they need. In the year before arrest, a disproportionately large number of people who were arrested had been homeless, a fact that suggests that they were indigent and/or mentally unstable.[141] The American Psychiatric Association has estimated that every year our criminal justice system processes more than 700,000 people (20 percent of those processed) who are mentally ill.[142]

In effect, the jury in LeGrand's case reflected a viewpoint that is widely held: people are culpable and therefore responsible for their behavior so long as they knew what they were doing and chose to commit the crime. This issue is the foundation for the system of "degrees" in criminal charges and it enables juries and judges to consider what are called "mitigating factors" in deciding the severity of sentences. It should be noted that most capital defendants do not have the resources to hire a private attorney and court-appointed attorneys are notoriously inadequate. There are a limited number of pro bono attorneys who represent death-row inmates and the cases that are taken are carefully chosen to maximize the chances for success.

In a precedent-setting ruling (*Ford v. Wainwright*, 1986), the Supreme Court cited the Eighth Amendment prohibition of "cruel and unusual punishment" to ban execution of a person who does not understand the reason or the reality of the punishment. Determining just who understands what and under what conditions, however, can be complicated. Accordingly, three years later, the Court refined the ruling, declaring that mental retardation may be considered a mitigating factor, but adding that the Eighth Amendment could not be used as an outright ban on execution (*Penry v. Lynaugh*, 1989). These Court decisions, along with some of the restrictions and clarifications that followed, have limited those offenders who qualify as mentally insane and/or mentally retarded, in many instances because of jury instructions and understanding of the law. It is tragic that many mentally ill inmates do not qualify as legally insane, the result of which is that mentally incompetent people are still executed regularly.[143]

These problems are ongoing. As the prison population grows, its population of mentally ill inmates continues to grow disproportionately. Those with mental illnesses often have episodes of violence, leaving both untrained prison personnel and inmates vulnerable. Recent court cases demand medical services for the mentally ill, but in prisons strapped for funds it's an uphill battle to get them.[144] Though mental retardation and mental illness are not the same, both conditions limit an individual's understanding of crime and its consequences, thereby undermining the concept of personal responsibility. Legally, the conditions are not as distinguishable as one might think. The issues raised by these questions often are not clear-cut during a trial and sentencing. The nature of mental capacity further complicates the administration of justice. The courts call on doctors, usually psychiatrists in these kinds of cases, to evaluate defendants and determine their condition and thus their culpability and exposure to a death sentence.

With the advent of psychotropic drugs, medicine has the capacity to help many of those who suffer from some of the most severe kinds of mental illness. Major mental illnesses, such as schizophrenia and bipolar disorders, in many cases can now be successfully treated with medication. But we are just at the beginning of the learning curve on neurology and the chemistry of mental illness, and many of the psychotropic drugs are relatively new; some are experimental. Mental illness, as we understand it today, is not as clear-cut as other physical diseases since its manifestation is largely behavioral. Using these new drugs to manage mental illness is akin to taking insulin for diabetes; they are not cures but simply ways of managing the disease. If the patient stops the medication, the symptoms return with deadly consequences. In a diabetic, a increase in the patient's blood sugar can cause severe problems, resulting in seizures and unconsciousness; for mental illness the symptoms—delusions/hallucinations/suicidal depression, etc.—return, causing all the concomitant aberrant behaviors.

BECAUSE OF THE NATURE of mental illness, we tend to be less tolerant and less sympathetic toward those who are afflicted with such conditions. It is another example of shunning the "other" without understanding the dynamics and the facts of the disease. Those with mental illness can't usually hide their illness the way my colleague and I were able to hide our myasthenia gravis. So long as a person's behavior conforms, we don't look further and seek understanding of the underlying problems. When it does not, we pretend it doesn't exist and send people with these problems to prisons or mental institutions where we don't have to be reminded of their existence until we are asked to help pay the costs of their care.

Medication can and often does alleviate mental disease, but it can be a double-edged sword for it raises as many questions as it does answers. There have been several recent cases in which medication has played a role in the outcome and has called into question medical ethics, much like that of the lethal injection controversy.

A case in point was Charles Singleton. Sentenced to death for murder in 1979 in Arkansas, he languished on death row for years and began to suffer from delusions, including describing himself as "God and the Supreme Court." He was diagnosed as schizophrenic and was put on antipsychotic medication. When he refused medication, it was forced on him because the state claimed he posed a danger to himself and others. Once back on medication, his symptoms dissipated, thus setting up the path for his execution. In his defense, Singleton's attorneys argued that the state did not have the right to force him to take medication that would in effect restore his legal competency in order to make him eligible for the death penalty. The state supreme court agreed, but that decision was overturned by a federal district court, whose decision then was upheld on further appeal. On appeal, a dissenting judge wrote:

> I believe that to execute a man who is severely deranged without treatment, and arguably incompetent when treated, is the pinnacle of what Justice Marshall called "the barbarity of exacting mindless vengeance" . . . Physicians are duty bound to act in the best interests of their patients. Consequently, the ethical standards of both the American Medical Association and the American Psychiatric Association prohibit members from assisting in the execution of a condemned prisoner. Needless to say, this leaves those doctors who are treating psychotic, condemned prisoners in an untenable position: treating the prisoner may provide short-term relief but ultimately result in his execution, whereas leaving him untreated will condemn him to a world such as Singleton's, filled with disturbing delusions and hallucinations.

Singleton was executed in 2004. In what seems like Kafkaesque reasoning, the court said that it was in the state's interest to have "sane" inmates and the side effect of sanity resulting from Singleton's medication should not affect his sentence. "Eligibility for execution is the only unwanted consequence of the medication," the court declared.[145] Could the "insane" Singleton, while medicated, have been making a "sane" decision to cease taking his medication to preserve his life?

Such cases again leave physicians in an ethical bind and as a consequence, the courts have trouble finding psychiatrists to evaluate and treat patients on death row. The dilemma gets even more complex. One could argue that if a physician were treating an inmate on death row, he or she would be ethically bound to withhold treatment, since that would be the only way to spare the patient's life. How would a doctor decide what is in the best interest of the patient in this case? Which treatment does "no harm"? It should be noted that the mental illness that causes delusions may also cause the individual to have totally fantastical ideas and thoughts about death. Singleton in his delusional state declared that execution would stop his breathing but that a judge could restart it again. Obviously, he lacked comprehension about his own reality and had limited mental capacity to consider the nature of execution, his own included.

In these cases, if physicians and psychiatrists determine that a defendant/patient is competent enough to decide on his or her course of treatment, the consequence of choosing medication is electing execution. In this instance, is the physician assisting in the patient's suicide? There have been no legal tests of this premise but that doesn't erase the ethical problem it poses to the medical community.

The American Bar Association, the American Psychological Association, and the American Academy of Psychiatry and the Law are among professional organizations that have called for moratoriums on the death penalty in cases involving defendants who are mentally retarded and/or mentally ill.

PERSONS WHO ARE MENTALLY retarded have severely impaired capacity to reason, yet there is a range of behavior and ability within the category. We just don't know enough about brain function to pinpoint a specific gene or even a physical brain dysfunction to help us define this kind of impairment, though it is clear that people in this category have limited mental capacities and an insufficient ability to distinguish between right and wrong, although not in every case.

In light of the insurmountable problems in determining mental conditions, the calls for a moratorium from so many professional organizations are not surprising. Modern medicine has brought many benefits, some of which we take for granted. But it has also brought with it a host of unanswered questions. The death penalty compels us to focus on deep questions of life and death. We must be willing to think about what value we put on life itself and who gets to make life and death decisions about our fellow humans, and why some lives are deemed more valuable than others. Should they be? Those broader questions naturally lead to the more practical applications embedded in the answers: state versus individual rights and powers, medical treatment and its limitations and applications, and allocation of societal resources. These issues get played out in the political arena, but they derive from our answers to the original questions. Not to think about the foundations inevitably leads to the same kind of misguided thinking that underlies racial prejudice.

In dealing with the thorny issue of mental retardation, after the *Penry* decision, states had to consider the issue as a mitigating factor, but decisions were not uniform, not only because states varied in their approach to capital punishment, but also because there is no agreed-upon definition of mental retardation. In 2002, the Supreme Court was again called upon to rule in a capital case in which the defendant was determined to be mentally retarded (*Atkins v. Virginia*). Notwithstanding the problems with defining the condition, which are numerous, Justice John Paul Stevens, in the majority opinion, cited public consensus of the morals involved in executing someone who "because of their disabilities in areas of reasoning, judgment, and control of their impulses, do[es] not act with the level or moral culpability that characterizes the most serious adult criminal conduct."

Stevens was appealing to a universal moral precept that would consider it wrong to execute someone whose mental capacity was so limited that he could not distinguish right from wrong. "Their deficiencies do not warrant an exemption from criminal sanctions, but they do diminish their personal culpability," Stevens wrote in the majority decision. He concluded that the death penalty was inappropriate punishment for the mentally retarded, citing the Eighth Amendment prohibition of cruel and unusual punishment and calling it "excessive." The ruling effectively banned execution of the mentally retarded.

Since *Atkins*, states have had to come up with their own definition of retardation—an invitation for problems and noncompliance; some states have enacted their own laws prohibiting the execution of the mentally retarded while others have in effect ignored it. Before *Atkins*, forty-four inmates characterized as mentally retarded were executed. The largest effect of *Atkins* was the removal of a number of inmates from death row due to their prior diagnosis as mentally retarded. In Texas, five inmates were taken off death row and fifty were going back to trial for claims as of October 2006.

In January 2008, a new ruling found prosecutorial misconduct in the original *Atkins* case and Daryl Atkins's sentence was commuted to life without parole. It was revealed after many years that the prosecutors had coached a witness against the defendant to make his story match the evidence.[146]

In subsequent trials, *Atkins* has become less of a factor, particularly since defining mental retardation is so amorphous. Confounding the legal determination are issues like: Which IQ test should be used to determine mental ability and what is the cut-off score? Who should diagnose mental illness and which diagnoses are to be used and to what degree are they relevant to capital cases?

These are complex questions legally and morally, and unlike a DNA test, they have no definitive answers. Our legal system applies laws to behavior in line with social norms. In the case of mental illness and mental capacity—where the shades of human differences in capability and understanding in behavior and motives can't be neatly laid out and clinically applied—it is even more difficult to establish legal parameters that can offer absolutes or even uniform guidelines. Humans are simply too messy; they don't fit neatly into categories and our behaviors are often hard to analyze. This is particularly true of those who are mentally ill or mentally retarded.

Given the limits of our understanding of the science of mental capacity and mental illness, how can we make a determination about culpability of such an offender? We are consumed with a political environment that talks about "personal responsibility." Yet we live in a culture where at every turn we see role models who take little if any responsibility and are quick to deflect blame, point fingers in the other direction, and ultimately, when the evidence is irrefutable, pay a perfunctory apology and blame alcohol or drugs or some other malady. These conditions certainly can cause aberrant behavior, but we seem more open and accepting of that fact when the offender is white and/or a celebrity. High profile offenders are accepted as folk heroes in some quarters. They apologize when pushed, keep a low profile for a while, and then are forgiven by the public. These people may or may not be genuinely sorry about their behavior, but are no more or less so than the others who we don't hear about and are not forgiven.

It's hard to imagine someone like Charles Singleton or others like him faking their condition for the benefit of trial, yet in his dissent in *Atkins*, Justice Antonin Scalia expressed concern that "the symptoms of this condition [mental retardation] can readily be feigned."[147] Is it a surprise that Atkins is black, as is his co-defendant who was given a life sentence in exchange for his testimony against Atkins, and that their victim was white?

WHY IS IT THAT some people get a pass and others barely get the benefit of the doubt? Is it our discomfort with mental conditions and disease, which we try to hide from view and pretend don't affect us? Or is it our discomfort with and disregard for the race of the violator that is part of our latent prejudice? It seems that we are often more comfortable with vengeance if the targets are black, minority, and/or poor than if they are white and wealthy.

While most of us go about our daily lives, we don't want to look at these segments of our population; we want them to be invisible so we can forget they are there. When they become more visible, we urge our politicians to take action and "clean up our streets," as if these people were part of the trash picked up routinely and carted off to the dump. We don't think about what happens to them after they are picked up; we just want them out of sight. Although this is not necessarily a racial issue, the poor are disproportionately black.

As de Tocqueville observed, equality must be at the heart of the laws of a democracy and the lack of it leads to crime. When the wealthy grow farther apart from the poorest among us in mind, spirit, and geography, and the poor no longer feel hopeful about their ability to move up in the world, equality is not assured. The system of criminal justice is skewed toward the wealthier citizens, most of whom are still white. By not acknowledging the inequality and bias, it festers and grows.

Just recently, reports of a new ordinance in Orlando, a growing city that we associate with the all-American icon of Mickey Mouse, made me sad and angry. In a move to counter a court ruling on the city's unsuccessful efforts to ban panhandling, the city rewrote the law and banned feeding groups of twenty-five or more people without a "Large Group Feeding Permit." Organizations that routinely try to feed the homeless will now be subject to criminal prosecution for violations.

"We've seen cities going beyond punishing homeless people to punishing those trying to help them, even though it's clear that not enough resources are being dedicated to helping the homeless or the hungry," explained Maria Foscarinis, executive director of the nonprofit National Law Center on Homelessness and Poverty. Many other cities have enacted similar legislation—all to get the "others" out of sight.[148] In Birmingham recently, a local church received complaints from nearby businesses when long lines formed to receive free meals provided to the hungry. I was glad to see that the church did not give in to the pressure.

Most of those we arbitrarily sweep up into the criminal justice system are poor; many are homeless; many have substance abuse problems; many would be good candidates for restorative justice programs. Yet we are more likely to support spending additional money on building prisons than on creating the kinds of programs that would contribute to the rehabilitation of criminal offenders. It makes us feel safer to lock people up, though that policy is not based on fact. Like the death penalty, it is less expensive in the long run to treat people and help them become useful citizens than to keep them locked up in prisons for years on end. It is also inhumane. "When they are diminished and brought low through oppression, trouble, and sorrow, he pours contempt on princes and makes them wander in trackless wastes; but he raises up the needy out of distress, and makes their families like flocks" (Psalms 107:39–41).

Over the last two decades, we have also adopted a series of more punitive laws that demand jail time for lower-level crimes, including the "three strikes" concept that continues to keep nonviolent offenders in prison for life. This mandatory policy has its roots in a 1736 Massachusetts decree that describes how the colony would deal with those who broke the laws: on first conviction a thief would be fined or whipped; on second offense the fines would be tripled and the convict would get the "gallows"—a public display during which the convict sat on a platform with a noose around his or her neck and would get thirty lashes at the whipping post; on third offense, the convict would be hanged.[149]

Although we often think of colonial laws as archaic and their punishments as harsh and rigid—particularly those that dealt with issues of morality—our current "three strikes" law is no less rigid. This law has contributed to the large number of drug offenders now serving life sentences for relatively minor crimes. As with other policies in our past, the punitive nature of mandatory sentencing for drug offenses has affected blacks disproportionately. And, as is the case with other policies, it is not because so many more blacks are drug users or drug dealers. It is a result of enforcing drug laws unevenly.

In a landmark study in 1991, it was found that black offenders were 21 percent more likely than whites to receive at least the mandatory minimum sentence; Hispanics were 28 percent more likely.[150] This data has been confirmed by subsequent studies.[151] The racial disparities found in studies of inmates on death row are also apparent in the general prison population; from plea bargains, assistance to the prosecution, jail time pending trial, to sentencing for similar crimes, black offenders disproportionately receive harsher sentences and fewer allowances for variables.[152]

WORKING IN THE PRISON ministries program, I've met many courageous inmates who have worked hard to overcome obstacles to their rehabilitation and reentry into society. One of the men I have become acquainted with is a former drug addict and what most people would label a career criminal. He is now one of many success stories, assisted by programs offered through drug courts. Billy's story follows:

Having been a statistic in the prison system for almost four decades now, I have yet to see anything even remotely resembling rehabilitation until I entered the Federal Crime Bill Drug Treatment Program. When I entered treatment in January, 1998, I had absolutely no desire to change; nor did I believe that it was possible. I had been in the program for a year and a half before finally coming to the realization that I could change if I would merely work the steps as laid out by the program.

As addicts we tend to drift away from the morals and ethics we were taught as children. All of my life I lived by the convict code, always trying to get over on anyone in authority. The treatment program changed all that. I am speaking from thirty-eight years of experience. I have had the privilege of watching many individuals progress, making changes in their lives and actually living recovery one day at a time.

After four months in pre-treatment, I moved into active treatment, which is divided into three two-month sessions. Phase One being SAP, an introduction to chemical dependency; Phase Two, criminal thinking, identifying your criminal thinking patterns and changing them with new responsible ways of thinking; Phase Three relapse prevention, learning to recognize what your triggers are and what to do so you don't relapse. Following the completion of active treatment and graduation, I was moved into Aftercare, where I was expected to continue working on myself. This is when I came to the realization that recovery is a life long experience and we[I] must continue to work on [my]self every day.

When I first entered the system in 1966, at the age of sixteen, the rage was technical education as the ticket to rehabilitation. Believing this, I enrolled in trade school, studying auto body and fender repair, thinking that by learning a trade I would be able to stay out of prison. Wrong! When I got out in November, 1970, I never once worked at this trade. However, I did go back to using drugs just as heavily as before, which in turn finally led to criminal activity and the cycle started over again. I lived on this merry-go-round for another seven years—prison, out, drugs, prison, out, drugs—and then back to prison until 1980 when I took my final fall. Now I am serving life, life without parole and 124 years.

Drug courts are an effort to coordinate the various social systems with the goal of breaking the kind of cycle experienced by Billy. Drug court programs intervene in the system immediately after sentencing to identify an inmate who is a drug abuser. Once the inmate enters the drug court program, he or she is placed under court monitoring and community supervision with long-term treatment services. It is one of many similar attempts to offer alternatives to the standard incarceration of convicts. With over half of our prison population consisting of inmates who have violated drug laws, it would seem to be an obvious change. As of 2005, drug offenders accounted for 55 percent of the federal prison population. About 45 percent were in prison for possession, not trafficking.[153]

There are many varieties of the drug court model, each specialized to address a specific population; they include mental health courts, juvenile courts, and family courts, among others. All are attempts to use community resources to coordinate the process of adjudicating crime, from courts/judges, probation officers, drug counselors, job counselors, and drug testing personnel. All or some of these resources may be called upon in specific combinations, depending on the need, in an effort to keep inmates from getting lost in the system. Use of drug courts has grown from one in 1989 to more than sixteen hundred in 2004. More than seventy thousand drug court clients are being served at any given time. Most adult-based drug court programs have had lower recidivism rates over a substantial period of time after completion of the program, according to a February 2005 U.S. Government Accountability Office review.

Like other programs that are more punitive in nature, drug courts rarely have the resources needed to operate fully, despite of their success record. Many states with thriving drug court programs have not allocated separate funds for the drug courts. Funds used for drug courts may come from the budgets of state agencies like corrections, substance abuse treatment, or even administrative offices of the courts. Alabama has set up drug courts in most counties, but adequate funding is still an issue even though it has been shown that their use has reduced prison overcrowding and lowered costs.[154]

Drug court participants undergo long-term treatment and counseling, sanctions, incentives, and frequent court appearances. Upon successful completion of the treatment program, participants' charges may be dismissed or sentences may be reduced or set aside.[155]

Should the corrections system embrace treatment and the two begin working together, we would see a gradual change in the system as we know it today. Prison would no longer be the breeding ground of criminal behavior. Rather than a man being released to return to his old way of life, he could go back to society with a new concept of living. His thinking patterns would have been altered, his decision-making skills honed and his willingness to be held accountable for his actions strengthened. You would have a man coming out of prison ready to become a responsible, productive member of the community.

Sadly, Billy will never be able to use his abilities on the "outside." Had he been able to access this kind of program earlier . . . There are lots of what-ifs in Billy's case and thousands of others like him. We do have alternatives to incarceration, alternatives that work. What we don't have is the will to create and fund the programs that offer these alternatives on a wide scale. Is it because this, too, is perceived as a "handout" to minorities and the poor who would be the largest beneficiaries of such programs? Is it really "soft on crime" to have empathy for those who are indigent and/or "other"? Why is it better to build prisons rather than mental institutions or drug and alcohol rehabilitation centers? From 1987 to 1995, the state of California increased expenditures on prisons by 30 percent while spending on higher education decreased by 18 percent. Has society gained from that policy?[156]

While we pour more money into what is now accurately called the prison-industrial complex because of its size and scope, thousands of the mentally ill go without help and remain untreated. Mental health professionals report that there are so few available appropriate care facilities that they can't admit new patients unless it is mandated by their sentence in a criminal conviction. Instead of helping people before they get to that point—giving them therapy, medication, drug treatment, and assisted living facilities in the community—we arrogantly think that people should "make it on their own" and should be responsible if they can't and resort to crime in the process.[157]

In the days of our experimental democracy, de Tocqueville was very clear in his analysis of the problems of the unequal members of society, and he wrote about the terrible blight of slavery on an otherwise laudable system. His caveat about equality is still prescient. Getting rid of the vestiges of racial prejudice and its inherent inequality will not be an easy task.

Prisons have become a large, profitable and fast-growth industry. Those invested in such businesses do not want to lose their livelihoods; they have a vested interest in maintaining a high inmate count. The push for privatization of prisons is part of the trend, and companies would not be pitching for the business if it were not profitable. The location of new prisons has become part of a bidding contest with the number of inmates used as fodder, reminiscent of the old slave trade. In those days, slaves were counted as three-fifths of a person for the purposes of taking a census. In an odd twist on history, prison populations today are counted as part of the census in the location of the prison. Legislative districts often compete to obtain funding and grants based on their population. Increasing the prisoner population makes the district eligible for more money. This funding then gets distributed within the district and not necessarily to the prison. When a prison has empty beds, it starts to lose money. If it is forced to close altogether, it leaves in its wake an economically depressed community, ironically one that is ripe for increased crime. These factors remain pertinent to the difficulty of changing the system.

I am not advocating opening up all the prison gates; we have to balance public safety and the usefulness of keeping someone locked up. Humane treatment is what God tells us is the right and moral response to people who are indigent and sick and cannot help themselves. "As God's chosen ones, holy and beloved, clothe yourselves with compassion, kindness, humility, meekness, and patience" (Colossians 3:12).

I have found that inmates want to be productive and self-sufficient but they don't know how to get there. Wouldn't we be better off as a nation if we could offer a way for those who have committed criminal acts to make restitution and to change their previous behavior patterns? Even if we have determined that an inmate's crime was so heinous he or she should never be released, aren't we all better off benefiting from the contributions that the inmate could make from within prison?

Those who are not capable of living harmoniously within our social structures, and that includes the mentally handicapped and/or mentally ill, should be given medical care and close supervision as appropriate for each person. The rough and tumble atmosphere of most prisons serves no purpose other than to incite more negative behavior and violence, as de Tocqueville observed more than 160 years ago. A large part of those now held in our nation's prisons fall into this category.[158]

If we were to filter out the mentally ill, mentally handicapped, drug and alcohol abusers from among the inmates, it would empty more than half of the prisons and alleviate the overcrowding problem. But there have to be alternative places to send those who are released, places that could offer rehabilitation and a path out of the mindset of crime and into the mainstream. And yes, there are some individuals for whom reform is not possible; they must be kept away from the rest of society, either in prisons or alternative institutions, but certainly treated humanely. Isn't that the better object lesson?

We hear stories now and then about people who commit crimes in order to get caught and sent back to prison! Why? Because they feel hopeless about their lives within a society where opportunity is not always equal, where they can't get a job and support themselves and a family, where they are shunned because of their prison record. The lessons of Jesus are in humility and kindness, love and hope, not in vengeance, hate, and arrogance. An offer of hope and redemption for the millions of people who languish in our prisons would do much more to change the dynamics of crime and spread the lessons of Christ than instilling fear and inciting vengeance. "Finally, all of you, have unity of spirit, sympathy, love for one another, a tender heart, and a humble mind. Do not repay evil for evil or abuse for abuse; but, on the contrary, repay with a blessing. It is for this that you were called—that you might inherit a blessing" (Peter 3:8–9).

16

WHO'S YOUR LEADER?

An odd paradox set in during my medical crises. When I was debilitated, I probably had more time on my hands than ever before; yet I was acutely aware that the clock was ticking off the remaining days of my life and I no longer had the luxury of a lifetime ahead of me. I realized that I was now "playing the back nine" in golf lingo, and I recalled what an older and dear friend had said to me about time flying as you get older: "It is because each day is a bigger part of the rest of your life." During this period, I read a lot in my quest for answers and one of the voices I found most comforting was that of John Wesley.

Dr. Crawford Owen, who had been my personal physician as well as my Sunday school class teacher for many years, is also a Wesley scholar. Crawford introduced Wesley to me and I began to read more about the man who was the founder of Methodism; his message for me was both comforting and stimulating. Wesley talks about meaning and purpose, and I took comfort in the precept of living a life to please God and prepare for the afterlife. I also was attracted to Wesley's notion of "holiness" as that which is manifested by doing all the good you can for fellow humankind through "acts of kindness" and doing good things for the sake of others, termed "outward Holiness." Wesley describes it as the purpose of life and it was one of the concepts that led me to get involved in the prison ministries. Inward holiness also includes loving God as proscribed by none other than Jesus ("Love the Lord your God with all your heart, mind, and strength"). Love of God underlies love and compassion for all humanity—rich and poor, sick and healthy, regardless of color.

One of Wesley's most famous sermons is entitled, "Circumcision of the Heart," for which the scriptural basis is found in Deuteronomy 10:16): "Circumscribe then the foreskin of your heart, and do not be stubborn any longer." Open your mind and let your will be God's will, the text is saying. Wesley emphasized that true transformation comes not from just change in behavior or conforming to God's Law, but from a real change of heart. "You shall put these words of mine in your heart and soul, and you shall bind them as a sign on your hand, and fix them as an emblem on your forehead" (Deuteronomy 11:18–21).

And so I began a different journey, not just to heal my physical being, but to heal my heart and soul as well. While my sins are not in the same sphere as those on death row or even inmates who are guilty of less egregious crimes, none of us is completely free of sin since we are human and suffer from the frailty of the human condition. The question isn't can we lead a perfect life without ever making mistakes; the question is how do we amend our ways when we do make mistakes, and how do we seek to reconcile with the objects of our sins? There is a large range of sin: many shades of gray lie between forgetting a loved one's birthday and murdering someone. The restorative justice programs seek to address some of these questions and help heal both the offender and the victim in the process.

A life in and through God had been incubating in my mind for some time, but it was reading Wesley's words that led me to my aha moment. God, through Wesley, through his church, through his servant, revealed himself to me. I now felt that I knew the direction my life would follow—must follow.

My search for truth and deeper understanding continues to evolve. My progress has been rapid. My human frailties notwithstanding, I have become empowered through Jesus Christ. I gave him a toothpick and he built me a house from it. May I never stray, but when I do, I am impelled to forgiveness and penance to return to his good grace and my truly good life in him. I am not an exceptional person, but a mere mortal transformed by the power of God. I am but one of millions who have answered his call. I am but one of many to whom he provides the guiding light. While I do not set myself above others who hold different beliefs or conceptions,

I do feel a purity of purpose and understanding.

Wesley was sensitive about poverty and spent a lot of his time ministering to the poor. He was one of the few in his time to speak out against slavery, which he thought morally wrong. I was looking for a path that would follow in the Wesley tradition, doing good for humankind. And here it was. I couldn't ignore the evidence of inequality. It is clear to me then that racism permeates the whole criminal justice system, and the layered depth of it became part of my focus. More recently, the prison facilities I have observed around the state have also heightened my awareness and fanned the flames smoldering beneath the surface of my quest. My mission had been clear for some time, but now the path for working toward it had opened.

As Christ tried to spread justice and fairness in treating fellow humans, so, too, is that my message. I have complete faith in God and in the path provided by my faith as guided by Jesus Christ. I know that the transformation I experienced was powerful. I look at the criminal justice system and have to say justice not served is justice denied. The intensity of one's religious belief (or lack of it), is irrelevant to the administration of justice. After all, those who claim Biblical dictums as justification for capital punishment are firmly convinced that their strong religious beliefs give them the moral high ground. Whatever our religious belief system, shouldn't we be concerned about justice? Wasn't the execution of Christ in itself unjust? Isn't what is just, moral, and what is unjust, immoral?

Our legal system is derived not only from moral principles but implemented by humans who often err in their judgment of themselves and of others—whose attitudes and beliefs are as often shaped by their heritage and faulty assumptions as by reasoned views of justice. Our legal system was pieced together by the times and by those who dedicated their lives to creating a more just and equal society. Legal and moral are not the same, though they often drive each other and serve each other. Morality can act as a pressure point in changing the legal framework in a democracy, but it cuts both ways. The tyranny of the majority is a danger that de Tocqueville warned about and saw as an inevitable part of a democratic government. He believed that the majority would always attempt to subjugate the minority and the court of public opinion is one strong pressure point. This paradox is one of the unsolvable problems in a democracy. Minority rights and minority voices must be protected for democracy to sustain itself. Our system of checks and balances was designed to alleviate this risk. Sometimes it does, but not always.

We can see in our own history how minority voices sometimes do get heard and eventually become majorities, paving the way for change. From the abolition of slavery to prohibition, from women's suffrage to civil rights, from the right to unionize to the demand for food safety and government oversight of the banking system and the stock exchange—none of these issues were first led by politicians. The demand for change came from the people and the politicians eventually followed. The majority was not always on the right side of morality—for example, in the case of slavery—but for the most part, the majority got it right. And when they didn't, they went back to the drawing board and fixed it—for example, prohibition.

The polls are now showing that the majority opinion is wavering on the death penalty, the caveat being how the question is framed. If the question is posed as a choice between death and life without parole, there is now much more support for the latter. In the last twenty years, solid majorities have supported capital punishment. It was part of the law-and-order mentality engendered by fear and a growing crime rate that was frequently exploited by politicians. The "tough on crime" image was fostered as more and more "criminals" were rounded up and removed from sight. But while overall crime waned, the murder rate in those states that had a death penalty in place was often higher than in those that did not. Coupled with the distaste for the killing of innocents, the majority has slipped into a split that mirrors the conflict. In 1994, only 32 percent of the public favored life without parole; 50 percent supported death—more if the option for life without parole was not offered. By 2006, support for life without parole had grown to 48 percent.[159] That slim margin in public opinion is reflected even here in Alabama, home to the most zealous supporters of the policy. A *Birmingham News* editorial in 2005 illustrates the shift:

> After decades of supporting the death penalty, the editorial board no longer can do so . . . We have come to believe Alabama's capital

punishment system is broken . . . First and foremost, this newspaper's editorial board is committed to a culture of life . . . We are not turning soft on crime. Remember, the alternative to the death penalty is not leaving predators free to kill again. The alternative to execution is life in prison without any chance, ever, for parole. That is enough to protect the public.[160]

Part of this change is rooted in the discomfort of supporting a policy that not only *might* be killing innocent people, but had been proven to have done so and was likely to continue making mistakes. Not even the staunchest proponents of capital punishment think it's okay to execute someone who is not guilty of the crime. A few proponents shrug off the inevitability of mistakes as the price we pay for safety, but I think these are exceptions, and certainly a minority.

When people are asked the question differently by offering life without parole as an alternative to the death penalty, the thin majority turns into a slight majority in favor of life without parole. People pay attention to headlines about an impending execution (or some sensationalizing of it) or to the discovery that someone innocent has been killed or exonerated. Other thoughts about crime are related to fears about personal safety. The fear of crime is countered by the fear of erroneous execution. The guilt gets transferred from the presumed criminal to the public. It becomes a moral issue when people start to feel responsible for executing an innocent. That collective guilt is part of what is driving the public toward looking at alternatives. With few exceptions, it has been the public that has made the switch, not the politicians.

So THE QUESTION IS which comes first? We think of our elected politicians as leaders, but are they? Leadership often comes from the ranks of the people—Martin Luther King Jr., Eleanor Roosevelt, Cesar Chavez, Helen Keller, among many others. These are not people who were elected, but they worked through the political system to effect specific changes in the law so that the minority would be heard. Eventually, the minority turned into a majority.

In general, the public is ahead of the curve and the politicians follow, which is why we see so much emphasis on public opinion polls. It is, after all is said and done, the way our system works. Officials are elected to follow the will of the people. But what happens when there is a clash of wills, when the politician doesn't agree with the poll or doesn't think the policy is right? This is not a defense of politicians—some are invariably more responsive and have more integrity than others—but a question of expectations. If we want laws and policies to change, politicians have to be pushed to make the changes. Eventually, they do or they get thrown out of office. Often, politicians tread a fine line in trying to get their public image in sync with the public will.

We've seen the populist view played out before. George Wallace changed when it was clear that support for segregation was seriously eroded. In California, Proposition 36 passed in November 2000 with a 61 percent margin, mandating treatment and probation instead of jail time for nonviolent drug offenses. Governor Arnold Schwarzenegger disagrees with the policy and has subsequently cut its funding from the state budget, basically voiding the proposition. The issue is in court now while Schwarzenegger shifts the debate from the policy to the legality of the proposition itself. It is just this sort of manipulation of the power structure that so often prevents justice from prevailing, regardless of the laws in place.[161]

We now meet the resistance of politicians who are supposed to be following the will of the people and acting in the public interest, when in reality what they are following is their own attitudes and views, full of their own fears and latent prejudices. It will take more people becoming more vocal before there are legal changes to the criminal justice system and to the death penalty policy. Popular wisdom is that someone who advocates for prisoners is "soft on crime" and therefore can't get elected. We need to change that mindset by educating and mobilizing the public.

Often, the public is less punitive than politicians, particularly when given choices. This is most evident in Alabama where a judge can override a jury's decision in capital cases. Of the 205 convicts currently on death row in Alabama, as many as 22 percent are there because a judge overrode the jury that voted for a lesser sentence.[162]

In 2007, an Alabama circuit judge overruled a ten to two jury decision of life without parole, changing the sentence to the death penalty. Referring to the jury decision Judge William Cole said, "I weighed that very heavily in favor of the defendant. But everything tells me the jury did not make the right decision."

By Alabama law Judge Cole had the right, but no obligation, to change the jury decision; but it seems that he would rather not have had a choice. "I never saw myself as someone who would override a jury's decision, especially a nine to two decision," Judge Cole said. "Maybe the courts will do away with overrides. If they do, it won't hurt my feelings at all." Judge Cole's actions speak loudly. This seems a bit disingenuous to me. That criminals must take responsibility for their behavior is always a given, but Cole says he would rather not have had that responsibility. Yet no one forced him to make that decision. Need I add that the defendant is black and in this particular case, the white victims' families played a prominent role?[163] Other cases have followed the same pattern.

In Alabama, judges are elected officials and are thus more subject to their own fear—that of losing their jobs. In the process of considering a jury verdict, judges in these situations also, consciously or not, look at how they think public opinion will play out. In an attempt to analyze the issues and perhaps to provide palatable solutions, judges may render decisions that they think will be more popular. The message sent by such override decisions is both the inherent power of the judge to rule and the harsh penalty affecting blacks as the object lesson to the community. The judge's message is, "I know better and my judgment will keep you safe from the blacks who might harm you; we know they are criminally prone so we'll get them off the streets. Vote for me and I'll continue to do this—even if you don't want to say you don't like it. I know you agree with me—you just can't say it in public anymore." This is the arrogant thinking that is behind these kinds of judicial decisions in the state. If this unspoken message is not what drives it, where is the public outrage?

Politicians too often respond by offering simplistic solutions to complex issues. Their responses pander to the public's fear but do little to resolve the problem. The media report on what the politicians say and do, and the public reads and interprets the information. The public winds up being fed half-truths or false information or at least false impressions and then opinions are based on this misinformation. Frequently, crime is framed in terms of race, conjuring up images of the old hateful stereotypes. It's not always conscious or overt, but it serves to push alarm buttons. Not only does it encourage fear of crime, it also encourages fear of "other" and of racial differences in general.

For example, media portrayal of light sentences is often negative and critical without discussion of all the parameters of the case. In the information age, there is less time for reflection and more attention is paid to reaction. To gain audience, the media focuses on the sensational, and execution surely is sensational, as is fear. Although the medium has changed greatly in the past century, I often wonder how much progress we have really made in the dissemination of truth and our willingness to follow along without question. Mob rule and the politics of fear supported the execution of Christ and it is mob rule and that same fear that today's politicians count on to continue support of "populist" policies.

In reaction to the infamous 1938 radio broadcast adaptation of H. G. Wells's classic *The War of the Worlds*, there was mass hysteria because people thought the show was real and were afraid. It seems silly now to most of us given the subject—the Martians are coming. But the hype and the public susceptibility in believing things that are simply not true is still very much with us. Our present-day hysteria about crime is used to the same ends by media portrayal of crime being solved by brutal treatment and execution of the "bad guys."

I HAVE BECOME SOMEWHAT of a maverick among my friends. They have grown used to me being more vocal about views that differ from theirs, mostly about capital punishment, but also about racial issues. I understand that more often than not they will choose to ignore the facts, regardless of the sources, and will refuse to acknowledge that discrimination exists in our criminal justice system. While this saddens and disappoints me, I feel as if I am straddling the crossroads of a different kind of segregation. Those in my immediate environment accept my new views, regardless of their disagreement. They know that I will not judge them or jeopardize our relationship because of our differences in opinion. They listen to me because they care about me, they trust my judgment, and they sincerely enjoy engaging in a conversation about the issues. Then there are those who disagree with my views and may be hostile toward them. This always hits me from left field. I never seem to anticipate it, perhaps because I am overly optimistic, or naïve. Yet after all these years, I am still surprised when someone expresses the kind of hatred, bigotry, and ignorance shown by a fellow church member not that long ago.

I now have few inhibitions about articulating my views, tempered of course by the situation—creating enemies doesn't serve my cause. While I can't force anyone to change an opinion, I have on occasion been able to puncture a small hole in the armor. Some have confessed that information I provided gave them cause to re-evaluate their feelings. Others, I think, have found some resonance with what they have felt but hadn't previously been able to express. One acquaintance told me that if the facts are as I explained them, then the death penalty is a sin and those that support it are sinful. He followed that with, "I certainly do not want to carry an opinion that would be considered a sin." I know that if I can bring just a few people along and help them to accept the facts, they may start to form fact-based opinions. This seems like it would be simple but the truth is that most of us have deeply held beliefs that have little to do with facts.

When there is no reason to question our beliefs, we simply ignore and/ or deny conflicting facts. Opening the door to those truths and making changes doesn't come easy; nor does confronting the demons of death. While we are in good health, we deny the fact of death, yet it is inevitable. Perhaps this denial is merely human nature. But when facing my own death, I found another truth that stood apart from myself and my own struggles. Death was to show me the reality of man's inhumanity to man. A look at my own truths stimulated changes that were so profound I felt like I had no choice but to make it my responsibility to help others see through the fog of emotion. I have arrived at this point clear in my conviction that capital punishment is morally wrong and should not be codified in a system that is supposed to represent liberty and justice for all.

In my own small way, by leading Sunday school or Bible study classes or talking to lay groups, and speaking up instead of remaining silent—whether among friends who accept my views as part of who I am now, or strangers who dismiss my views and grow hostile in their own defense—I am intent on staying on this path. As Abraham Lincoln once said, "To sin by silence when they should protest makes cowards of men." While I consider myself neither a missionary nor a messiah, what I learned in the process of becoming one with God profoundly affected how I wanted to live the rest of my life. I made up my mind to devote myself to doing what I can for my fellow humankind, especially for those who are less fortunate.

Our Constitution and Bill of Rights was designed to protect everyone equally. I grew up believing in that system and its virtues, never thinking that those who administer it could be using it for their own purposes or acting according to their own biases, whether blatant or latent. Of course at the time, I did not understand how my own flawed beliefs played a role in perpetuating and protecting the entrenched belief system that underlies our current legal and social mores. They are all related but they are not things we think about much; they are things we assume.

I held on to the belief system I grew up with, much the same as most of us do. As a society, we have made changes over the years which have paved a more moral path for the generations to follow. Ideas governing social issues evolve and people do change. But big changes do not usually occur without a struggle, whether personal or global. Though my own change came about because of my own personal threat, death is universal and social issues are global. Perhaps sometimes the personal really is political, or at least has political implications.

But there is also a moral issue here, whether one believes that morality is derived from God and Biblical precepts or from other sources. We expect our politicians to govern not just from legal precedents but also from moral ones. In fact, I think we want them to be obligated to do so and when they don't, they betray the public trust. One of the reasons politics is held in such low esteem by the public is because of that betrayal. We expect politicians to act ethically, if not morally, and to fulfill their public duties in the interest of the common good. While defining that common ground is the foundation of political debate, ethical standards need not be compromised in the process. Because there is opportunity to act, there is no obligation to do so.

Judge Cole had no obligation to impose the death penalty and seems to have dictated a decision suited to his own beliefs and perhaps his own sense of morality rather than either a social change or a greater societal good. Unfortunately, this practice is widespread in Alabama and probably elsewhere. In Jefferson County (Birmingham), death penalty convictions have a 77 percent error rate as returned by the Supreme Court of Alabama—a court comprised of many social conservatives who would probably like to see capital punishment preserved. In attempting to impose their own personal morality, the legal system does a disservice not only to those caught in it but to the public who has entrusted those officials to run the government "for the people." Almost a century ago in 1916, Theodore Roosevelt said, "Justice consists not in being neutral between right and wrong, but in finding out the right and upholding it, wherever found, against the wrong."

We have an obligation to root out wrongs, whether individual wrongs or global ones. Those in power and those working on behalf of those in power must follow the same code of ethics. I understand that the law is not yet in accord with my code of ethics on this issue. But just as I must work within the confines of the current law to seek change of both law and attitude, those working on the other side of the debate who are in a position to decide on life or death issues, must do the same. They must follow the law and a code of ethics compatible with democratic principles; they must separate their own personal morality from the national good. Sometimes the two are merged; other times they are not. Understanding the difference and operating on that premise is the basis for democratic institutions that have longevity and integrity.

OCCASIONALLY I HAVE HAD lively discussions with friends. Knowing my position, they would tease me, mostly in good faith. "Hey, Baldwin's gone soft on crime," I would hear someone yell across the golf course after some off the cuff remark I made about inmate rehabilitation. Other times, I'd engage people in a more serious dialogue—friendly, but decidedly more serious.

Recently, after having spent some time visiting with and counseling prisoners, I was relating a conversation I had with a young inmate. Gene had been involved with drugs at an early age. Life was not something he cherished, so he figured out at the age of twelve that the beer in the refrigerator tasted pretty good but, better yet, took the edge off feeling empty. By the age of sixteen he was popping pills and drinking and ingesting whatever else he could manage to buy. Yes, money was always a problem—these are expensive habits. At first, Gene just wanted the high to get through the school day; then he wanted it to have fun and feel better around girls; then there came a point at which he didn't care at all—he just needed a fix. If he had to empty someone's cash register to do it, it didn't matter. Predicting the inevitable results of this lifestyle are easy; changing them is hard.

A young teen with few social skills, little self-esteem, and no self-control, he had already seen his share of the juvenile justice system. After his sister was raped, he turned his anger to kill the accused. He was tried and convicted and sentenced to ten years—the shorter sentence because of his "temporary insanity" defense. After all, he told me, "He raped my little sister." After serving his time, Gene was released.

By the time Gene was nineteen he had been in prison several times, mostly for petty crimes, but by the time I met him, he was slated for death row. In his last round of desperate need to support his habit, he and some friends were waiting to score some drugs, but the deal went bad. The forensic evidence showed that Gene's friend fired the weapon that killed a bystander. Gene also had a gun but it was apparently not the weapon that killed the victim. Although neither Gene nor his pals intended to use their weapons, somehow it happened anyway.

Because none of the other teens had criminal records, the investigation focused on Gene. The others "flipped," and Gene was charged with and convicted of capital murder. The other three were set free. Gene is convinced that his previous record made it easier for the prosecution to make their case, and that is why he was convicted despite forensic evidence that basically exonerated him. In addition, the state-appointed attorney, Gene said, spent little time with him, using most of their pre-trial preparation time attempting to get him to plead guilty.

When counseling inmates like Gene, I have to exercise caution in discussing his case, else I could be called to testify and that testimony could be used against him. So in listening to his story I was careful not to broach issues of legal guilt. Knowing what I do now about the zeal of some prosecutors, I have no reason to doubt the circumstances Gene described to me, or his conviction, which is currently on appeal.

The amazing thing about Gene is that he has been on death row for years but is at peace. Like the majority of other inmates I have encountered as part of the prison ministry program, Gene is friendly, outgoing, and easy to talk to. As is often my practice when visiting inmates, Gene and I prayed together and we talked a bit. He teared up when he tried to tell me about the incident and that he was sorry that the bystander was killed. This was the first time I had seen him express emotion; the fact that he was expressing remorse, I thought, was quite remarkable.

"You mean you really feel bad about what happened?" I asked him.

"I feel awful that an innocent person's life was taken and I have related that to his family," Gene replied. "In fact, we have met and they have forgiven me for what happened. I think that they know what really happened also."

Both Gene and the victim's family have closure and the family is willing to testify on his behalf, should the opportunity and circumstances arise. Gene attributes his ability to move toward remorse to his acceptance of God. Gene came from a religious family and his mother and aunt had maintained contact with him during his time in prison. They had been encouraging him for years to turn to God to help straighten out his life. After a visit from them one weekend, he returned to his cell and felt that he had to do something. His mind was clouded by the incident, the trial, and now his impending death. All of these things had left him agitated, angry, and unable to sleep, he explained. Over the years, they had taken a toll and now he was ready for a change. That night Gene got on his knees and prayed for forgiveness and peace.

"For the first time in years I woke up the next morning having slept all night. I was free, man," Gene told me calmly. "Oh, what a feeling that was and it has stayed with me. In fact it has strengthened as I have learned more about a life with God in charge. Even if they call me up [to the death chamber] tomorrow, I will still be at peace."

I understood exactly how Gene felt. Although my death sentence had a difference source, we have both made peace with God and are ready to receive him. I was moved by Gene's reconciliation both with the victim's family and with God. The next day, I still couldn't get it out of my mind. I was on my way to a Rotary meeting when I ran into Charlie. I had known Charlie for a number of years, but our paths rarely crossed. He is a bit older than I am and ran in social strata well above my own. Always the coarse and outspoken one (most thought of him as a loudmouth) he has been known to interject his opinion on anything from the church to street sanitation; all he needs is an audience. And, of course, Charlie is always right. Though we are both members of some of the same organizations, he seldom attends the meetings, so I don't see him much. But he always knows what's going on with everybody.

"I hear you're working on the chain gangs these days," he said with a grin. I'm sure he thought he was being funny—Charlie always was a kind of smart aleck.

"I guess you could say that," I told him. "But mostly I'm exercising my brain muscles. I look at inmates in a whole different light these days."

"How's that?" Charlie asked. "Seems pretty simple. Do the crime, serve your time."

"It's not quite that easy, Charlie," I told him.

"I know you think we should abolish the death penalty, and some people agree with you these days," he said, striking a more serious demeanor. "But I'm not one of them! I am one who believes what the preacher says when he talks about the sanctity of life, and I agree. But your pals didn't consider that when they murdered their victims. Nor did they consider the victim's family. I think we have to look at that side of the equation for once and stop pandering to the criminals."

"Well, you know, a lot of times they don't really stop to consider anything. Many of them are addicts and don't know what they are doing. And some are really still kids," I explained.

"Old enough to know better," Charlie replied. "That doesn't make them less culpable. They need to be responsible for their actions. Don't you think people should be punished for their crimes? And you should know better than I that the Bible clearly states how criminals should be dealt with. Listen to the preacher, son!"

I ignored his admonishment. "I guess it depends on the punishment," I said. "I just talked to one of them recently and what he really needed a long time ago was drug treatment and rehab. And now we're going to kill him because his addiction won that battle?"

I think at this point Charlie was considering whether or not I had totally lost my marbles. Besides, it wasn't that long ago that I'd heard that his own son had been picked up for driving under the influence. I didn't want to go there, but I was prepared to do so if I had to.

He changed tacks, saying, "Look man, we also have to consider the closure that the death penalty brings to those poor families who have lost their loved ones. Don't they deserve some peace of mind?"

"Of course people need closure," I told him. "But they don't get it because the state kills someone. It's a myth." Before he could interject something else, I went on to relate my experience with Gene and told him how that reconciliation affected everyone, not just Gene, who seemed truly transformed. I'm not certain that Charlie really believed me. At the least he thought I was exaggerating or describing an exceptional case. "Well, I, for one, could not forgive someone who murdered someone in my family," he proudly told me. "The way I feel about it is give me a gun and I would take care of justice if my family was involved in a situation like that."

"I certainly hope you never have to find out," I said. And at that, another acquaintance joined us.

"Either one of you gentlemen want to volunteer to give me some tickets to the Alabama-Auburn game this weekend?" Ben asked us. That abruptly changed the subject.

"Well Robbie here would like to suggest that you give them out to the killers in the prison. Get 'em a weekend pass, and then he can take 'em to the game with him!" Charlie said grinning. What I felt was disparaged. Ben looked a bit confused and then continued his pitch before I had a chance to respond. I wasn't happy with Charlie's sense of humor but I didn't think there was much hope of him changing his mind anyway. It is always frustrating to have this conversation repeated again and again with many others who may not be as coarse as Charlie but are in accord with his attitude.

Nevertheless, the conversation rankled me and I couldn't help thinking about it later. "They deserve to die for what they did" is a continuation of the feeling of revenge, not an effort to look for ways to forgive. Isn't the message that Jesus sends us in forgiveness and compassion? Isn't it enough that Christ was made to suffer out of vengeance for our own sins? "Beloved, never avenge yourselves, but leave it to the wrath of God, for it is written, 'Vengeance is mine, I will repay, says the Lord'" (Romans 12:19–21). From my reading and from the brief training I'd had in the ministries program, I have come to understand that forgiveness and forgetting are not the same. Forgiveness doesn't erase the memory, but it allows one to stop the cycle of desire for revenge. Revenge merely continues bitterness and prevents the hurt from healing. The Bible tells us that God will forget our transgressions if we seek forgiveness and repent. How can we do any less for our fellow man?

Those who seek closure through revenge rarely get what they bargained for. Aba Gayle, an Oregon mother whose daughter was murdered, explained it this way: "It's amazing to me to think that anyone could truly believe that sitting and watching another human being be murdered could heal them, but I did. I was in such a state of anger and rage, I was lusting for revenge."

Strangely, it's the government that is apt to encourage victims to seek revenge, perhaps hoping to maintain a policy that is beginning to be at odds with the majority. Gayle says the prosecuting attorney actively tried to stimulate those feelings. "The district attorneys are very careful to let you know they're there for you. They tell you, 'We're going to convict him, and when he is executed, everything's going to be okay.' It's a magic bullet they're offering to all of these victims' families."[164]

It doesn't usually work that way, however, and it leads to further rage and victimization—a never-ending spiral of bitterness and revenge. To the contrary, Jesus tells us, "If your enemies are hungry, give them bread to eat; and if they are thirsty, give him water to drink; for you will heap coals of fire on their heads, and the Lord will reward you" (Proverbs 25:21). "Do not be overcome by evil, but overcome evil with good" (Romans 13:8–10). Christ teaches us to forgive, so why is it that, where they can, we have judges overturning juries and prosecutors encouraging jurors to seek the death penalty? If these government representatives were secure in their judgment about this issue, they wouldn't need to exert pressure on anyone, especially those who are vulnerable victims. It feels eerily similar to those who continued to try to rally support for segregation in the 1960s. Perhaps this is an example of tyranny of the majority.

HERE AGAIN RACE ENTERS the picture. Most of those who hold positions of power and have decision-making authority in the state criminal justice system in Alabama are white.[165] As in earlier decades, the white power structure is dominant and the criminal justice system reflects this, from the disparity of inmates (59 percent of the state's inmates are black but the total black population in the state is only 26 percent), through the state judiciary. Currently there are no black appellate court judges; and only one black out of forty two state district attorneys. Both of these are elected positions. Black men are incarcerated at eight times the rate of white men. This isn't a surprise given the parameters of the system.

The contrasts are stark. In multiple studies, the statistics show clearly that whites are favored in the sentencing process. Controlling for all the variables, blacks get longer sentences, less consideration for testifying against co-defendants, fewer options for bail, and a harsher sentence for a crime if the victim is white. Regardless of the crime and prior criminal record, white men between the ages of eighteen and twenty-nine (the largest group of offenders) were found to be 38 percent less likely to get jail time than black counterparts for similar offenses. The system itself makes it more difficult for blacks to break the cycle than it is for similarly situated whites. This may be more because of the latent prejudice that has been historically built into the system from the ground up. It is time to reexamine this practice and attempt to make it more equitable.

Before my illness I was no different from my friend Jim, who continues to believe that his personal safety is enhanced by capital punishment—that underneath it all, blacks have some kind of "innate criminal tendency," and that his hard-earned tax dollars shouldn't be wasted on feeding and housing people who have committed terrible crimes. That the system feeds upon itself and is inherently unfair is of no consequence if it punishes those who are "deserving" of punishment, even if those found to be "deserving" are more likely to have black faces. That reasoning provides cover for the racial prejudice at its core: people should be responsible for their behavior; blacks are less "civilized" and are more likely to commit crimes and must be held accountable; it is reasonable that more blacks will be arrested and convicted and given the death penalty; society is safer with fewer blacks. Personal safety and the security of one's own convictions merge in this issue and it is a very powerful nexus. After all, we must hold onto that which keeps us safe. If facts get in the way of arguing our case, well, it just ain't so!

The latent prejudice exemplified by this disjunctive thinking fosters stereotypes of blacks and minorities as "criminal elements" and continues to separate "us" from "them." It also allows the continuation of the policy because those trusted with the power to make laws and lead our government also are humans who hold onto their own cognitive dissonance. Our political leaders also disregard facts in the face of contrary evidence, partly out of their own personal fears and convictions and their own latent (or overt) prejudice, which they believe are in sync with that of their constituency, and partly out of their own personal fear of losing their jobs. The two are often inseparable. If the perception is that being "tough on crime" is what the public wants, then public officials will strike that pose.

While this is not the forum for in-depth political discourse, I must say that it's not always easy to determine the real agenda of politicians. In an ideal world, public officials would be driven by a quest to seek justice. But our system in practice is far from ideal. Prevalent in the general population as well as among elected officials is a willingness to dismiss solid data and statistics, especially when they point to unpopular conclusions. Some are unable and/or unwilling to analyze data; others simply misuse it to prove a point. This is a living example of the tyranny of the majority and it cuts across many social issues, including capital punishment, stifling most attempts at opening a more reasoned discussion. And we can't forget that those who vote for and empower the elected officials are often those who are least affected by the policy embodied in the death penalty.

Changes come slowly as seen in our own history. We are living in a society that passed the Civil Rights Act over forty years ago. Subsequently, our government enacted many additional laws aimed at ridding our county of the vestiges of racism and discrimination. These laws are and should be a reflection of the people's will, so we must assume that the country was ready for a change by the time those laws were passed. Those who lived through the civil rights era know that whatever changes were exacted didn't come easy and many paid the price during those tumultuous times. Just as the time had come a century earlier to end slavery—though its demise was certainly not universally accepted—the time had come to end segregation. Dr. Martin Luther King Jr., during a training meeting for the Southern Christian Leadership Conference, told the audience about a question that had been posed to him. He had been asked if he thought he should reconsider his position on the Vietnam War because it was causing him to lose some support. King recognized immediately that the question really was about moral imperatives. He explained: "That was a good question, because he [the reporter] was asking me the question of whether I was going to think about what happens to me or what happens to truth and justice in this situation."

I believe that is a precept that we all ought to follow. I don't mean to compare myself to King; my mission and my means are different, and I don't harbor ambitions that compete with his. Nor do I possess his ability. Yet I must ask the same questions of myself and of the society we live in, when he said, more eloquently than I ever could:

Cowardice asks the question, is it safe? Expediency asks the question, is it politic? Vanity asks the question, is it popular? But conscience asks the question, is it right? And there comes a time when one must take a position that is neither safe, nor politic, nor popular; but one must take it because conscience tells him it is right.

Abolition of the death penalty may not be a safe position; nor is it politic in the Deep South even in the twenty-first century; nor is it particularly popular. But my conscience and my core tell me capital punishment is wrong, and the resolve with which I address it renders me immoral if I stand by in silence. The time has come to end the immoral practice of capital punishment. While I don't expect to be starting another formal abolition movement, I hope my decision to devote my energies to effect change meets with some success. Though I was summoned to my changes and understanding of the errors of my past through my belief in God and the example set by Jesus Christ, others may find a different path to help them seek the truth. It can be a rational and logical decision, but, looking back to the message of the Wesley sermon, it helps if your heart takes the lead.

Epilogue

Birmingham, Alabama. May 5, 2007. I awoke with a jolt, anxiety taking over what is normally a peaceful moment in the process of early morning consciousness. The day I had been anticipating for some time now was upon me. I had taken on this mission with open eyes, and now as I opened my eyes to the day of the scheduled execution, I was trying hard to maintain my sense of optimism. Whatever the day would bring, I felt prepared and eager to serve as best I could.

My wife was still having trouble believing that I was going to an execution. Perhaps it would be more accurate to say she had trouble understanding how I had gotten so heavily involved in this activity; it was so different from what I did in my prior life. "You would have been scared to death to go into a prison," she reminded me. She does not want to hear about any gory details of death and executions, and although she is very supportive of what I am doing, I think sometimes she gets tired of hearing me talk about how inmates are treated, their unfair trials, etc. We do not always see eye-to-eye on the death penalty, which makes it even harder for her to understand.

The early morning light filtered into the bedroom, as if to proclaim that God was with me; I would need him today and I silently gave thanks to his presence in my life. The spring air was crisp with hope and promise, and I wanted to keep that hope alive. But I also had a sickening feeling of free-floating anxiety—the kind that hits you in the gut to announce some impending personal doom, and the feeling that you know that your life is about to change for the worse and you are helpless to counter it. There were only a handful of times in my six-plus decades that I've had such feelings; the common thread in each was that big dark cloud of the unknown signaling a change in life as I knew it. The first time it hit me was at the age of fourteen when I was told that my mother had died. It took a long time to recover from that punch. Perhaps I never have completely. It's not an experience one forgets, and luckily I didn't have to face such extreme discomposure again until much later in my adult life, when I was ill with MG and didn't know what was wrong, and then again a year later when I received the test results of my prostate cancer biopsy. When my illness forced me to dissolve my medical practice, similar feelings overwhelmed me. I wasn't prepared for early retirement of either my career or my life. Giving up practicing medicine made me confront my own life and death issues.

I went through the motions of preparing for the disquieting day ahead, unable to shake this odd combination of feelings. In some ways my senses seemed sharpened. I was struck by the beauty of the early morning light streaming through the stained glass window of the bathroom as I shaved. I had faced my own death but had been spared. Would Derrick be as lucky? I said a silent prayer knowing that it was all in God's hands now.

I got into the car for the three-and-a-half hour drive ahead of me. Plenty of time to reflect. I would meet up with several other members of the prison ministry program at the site of the state's infamous execution place. Once on the highway I settled in for the trip. I mulled over the day ahead and was somewhat comforted by the fact that I knew Derrick was prepared for this day as much as anyone can be. Over the time in which I had gotten to know him, Derrick had found peace and comfort from God and he would be able to call upon that for the strength needed for his final moments.

I am the perennial optimist, but even I was finding it difficult that day. There was a remote chance that Derrick could get a stay of his execution. All he wanted was to delay it long enough so that his case could be included among the small handful of other capital cases now pending a ruling that was expected in a few weeks on the constitutionality of lethal injection. Other states had already found the method unconstitutional. In my heart, I doubted that Alabama would go that route, but I desperately wanted to be wrong on this count. Derrick's attorneys had previously appealed to Governor Bob Riley; so far, however, Governor Riley had refused to grant a commutation or other delay in Derrick's sentence.

Derrick had been on death row for twenty-seven years. Why hurry now, I wondered. Why this sudden rush to justice? How can we call this justice? The highway billboards flew by: McDONALD'S—would that be his last meal? 1-800 LAWYERS—too little too late for that; LURLEEN WALLACE COMMUNITY COLLEGE—opportunities Derrick surely never had. All the things we take for granted when we are free and have our lives in front of us, waiting to reach out and grab the world and make a difference. Derrick and others like him grabbed the wrong things, got in trouble, and paid a heavy price. Who knows if he is really guilty? Does it matter at this point? He has been punished; he is transformed—a changed man. Yet as a society, we are willing to kill him anyway, regardless of his threat level. Wasted lives just don't make sense.

I had spent as many years practicing medicine and helping people with their hearing as Derrick had helping other inmates on death row. It was hard to imagine languishing in that environment for all that time. And yet, in all these years of observing with pride and satisfaction as patients gained or regained their ability to hear, I have found few politicians who have been willing to listen. How do they become so anesthetized to the people they are supposed to serve? Is it solely because of the preponderance of the poor and mostly black faces like Derrick's on death row? Is it all simply about money? Purely politics? Or fear? Or bogus myths about who we are and what we represent as a nation?

I have only known Derrick for nine months now, but others in the ministry have known him for fifteen or more years. In the short time that I've known him, he has become part of my extended family. I will miss him and the broad smile he always gave me. And his laugh—how could I ever forget his unique laugh. It made me smile just to think about it. But then I grew sullen, reminded by the grim event scheduled for later in the day. I had to stop myself from getting teary—I still had another two hours of driving.

I turned on some music and started to sing along. Since my last major bout with myasthenia gravis and the eventual return of my voice, I was delighted to take whatever opportunities I could to let loose in song. Being in the car alone was one of them—no one to complain and give me snide looks politely suggesting that I stop. As a member of the church choir band, I had a regular outlet, but in this environment, I had my own stage. I went through my whole repertoire, from "Elijah's Coming," adding my own verses, to "Onward Christian Soldiers." Singing is such a great cleansing of the soul; before I knew it my exit was coming up.

I WAS FEELING A bit better, more resolved, by the time I pulled into the small prison parking lot just outside the gate that led to the death row visiting area. I looked at my watch. It was almost noon. Six hours to countdown. As I got out of my car, another car was pulling into the lot. Two of Derrick's sisters emerged. I had first met them last week when I was visiting; we smiled and exchanged greetings and hugs. Everyone was subdued.

Another brother accompanied them and they introduced me to him. I had been told that he is a police officer. I didn't know how he felt about capital punishment in the abstract, but it's always a different story when it becomes personal. We were all sad, and it showed, but he seemed more chastened and a bit edgier than the others. From what I had been told, he had not had much contact with his brother over the last fifteen years, but I didn't really know more than that. There was so much one could brew about in these circumstances, from the unjust system itself to the love of a brother whose behavior shamed you, but I could hardly ask him about such things.

I guessed that from his position as an officer of the law, the conflict went even deeper; it would be natural for him to have wanted to protect his brother and to feel guilty and helpless when he couldn't. I knew those feelings, too. As a child, I had wanted desperately to protect my mother from my father's violent outbursts and of course I couldn't. I was still haunted by those ghosts on occasion. My mother died of cancer; Derrick's death would not be of natural causes. I thought about how it would impact his family, the emotional turmoil it would create. I had no way of knowing how it would play out, but it made me think again of the ripple effect of not only the original crime that occurred in 1975, but also of how the unjust process extends all its victims into the next century.

As we walked toward the prison entrance, we turned upon hearing a voice shouting from the low tower adjacent to the entry gate.

"What'ch ya'll doin' today?" the officer asked. I yelled up to him and explained the purpose of our visit. He picked up the phone to summon another officer to come and let us through the gate and lead us to the death row check-in area inside the prison.

Once inside, we passed through the metal detectors and were routinely searched before being allowed to enter a small, plain room containing a couple of gray well-worn metal desks and a few heavy wooden-back chairs. Two officers were sitting at the desks, both busily writing. I later learned that, among other things, they were charged with recording every movement of the condemned during his last day here on earth, including this visitation. I still don't know the purpose of this procedure. They barely looked up as a third officer methodically checked each of our credentials. We were already on the list of visitors that Derrick had selected to be here for today's proceedings.

Adjoining this room was the visiting area, exposed through a large plate-glass panel window and glass door entryway. This area was reserved solely for those visiting death row inmates. Our little group had to wait until we were all duly signed in before we could join the others who were already here.

As part of the official check-in, one of the officers advised us to "take our potty breaks" now as there were no facilities in the visiting area itself. The old, spartan institutional bathroom reminded me of a "colored only" bathroom I had entered by mistake as a teen. The officer waited for our group to assemble to allow simultaneous entry, saving himself a little time and effort in dealing with the locks on the door. As we entered, we were each given a large metal token with a number on it and were instructed to turn it in upon leaving for the day. I assume it was an arcane way to keep count of the visitors.

There were about fifteen other members of the ministry present as well as Derrick and his two attorneys. The fluorescent lighting cast a dull pall on everything in the room; the brightly colored lights from the vending machines glowed in contrast. The offerings buried in these machines would serve as our temporary mess hall; the ministry volunteers had kindly provided neatly stacked piles of quarters, now placed on the plastic tables that adorned the room.

It was a good-sized room, certainly large enough to accommodate this group comfortably. It was a definite improvement over the small, bare, hot and stuffy death row cell where I had met with Derrick prior to his transfer to this facility. Neither afforded any privacy, but at least this room was air-conditioned, compliments of the ministry. It had large plate-glass windows cut into three of the walls, a separate entrance for the inmates, and an adjoining observation booth where officers kept watch on those inside death row itself. Although the officers went about their business—it was a normal day for them—with little attention paid to the guests du jour, I couldn't help feeling like we were in a fishbowl.

Those in the room had already pushed a few tables together in an effort to form a makeshift mini-community. There was nothing to see out of the windows but dull, nondescript hallways; we wanted to face one another. Derrick was seated more or less in the center, freshly dressed in his crisp white prison uniform. I was glad to see him but I couldn't help thinking of the symbolism of his journey. The state had swapped the figurative black hat he wore on his way into the prison system with the sanitized, crisp white duds they provided for his way out, as if the act of execution would erase his presumptive sins as well as the sins of vengeance that plagued those who were seeking his demise in the name of justice.

As a young black man, Derrick had entered the criminal justice system with the odds against him. His first attorney never even defended him in court against the murder for which he was charged. All of his appeals had been denied; the system was just too difficult to wade through without proper legal counsel from the beginning. Legal errors, like crimes themselves, are hard to undo. At this very moment, competent legal counsel was still attempting to defend this fifty-five-year-old man, but the options were few.

Derrick stood to greet us, smiling at and hugging each person who had come to see him. It was hard not to think about the inevitable, but Derrick seemed calm, actually calmer than some of the rest of us. I know I was trying very hard to maintain a warm and serene exterior despite the turmoil I was feeling.

I was amazed by Derrick's composure, though he was less talkative than when I last had seen him. We all, of course, sensed the tension and sadness that filled the room and tried hard to be natural and upbeat. It was a difficult balance to reach without being totally phony. Derrick, on the other hand, was the one who wound up consoling the rest of us. "I'm all right now, so don't ya'll worry none," he piped up when someone expressed concern for him. It was hard not to cry, but it made me understand ever more intimately the power of salvation and God's comfort in our final moments.

We spent the afternoon in mostly idle chatter and seemed successful in our attempts to keep the mood upbeat. In the back of my mind I was still holding out hope that a warden would appear with news of a stay and periodically glanced at the door. Nothing yet. It was going on three o'clock.

I tried to push that thought out of my mind and soon found myself caught up in some of the conversations in the room: family stories, biblical tales, sharing of past adventures and defeats. I was amazed at the display of love and the comfort that all of it seemed to bring both to Derrick and the members of his family. The tension that usually surrounds the process of dying and impending death was dispelled by the unconditional support of the caregivers in that room. In a situation in which one expects to be at a loss for words, someone always had some. When a question or concern was raised, a loving and thoughtful response followed. And when appropriate, someone always had a funny story or a joke to help quiet the tension. I thought how truly blessed we all were with the abundance of God's love. It was easy to get swallowed up in it and feel the joy rather than the sorrow at hand. As perverse as it might seem, I kept feeling like I was at an in vivo, or live, funeral, or a wake, only the deceased walked among us.

The mood was rather upbeat most of the day, so much so that I had early on lost much of the anxiety that had enveloped me this morning. As a physician and as one who has experienced life-threatening illness, I have given thought to the medical aspects of pain management, terminal illness, and doctor-assisted suicide. I never thought the latter was a good idea but it occurred to me that this might be what such an event would look like. There we were, exchanging farewells, dispensing love and comfort as best we could, trying to put a smile on death. The lethal injection that would be used on Derrick was similar to that used by Dr. Kevorkian when he was still practicing his craft, though because Kevorkian had medical training and had perfected his techniques he was a lot less likely to inflict pain in the process. I shuddered slightly and tried to think of something positive to focus on.

It's hard to think positively about anything associated with death, especially a death that is pre-ordained, but there is one benefit. Knowing the exact time of your death affords you the time and opportunity to make your peace with those who will be left behind and to anticipate your communion with God. Not many of us have that advantage and I knew that Derrick was not going to leave this earth with anything left unsaid or undone. This time period has allowed him the kind of closure most of us don't get. He told me that he felt comforted by his covenant with God; where he was going there would be no more pain, no more worries, no more freezing nights without sufficient heat, no more sweltering days without air-conditioning; just peace and serenity. My faith allowed me to trust that God had a hand here and that Derrick really would be taken care of.

Rather suddenly the warden appeared at the window by the door, beckoning the two lawyers to come out. We all knew what he wanted but of course we didn't know the answer to the big question. His face had no expression and gave nothing away. I wondered if he was a card player.

I watched through the window as he led the attorneys to another room down the hall. The small digital clock on the wall—the only reminder that we were in the twenty-first century—read 3:36 p.m. Two minutes later, we spotted the lawyers in the hallway as they made their way back toward the visiting room, their heads down, looking at the floor. The warden unlocked the door to allow them to reenter the room. We knew by their demeanor what the ruling was; the room went silent.

The attorneys approached Derrick from behind as he sat at the table, grasped his shoulders firmly but gently, and looked down from behind him as we watched horrified. It wasn't what we wanted, they told him, and there is no other recourse. Derrick didn't react. He sat stiffly and then said, "That's all right, don't y'all worry none. Everything's gonna be all right."

I heard a muffled sob but ignored it and grasped Derrick's hand from across the table. Others followed until he was being held by everyone, enveloped by people who loved him. Words of comfort. A short prayer. A lot of silence. Some tears. Many sullen faces, and some visible signs of anger.

The clergy there prepared for Derrick's last supper, consisting of a brief homily of comfort, and then a sharing of the "body and the blood of Jesus Christ" in Holy Communion. I mused about how news reports on executions inevitably included a detailed description of the inmate's last meal, one that Derrick would eat later in his cell, accompanied by his brother and a member of the prison ministry whom he had known for years and had selected to be with him. These were the only two individuals allowed to accompany Derrick into the pre-execution cell, though family members and a few others are allowed to watch the actual execution.

There's a myth that the condemned inmate can just order up whatever he wants—filet mignon, medium-rare please, and yes, I'll take some fresh pepper on that. The reality is that the choices have to fall within the parameters of the prison kitchen and budget, which varies from state to state. While they do try to provide for the inmate's wishes, it is also dependent on the good will of the prison warden and kitchen personnel. Some surely are better than others, but none serve up our fantasy meal. Believing that they do perhaps serves to absolve us of some collective guilt.

The quarters clinked as they were deposited into the vending machines. No one was truly hungry, but we wanted to provide some kindred spirits for Derrick. I reminisced about childhood visits to my grandfather in his shoe-shine shop. He would give me a nickel to get an ice-cold Coke from the machine down the road at the news shop near Mobile Square. It always seemed to taste better when it came out of that big old red dispenser, especially on a hot summer day. Food is equated with comfort and so when we don't know what else to do, we offer it up as a way to nourish the soul as well as the body.

I tried to put aside the image of Christ and his last supper. I didn't want to make a martyr out of Derrick, or anyone for that matter. The scene in the room, however, was so evocative of the words in the scriptures as well as all the marvelous artwork depicting the event through the ages that it was hard to put it to rest. It seemed like justice hadn't changed all that much more than two thousand years later.

I didn't know how punctual the prison officials would be, but the clock was ticking in my head. More hugs, tears, prayers, and words of reassurance from Derrick. "Don't you all worry. I be all right. God is with me," he said. We were quietly singing "Amazing Grace" as the warden came to take Derrick into the preparation room. We all joined hands and continued with the refrain of "Amazing Grace." It helped to keep our voices strong and in unison and from breaking down in pain and sorrow as he silently left the room.

The ministry had prepared Derrick for even these last hours in case the ruling didn't come out in his favor. Derrick had pre-selected the two individuals from the group—men who would see him through to the end. They left the room with him and the rest of the group filed into another room where the pastor led us in prayers, which we recited through our tears. It was a sacred moment.

And then, we made our way back to the parking lot where the sun was starting to set over the razor-wire fence. The group stood mutely in the parking lot, not sure of protocol. There was quiet discussion about the day, the sad circumstances, and our dismay about the injustice of the death penalty. We all expressed gratitude at being able to be of service on such a solemn, some would say even holy, occasion and we were all glad that we could offer Derrick comfort. Then we each got back into our cars and headed back home, left with our own thoughts.

As I drove home, I couldn't help but to look at the clock and imagine what was going on in the execution chamber. Other than prison personnel, the only individuals who would be witness to the actual execution were the people Derrick had selected, Derrick's family, and the family of the victim of the crime. Two hours after Derrick was taken out of the visiting room, they watched through the glass window as he was wheeled into the room next door, his body splayed out on the gurney, attached to I.V. lines connected to plastic bottles of the poison that eventually would stop his heart. The prison personnel remained hidden behind a screen, shielding them from any potential emotional outburst of a viewer, leaving only Derrick exposed. I was later told, confirmed by the local newspaper, that Derrick lay quietly looking up at the ceiling the entire time, no looking over, no obvious tears, just acceptance that his time had come and death was inevitable.

NOT BEING PRESENT IN the room allowed my thoughts to wander in different directions; the surgeon in me imagined a patient ready to be healed; the Christian in me saw the image of Christ on a cross, being treated unjustly, inhumanely. While there was no mob here, there were witnesses who would never forget either the person or the moment. And of course as a human, I visualized a healthy man who had much good to give to the world being snuffed out by ignorance, revenge, and malice.

Since this was my first experience with preparations for execution, I couldn't predict how I would feel. In all my anticipation, however, I had not expected the well of anger that it roused in me. When Derrick was taken from the visiting room to go to his death, a surge of anger and disgust filled the void and intensified my passion and desire to make things change. I had truly expected that this experience would be a holy mission, one ordained by God with me as his disciple. In spite of all my preparation—and certainly I understood the laws and the process—my dominating thought was that it was all so un-Christian; this was not congruous with the spirit of Christ and his message. I was angry at the injustice of the system and the complicity of the politicians in perpetuating the myth that capital punishment deterred murder and provided closure. This was simply the killing of another human being. I wanted to overturn the tables and throw the cheap plastic chairs, remembering Jesus as he ran the moneychangers out of his Father's temple in anger and disgust. As Jesus shed his blood for us, unjustly accused and willingly crucified, so this inmate suffers at the hands of what we call justice.

It had been a very long day and I was tired, but I was also energized by the strength of my anger. I was surprised by this emotion, but I knew that by the time I arrived home, Derrick would have met God and would be beginning his life everlasting. He would be taken care of and would be at peace in eternal bliss with God. I felt comforted by that knowledge. It took the edge off my anger.

I guess in truth I was also disappointed that the appeals ruling had been negative, though I should have known better than to expect any other outcome. I reflected about the contrasts of the day. The heavy emotions on the surface of all the visitors compared to the routine attitude of the prison staff. Not that they were rude or unprofessional; they were neither. But they were unfazed. Of course there was a part of it that I understood: doctors, too, have to remove themselves from the emotional aspects of caring for patients in order to be objective. But we don't remove our emotions to defend against reacting to someone's death; we do it so we can best treat patients to offer them better lives. It all seemed so perverse.

And yet, there was once a time when I thought that the death penalty was not only perfectly acceptable, but moral and right, though I admit that I didn't think about it much. Revisiting the billboards on the return trip, I thought about change—changes in the environment, changes in attitudes, and changes brought about by what we do with our time on earth. There was a time when cigarette ads filled these billboards, but now we know better about the risks of smoking and those signs are gone. I used to think that the fast food chains were great conveniences, and the kids loved them. Now I'm not so sure. Between the health risks of most of their foods and their impact on the erosion of family mealtimes, maybe they're not such great boons to culture after all. There was a time when Lurleen Wallace was governor of the state, fighting to continue segregation. Certainly there was a time when I wouldn't have thought twice about the execution of Derrick (or anyone else, for that matter); I assumed he and his ilk presented great dangers to me and to our country. I was wrong. And now I was trying to right those wrongs. I kept hearing the voice of Jesus on the cross: "Father forgive them, they know not what they do." I felt sure that Derrick was with God and at peace now. But what about those who participated in his demise? Would they too be forgiven? Would they ever recognize their errors, or even think about the contributions they were making to a system they hardly believed in? I hoped so, and I also prayed that I could forgive them, too.

Although I hadn't met the prison warden until that day, I had actually spoken to another warden several years ago when doing research for my thesis on capital punishment. He told me that he didn't believe that the death penalty served as a deterrent to murder because criminals don't associate their crimes with the punishment. "It just does no good the way it is," he had told me. I thought of Derrick's brother, the police officer, who had said much the same thing earlier that day. He had complained that the whole system was broken. I wondered if this warden also concurred about the futility of the death penalty, and if so, how he reconciled doing his job with that statement. I knew from reports, now confirmed by my own observation, that, in general, prison wardens tend to be friendly, efficient, professional, and dedicated to doing a good job. I couldn't challenge their life choices but it made me reflect on my own.

Most of my life was spent without questioning my choices and whether or not they were in line with my personal beliefs. In most cases, I hadn't even really analyzed my beliefs. They were just part of who I was at the time, like hair color that is inherited and changes over the years. Same thing with my religious changes; God was always there but I wasn't always open to his love and wisdom. I was grateful for the past few years—grateful for the knowledge and truths it had brought me, for my own moral reconciliation, my own communion with God, and for the opportunity to help right my own wrongs as well as more global ones.

The prison warden who facilitated Derrick's execution had told other members of the ministry team that he had come to appreciate the value of the ministry for the inmates. He witnessed the comfort it brought to them. Many inmates were not as fortunate as Derrick. They had lost contact with their families over the years, and only the ministry was there to bring some support and consolation to these inmates. I realized that day how grateful I was to be part of the program and I knew that would not be the last of my visits. I would go back to dealing with my world, but I would stew for weeks at my firsthand look at the penalty of death. I had expected to be sad but what would linger would be anger and strong resolve. I would continue to work for abolition, but until that time, I would also make this journey as needed. It was part of my own journey. The music of "Swing Low, Sweet Chariot" played though my head. Singing the line, "Coming for to carry me home," I pulled into my driveway.

NOTES

1   Statement of Proclamation of Governor George C. Wallace. University of Alabama. June 11, 1963. Alabama Department of Archives & History

2   Death Row U.S.A. Washington, D.C: NAACP Legal Defense and Educational Fund, Quarterly Report. Fall 2006.

3   U.S. Department of Justice, Office of Justice Programs, Bureau of Justice Statistics.

4   "Facts About the Death Penalty." Death Penalty Information Center, Washington, D.C. October 15, 2008.

5   Total does not equal 100.0 due to rounding. Note also that the U.S. census has a separate listing for Hispanic; that category is not included here because the Census Bureau considers Hispanic origin an ethnicity, not a race. In this context, Hispanics may be of any race. Many states, though, categorize their prison population by race using "Hispanic" as one of the categories.

6   Holland, Gina. "Court Stays Execution of Mobile Man." *Mobile Register*. January 25, 2006.

7   Spencer, Steven S. "Why Physicians Participate in Executions." Correspondence. *New England Journal of Medicine*. 355 (July 6, 2006): 99–100.

    Mentor, Kenneth W. "The Death Penalty Returns to New Mexico." Paper presented at the Western Social Sciences Association, Albuquerque, NM. April 2002.

8   Ryan, George. "The Death Penalty is a 'Shameful Scorecard in Illinois.'" Speech given to Center on Wrongful Conviction, Bluhm Legal Clinic, Northwestern University School of Law. November 30, 2000. Reprinted by Dobmeyer News Service, Dobmeyer Communication 5.20 (December 2000).

9   "The Medical Ethics of the Death Penalty." *Day to Day*. NPR. February 21, 2006.

10 Groner, Jonathan I. "Lethal Injection: A stain on the face of medicine." *British Medical Journal*. 325 (2002): 1026–1028.

11 American Medical Association, Policy E-2.06 Capital Punishment.

12 Bedau, Hugo Adam. *The Case Against The Death Penalty*. Capital Punishment Project. Washington, D.C: American Civil Liberties Union, 1992.

13 "So Long as They Die: Lethal Injections in the United States." Human Rights Watch. April 24, 2006.

14 Gay, Malcolm. "Uncomfortably Numb." *Riverfront Times* (St. Louis, MO). Dec. 15, 2004.

15 Corbett to author, telephone. January 2007.

16 Sturm, Daniel. "It Looks Like Medicine." *The Free Press* (Columbus, OH). Oct. 12, 2006.

17 Gawande, Atul, M.D., M.P.H. "When Law and Ethics Collide—Why Physicians Participate in Executions." *New England Journal of Medicine.* 354.12 (2006): 1221–1229.

18 Interview with Dr. Carlo Musso on the participation of physicians in capital punishment. Supplement to Gawande A. "When Law and Ethics Collide—Why Physicians Participate in Executions." *New England Journal of Medicine.* 354.12 (2006): 1221–1229.

19 *Letter from Birmingham Jail.* April 16, 1963.

20 Strum. Daniel. "It Looks Like Medicine."

21 As quoted in Groner, Jonathan I. "Lethal Injection: A stain on the face of medicine."

22 "Total Physicians by Race/Ethnicity—2006." American Medical Association, Minority Affairs Consortium.

"2006 American Community Survey." U.S. Census Bureau, American Fact Finder.

23 "Diversity in the Physician Workforce: Facts and Figures 2006." Association of American Medical Colleges.

24 Libby, D. L., Z. Zhou, and D. A. Kindig. "Will Minority Physician Supply Meet U.S. Needs?" *Health Affairs.* (1997): 205–214.

Rivo, M. L. and D. A. Kindig. "A Report Card on the Physician Work Force in the United States." *New England Journal of Medicine.* 334.14 (1996): 892–896.

25 "Minority Physicians' Experiences Obtaining Referrals." Editorial. *Medscape General Medicine.* 3.3 (2001).

26 Henderson, Ron, M.D. *Attacking Myasthenia Gravis.* Montgomery, Alabama: Court Street Press, 2003.

27 Covey, Stephen R. *The 7 Habits of Highly Effective People.* New York: Simon and Shuster, 1989: 82–83.

28 For a discussion of what's rational see Alasdair, MacIntyre. *Whose Justice? Whose Rationality?* College Bend, IN: Univ. of Notre Dame Press, 1988: 5–11.

29 Smith, Frank Elijah. "The Anti-Death Penalty Manifesto." Canadian Coalition Against the Death Penalty. http://ccadp.org/antideathpenaltymanifesto.htm

30 In 2006, there were 382 murders in Alabama and 1,208 traffic fatalities. www.disaster-center.com/crime/alcrime.htm

http://www-nrd.nhtsa.dot.gov/departments/nrd-30/ncsa/STSI/1_AL/2006/1_AL_2006.PDF

31 Death Penalty Information Center. January/February 2008.

32 Lee, Martin A., and Norman Solomon. *Unreliable Sources: A Guide to Detecting Bias in News Media.* New York: Carol Publishing Group, 1990: 242.

33 Reiman, Jeffrey. *The Rich Got Richer and the Poor Get Poorer: Ideology, Class, and Criminal Justice.* 6th Edition. Needham Heights, MA: Allyn and Bacon, 2000.

34 Data derived from Population Estimates, Census of Population and Housing, Small Area Income and Poverty Estimates, State and County Housing Unit Estimates, County Business Patterns, Nonemployer Statistics, Economic Census, Survey of Business Owners, Building Permits, Consolidated Federal Funds Report. Also U.S. Census Bureau. "State and County QuickFacts." January, 2, 2008.

35 www.doc.state.al.us/docs/AnnualRpts/2007StatisticalReport.pdf

36 U.S. Census, 2000. www.census.gov/prod/2001pubs/c2kbr01-1.pdf

37 "Inmates by Race." U.S. Department of Justice, Federal Bureau of Prisons. Sept. 27, 2008

38 "Racial Bias." Equal Justice Initiative. http://eji.org/eji/deathpenalty/racialbias

39   "Evaluating Fairness and Accuracy in State Death Penalty Systems: The Alabama Death Penalty Assessment Report." American Bar Association. June 2006.

40   The Equal Justice Initiative of Alabama. April 2007.

41   Baldus, David C., and George Woodworth. "Race Discrimination and the Legitimacy of Capital Punishment: Reflections on the Interaction of Fact and Perception." *DePaul Law Review.* 53.4 (2004): 1411–1495.

42   The federal government counts some categories, such as Hispanics, as an ethnic group rather than a race. Death Penalty Information Center refers to all groups as races because the sources for much of our information use these categories.

43   Number of Victims refers to the victims in the underlying murder in cases where an execution has occurred since the restoration of the death penalty in 1976. There are more victims than executions because some cases involve more than one victim.

44   The cases represented in this graph are cases of one defendant executed for the murder of one or more victims of one race. Cases involving multiple victims of several different races are not included here.

45   Racial statistics of executions and death row in the United States accurate as of August 18, 2006 following an execution in North Carolina.
"Death Row U.S.A." NAACP Report. Spring 2006.

46   http://www.aclu.org/capital/unequal/10390pub20031008.html

47   Hickman, Johanna M. "Recent Developments in the Area of Criminal Malpractice." *Georgetown Journal of Legal Ethics.* Summer 2005.
Appel, John G., Jr. "Legal Malpractice Is Tough to Prove in Criminal Cases." Blog of the law offices of John G. Appel, Jr.

48   *Talk Magazine* (September 1999): 106.

49   Steele, Tracey and Norma Wilcox. "A View From the Inside: The Role of Redemption, Deterrence, and Masculinity on Inmate Support for the Death Penalty." *Crime & Delinquency.* 49.2 (2003): 285–312.

50   "Fight the Death Penalty in U.S.A." www.fdp.dk/index.html#guatemala

51   "Study Finds More Than Half of All Prison Inmates Have Mental Health Problems." U.S. Department of Justice, Bureau of Justice Statistics. Sept. 6, 2006.

52   *The House of the Dead.* 1860.

53   "Criminal Offender Statistics." U.S. Department of Justice, Bureau of Justice Statistics.

54   "Creating More Victims: How Executions Hurt Families Left Behind." Murder Victims' Families for Human Rights. 2006.

55   Geringer, Joseph. "Karla Fay Tucker: Texas' Controversial Murderess." TruTV Crime Library.

56   Skruba, Angela. "The History of the Australian Penal Colonies." 2001. http://www.umd.umich.edu/casl/hum/eng/classes/434/geweb/AUSTRALI.htm

57   Abu-Jamal, Mumia. *Live from Death Row.* New York: Harper Perrenial, 1995.

58   Costanzo, Mark. *Just Revenge.* New York: St. Martin's Press, 1997: 50.

59   "One in 100: Behind Bars in America, 2008." Pew Center on the States. 15.

60   Born, Daniel. "In the Penal Colonies." *The Common Review* 5.1 (2006).

61   Colloff, Pamela. "The Sins of the Father." *Texas Monthly.* April 2000.

62   As quoted in TomPaine.com. December 22, 2006.

63   Barkan, Steven E. and Steven F. Cohn. "Racial Prejudice and Support for the Death

Penalty." *Journal of Research in Crime and Delinquency.* 31 (1994): 202–209.

64 http://www.gallup.com/video/28249/Death-Penalty.aspx

65 Liebman, J. S., Fagan, Jeffrey, and West, Valerie. "A Broken System: Error Rates in Capital Cases, 1973–1995." *Columbia Law School Research Paper.* 15 (June 2000).

66 Liebman, J. S., et al. "A Broken System, Part II: Why There is So Much Error in Capital Cases, and What Can Be Done About It." *Columbia Law School Research Paper.* 11 (February, 2002).

67 Ibid.

68 *Bill Bennett's Morning in America.* Salem Radio Network. September 28. 2005.

69 Kansal, Tushar. "Racial Disparity in Sentencing: A Review of the Literature, January, 2005." The Sentencing Project. Washington, D.C.

70 *Fox News Sunday.* October 2, 2005.

71 "Homicide Trends in Alabama, 1980–2001." Alabama Center for Health Statistics, Fact Sheet. January 2003.

72 Stevenson to author. Personal communication. April 2007.

73 Spohn, Cassia. "Thirty Years of Sentencing Reform: The Quest for a Racially Neutral Sentencing Process." *Criminal Justice.* National Institute of Justice. 3 (2000): 427–501.

74 Blumenthal, Ralph. "Faulty Testimony Sent 2 to Death Row, Panel Finds." *New York Times.* May 3, 2006.

75 Liptak, Adam. "At 60% of Total, Texas Is Bucking Execution Trend." *New York Times.* December 26, 2007.

76 Moran, Richard. "Wrongfully Convicted?" Paper presented at the annual meeting of the American Society of Criminology (ASC), Los Angeles, CA. November 1, 2006.

77 "One in 100: Behind Bars in America, 2008." Pew Center on the States. 5.

78 Sabol, William J. Courture, Heather, and Harrison, Paige M. "Prisoners in 2006." U.S. Department of Justice, Office of Justice Programs, Bureau of Justice Statistics. December 2007.

79 Liptak, Adam. "Serving Life with No Chance of Redemption." *New York Times.* October 5, 2005.

80 Dieter, Richard C. "On the Front Line: Law Enforcement Views on the Death Penalty." Death Penalty Information Center.

81 Bureau of Justice Statistics, Criminal Offender Statistics. www.ojp.usdoj.gov/bjs/crimoff.htm#recidivism

82 Abramson, R. "Emphasis on Values Is Needed to Stem Crime, Williams Says." *Los Angeles Times.* April 27, 1992. B1/4.

83 Mears, Bill. "Rape a Child, Pay with Your Life, Louisiana Argues." CNN.com. April 15, 2008.

84 Bedau, Hugo Adam, ed. *The Death Penalty in America.* New York: Oxford University Press. 1997: 11.
   "History of the Death Penalty in Delaware." State of Delaware. http://doc.delaware.gov/information/deathrow_history.shtml

85 Rachleff, Peter. "Lynching and Racial Violence: Histories & Legacies." Report from a Conference. http://www.nathanielturner.com/lynchingandracialviolencepr.htm

86 Beck, E. M., and Stewart Tolnay. "The Killing Fields of the Deep South: The Market for Cotton and the Lynching of Blacks, 1882–1930." *American Sociological Review.* 55.4 (1990): 526–539.

87   University of Illinois Press, 2004.

88   Liptak, Adam. "Despite Flawed Defense, a Death Sentence Stands." *New York Times*, November 2, 2006,

89   Messner, Steven F., Robert D. Baller, and Matthew P. Zevenbergen. "The Legacy of Lynching and Southern Homicide." *American Sociological Review.* 70 (2005): 633–56.

90   Consider also the work of Elizabeth Hines, Ph.D. and Eliza Steelwater, Ph.D. on "Project HAL: Historical American Lynching,"at the University of North Carolina at Wilmington. They recorded 4,730 incidents of lynching between 1882 and 1951, 59.3 percent of which took place in ten Southern states (AL, AR, FL, GA, KY, LA, MS, NC, SC, TN).

91   "Lynching by State and Race 1882–1962." *Chicken & Bones: A Journal for Literary and Artistic African-American Themes.* http://www.nathanielturner.com/lynchingbystateandrace.htm

92   Jacobs, David, and Jason T. Carmichael, et al. "Vigilantism, Current Racial Threat, and Death Sentences." *American Sociological Review.* 70: 656–677.

93   "Klan Confession Reported." *New York Times.* June 9, 1997.

94   "Death Row Inmates by State." Death Penalty Information Center. Jan. 1, 2008. "State Execution Rates as of March 27, 2007." Death Penalty Information Center.

95   Cornell University Law School, Legal Information Institute, *McCleskey v. Kemp* (No. 84-6811), Brennan, J., Dissenting Opinion.

96   "The Case Against the Death Penalty." American Civil Liberties Union. Dec. 31, 1997.

97   Gioseffi, Daniela. *Women on War: An International Anthology of Women's Writings from Antiquity to the Present.* New York: Feminist Press, 2003. 220. As quoted from an address given by John Temple Graves at Chautauqua, NY, in defense of lynch laws. *The Arlington Journal.* August, 20, 1903.

98   Neiwert, David. "Part VI: Strange Fruit." *Eliminationism in America.* Jan. 10, 2007.

99   "Negro Lynched to Avenge Assault on White Woman." *Washington Times.* February 18, 1903.

100 "Lynching." *Spartacus Educational.* www.spartacus.schoolnet.co.uk/USAlynching.html

101 Pesic, Andrei. "Sociologist Talks Race, Violence." *The Harvard Crimson.* Nov. 22, 2005.

102 "Death Penalty 101." American Civil Liberties Union, Capital Punishment Project. March 2007.

103 "The Death Penalty: Questions and Answers." American Civil Liberties Union. April 29, 2005.

104 Lee, M. R. "Concentrated poverty, race, and homicide." *Sociological Quarterly.* 41.2 (2000): 189–206.

105 Rondeaux, Candace. "Witnessing Execution a Matter of Duty, Choice." *Washington Post.* Dec. 1, 2006. 1.

106 Blasphemy was still a capital charge in the early American colonies. Another example of the way the law evolves to fit the times.

107 Gross, S. R., et al. "Exonerations in the United States 1989–2003." *The Journal of Criminal Law and Criminology.* 95.2 (2005): 523–560.

108 *Gideon's Broken Promise: America's Continuing Quest for Equal Justice.* American Bar Association Standing Committee on Legal Aid and Indigent Defendants. 2004.

109 "From Jesus to Christ: The First Christians. Arrest and Execution." *Frontline*. PBS. http://www.pbs.org/wgbh/pages/frontline/shows/religion/jesus/arrest.html

110 "The Innocence List" (as of September 18, 2008). Death Penalty Information Center.

111 Poulsen, Kevin. "Death Row Inmates on MySpace." Wired Blog Network. Nov. 16, 2006.

112 "Death Penalty Quotes." As quoted in *Family Circle Magazine*. August 6, 2002.

113 Brownlee, Shannon, et al. "The Place for Vengeance." *U.S. News & World Report*. June 8, 1997.

114 "Sentencing Standards Implementation: Emphasis on Data Quality, Collection, and Analysis." Alabama Sentencing Commission, 2008 Report. 39.

115 "The Hidden Death Tax: The Secret Costs of Seeking Execution in California." ACLU of Nothern California. 2007. 2.

116 "Performance Audit Report: Costs Incurred for Death Penalty Cases: A K-GOAL Audit of the Department of Corrections." Kansas Department of Corrections. December 2003.

117 "In New Mexico, Judge and Prosecutor Agree: No Funds Means No Death Penalty." Death Penalty Information Center. http://www.deathpenaltyinfo.org/node/2345

Chasey, Gail. "Death Penalty Costs New Mexico Millions, Justice." *Albuquerque Democrat*. Nov. 4, 2007.

Appel, Adrianne. "Death Penalty—U.S. Court Says, 'Pay Up—Or Let Live!'" *IPS*. April 23, 2008.

118 Greene, Judith, and Kevin Pranis. "Alabama Prison Crisis: A Justice Strategies Policy Report." The Drug Policy Alliance. Oct. 2005. 4.

119 Kroll, Michael. "The Unseen, Uncounted Casualties of the Death Penalty." New America Media. May 18, 2006.

120 Johnston, Norman. "Prison Reform in Pennsylvania." The Pennsylvania Prison Society.

121 "Prisons and Executions—The U.S. Model: A Historical Introduction." *The Monthly Review*, July–Aug. 2001.

122 Finckenauer, James O. "Prison." *World Book Online Reference Center*. 2004.

123 McKelvey, Blake. *American Prisons—A History of Good Intentions*. Montclair, NJ: Patterson Smith Publishing Corporation, 1977.

124 Beaumont, G., and A. Tocqueville. *On the Penitentiary System in the United States and Its Application in France*. Chicago: Vail-Ballou Press, 1964.

125 Jacoby, J. *Classics of Criminology*. 2nd ed. Prospect Heights, IL: Waveland Press, 1994. 374.

126 Jacoby. 379.

127 "Prisons and Executions—The U.S. Model: A Historical Introduction." *The Monthly Review*. July–Aug. 2001.

128 "Prison Design Boycott Campaign." Architects, Designers, Planners for Social Responsibility (ADPSR). http://www.adpsr.org/prisons/history.htm

129 "A Chronology of the Disability Rights Movements." In Pelka, Fred. *The ABC-CLIO Companion to the Disability Rights Movement*. ABC-CLIO American History Companions. 1997.

130 Lamb, Richard and Linda Weinberger. "Persons with Severe Mental Illness in Jails and

Prisons: A Review." *Psychiatric Services.* 49 (1998): 483–492. In Richard Lamb and Leona Bachrach, "Some Perspectives on Deinstitutionalization," *Psychiatric Services.* 52.8 (2001), the authors estimated the number of occupied state hospital beds had fallen as low as twenty-one per one-hundred thousand.

131 Harcourt, Bernard. "The Mentally Ill Behind Bars." *New York Times.* Jan. 15, 2007.

132 Nossiter, Adam and Christopher Drew. "In New Orleans, Dysfunctional Fuels Cycle of Killing." *New York Times.* Feb. 5, 2007.

133 "Mental Health: Culture, Race, and Ethnicity, a Supplement to Mental Health: A Report of the Surgeon General." U.S. Dept. HHS, U.S. Public Health Office. 1999.

134 Blow, Frederic C., et al. "Ethnicity and Diagnostic Patterns in Veterans with Psychoses." *Social Psychiatry and Psychiatric Epidemiology.* 39.10 (2004).

135 Teplin, L. A. "The Prevalence of Severe Mental Disorder Among Male Urban Jail Detainees: Comparison with the Epidemiologic Catchment Area Program." *American Journal of Public Health.* 80 (1990): 663–669.

Koegel, P. M., A. Burnam, and R. K. Farr. "The prevalence of specific psychiatric disorders among homeless individuals in the inner city of Los Angeles." *Archives of General Psychiatry.* 45 (1988): 1085–1093.

Breakey, W. R., et al. "Health and mental health problems of homeless men and women in Baltimore." *Journal of the American Medical Association.* 262 (1989): 1352–1357.

Vernez, G. M., et al. "Review of California's program for the homeless mentally ill disabled." Report No. R3631-CDMH. Santa Monica, CA: RAND (1989).

136 "Mental Health: Culture, Race, and Ethnicity, A Supplement to Mental Health: A Report of the Surgeon General." U.S. Dept. HHS, U.S. Public Health Office (1999).

137 "Guy Legrande Found Incompetent for Execution Due to Mental Illness." Amnesty International, U.S.A. July 2, 2008.

138 "Mental Illness and the Death Penalty in the United States." American Civil Liberties Union. Jan. 31, 2005.

"The Execution of Mentally Ill Offenders." Amnesty International, U.S.A. Jan. 31, 2006

139 "Study Finds More Than Half of All Prison and Jail Inmates Have Mental Health Problems." U.S. Department of Justice, Office of Justice Programs, Bureau of Justice Statistics. Sept. 6, 2006.

140 Ibid.

Koegel et al., 1988; Vernez et al., 1988; Breakey et al., 1989; Teplin, 1990.

141 Ditton, Paula. "Special Report." *Mental Health and Treatment of Inmates and Probationers.* Bureau of Justice Statistics. July 1999.

142 *Psychiatric Services in Jails and Prisons.* 2nd ed. Washington, D.C: American Psychiatric Association, 2000. Data from 2003 support the same premise.

Butterfield, Fox. "Study Finds Hundreds of Thousands of Inmates Mentally Ill." *New York Times.* Oct. 22, 2003.

143 "Mental Illness and the Death Penalty in the United States." American Civil Liberties Union. Jan. 31, 2005.

144 "ACLU Lawsuit Against Michigan Department of Corrections Resumes Today: Inadequate Mental Health Care Puts Prisoners at Risk." American Civil Liberties Union. April 28, 2008.

145 "Does the U.S. Execute the Severely Mentally Ill?" New Yorkers Against the Death Penalty. http://www.nyadp.org/main/faq#10

146 Liptak, Adam. "Lawyer Reveals Secret, Toppling Death Sentence." *New York Times*. Jan. 19, 2008.

147 Scalia, J. Dissenting, Supreme Court, 536 U.S. 304 (2002): 17.

148 "In Orlando, a law against feeding homeless—and debated over Samaritans' rights." *International Herald Tribune*. Feb. 3, 2007.

149 *Acts and Resolves of the Province of Massachusetts Bay*. Boston (1869): 52–56.

150 "Mandatory Minimum Penalties in the Federal Criminal Justice System." United States Sentencing Commission. 1991.

151 Lundman, Richard and Kaufman, Robert L. "Driving While Black: Effects of Race, Ethnicity, and Gender on Citizen Self-Reports of Traffic Stops and Polices Actions." *Criminology*. 41.1, 195: 220.

Steffensmeier, Darrell and Demuth, Stephen. "Ethnicity and Judges' Sentencing Decisions: Hispanic-Black-White Comparisons." *Criminology*, 39.1. 145: 178.

152 *Fifteen Years of Guidelines Sentencing: An Assessment of How Well the Federal Criminal Justice System is Achieving the Goals of Sentencing Reform*. Washington, D.C, United States Sentencing Commission. 2004. 127–135.

153 "Most Serious Offense of Jail Inmates, 2002, 1996, 1989." Bureau of Justice.

154 Brewer, David. "Chief Justice Says Drug Courts are the Way to Go." *Huntsville Times*. April 24, 2008.

Huddleston, C. W., Karen Freeman-Wilson, Douglas B. Marlowe, Aaron Roussell. "Painting the Picture: A National Report Card on Drug Courts and Other Problem Solving Court Programs in the United States." U.S. Department of Justice, Bureau of Justice Assistance. 1.2 (May 2005).

155 "Fact Sheet." Office of National Drug Control Policy, Drug Data Summary. March 2003.

156 *State Expenditures Report*. Washington, D.C: National Association of State Budget Officers. 1996.

157 Mauer, Marc. *Race to Incarcerate*. New York: New Press, 1999.

Weinstein, Henry C. *Psychiatric Services in Jails and Prisons*. 2nd ed. Washington, D.C.: American Psychiatric Association, 2000.

158 James, Doris J., and Glaze, Lauren E. "Mental Health Problems of Prison and Jail Inmates." Bureau of Justice Statistics, Special Report. Sept. 2006.

159 Gallop Poll Results. 2006

160 "A Death Penalty Conversion." *Birmingham News*. November 6, 2005.

161 Joseph, Brian. "Jail Time Sought for Drug Offenses." *Orange County Register*. June 26, 2006.

Russo, Frank D. "Judge Upholds Vote of Californians on Prop 36 Drug Courts Against Schwarzenegger Demanded Legislative Changes." *California Progress Report*. Sept. 15, 2006.

162 See, for example, the case of Oscar Doster. *Andalusia Star News*. November 22, 2006. "Judicial Override in Alabama." Equal Justice Initiative. March 2008.

163 "Matters of Life and Death." Editorial. *Birmingham News*. January 20, 2007.

164 Bunch, Kathy. "Does Seeing Execution Help or Hurt?" WebMD Feature. 2001. 2.

Goldberg, Michelle. "The 'Closure' Myth." *Salon*. Jan. 21, 2003.

165 *Broken Justice: The Death Penalty in Alabama*. American Civil Liberties Union, Capital Punishment Project. October 2005.

Appendix A: Ala. Department of Corrections, FY2007 Annual Report, On Hand Inmates—Sentences by Ethnogender Basis as of September 30, 2007

Sentence	Amer. Indian		Asian		African American		Unknown		White		Tot.	%
	Male	Fem.	Male	Fem.	Male	Fem.	Male	Fem.	Male	Fem.		
0–6 mo.	0	0	0	0	19	4	0	0	13	5	41	0.14%
6 mo.–1 yr.	0	0	0	0	80	16	0	0	101	17	214	0.73%
1 yr.	0	0	0	0	247	26	1	0	205	58	537	1.84%
1 yr., 1 d.	0	0	0	0	32	13	0	0	46	16	107	0.37%
1 yr., 1 d.–2 yr.	0	1	0	0	272	32	2	0	294	61	662	2.26%
2 yr.	0	0	0	0	616	57	1	0	445	93	1,212	4.15%
2 yr., 1 d.–3 yr.	0	0	0	0	88	9	0	0	62	12	171	0.58%
3 yrs.	0	0	0	0	1,370	118	3	0	889	138	2,518	8.61%
3 yr., 1 d.–4 yr.	0	0	0	0	47	3	0	0	54	9	113	0.39%
4 yrs.	0	0	0	0	303	15	0	0	207	37	562	1.92%
4 yr, 1 d.–5 yr.	0	0	0	0	23	1	0	0	21	1	46	0.16%
5 yr.	0	0	0	0	845	60	3	0	663	127	1,698	5.81%
5 yr., 1 d.–10 yr.	0	0	0	0	384	22	2	0	425	63	896	3.06%
10 yr.	0	0	0	0	1,206	86	2	0	1,210	176	2,680	9.17%
10 yr., 1 d.–15 yr.	0	0	0	0	241	13	0	0	178	24	456	1.56%
15 yr.	0	0	0	0	1,797	124	4	0	1,306	184	3,415	11.68%

15 yr., 1 d.–20 yr.	0	0	0	0	463	27	1	0	321	21	833	2.85%
20 yr.	0	0	0	0	2,214	103	4	0	1,047	88	3,456	11.82%
20 yr., 1 d.–25 yr.	0	0	0	0	550	23	0	0	208	15	796	2.72%
25 yr.	0	0	1	0	971	36	1	0	407	38	1,454	4.97%
25 yr., 1 d.–35 yr.	0	0	0	0	644	19	1	0	325	25	1,014	3.47%
35 yr.	0	0	0	0	121	3	0	0	59	6	189	0.65%
35 yr., 1 d.–999 yr.	0	0	0	0	592	10	2	0	303	15	922	3.15%
Life	1	2	0	0	2,314	46	7	0	1,206	61	3,637	12.44%
Life w/out parole	1	0	0	0	941	15	2	0	424	24	1,407	4.81%
Death	0	0	0	0	91	2	2	0	102	2	199	0.68%
Safe Keeping	0	0	0	0	0	0	0	0	0	0	0	0.00%
Totals	2	3	1	0	16,471	883	38	0	10,521	1,316	29,235	100%

APPENDIX B: LYNCHING BY STATE AND RACE 1882–1962

STATE	WHITES	BLACKS	TOTAL
Alabama	48	299	347
Arizona	31	0	31
Arkansas	58	226	284
California	41	2	43
Colorado	66	2	68
Delaware	0	1	1
Florida	24	257	282
Georgia	39	491	530
Idaho	20	0	20
Illinois	15	19	34
Indiana	33	14	47
Iowa	17	2	19
Kansas	35	19	54
Kentucky	63	142	205
Louisiana	56	335	391
Maryland	2	27	29
Michigan	7	1	8
Minnesota	5	4	9
Mississippi	40	538	578
Missouri	53	69	122
Montana	82	2	84
Nebraska	52	5	57
Nevada	6	0	6
New Jersey	0	1	1
New Mexico	33	3	36
New York	1	1	2
North Carolina	15	85	100
North Dakota	13	3	16
Ohio	10	16	26
Oklahoma	82	40	122
Oregon	20	1	21
Pennsylvania	2	6	8

South Carolina	4	156	160
South Dakota	27	0	27
Tennessee	47	204	251
Texas	141	352	493
Utah	6	2	8
Vermont	1	0	1
Virginia	17	83	100
Washington	25	1	26
West Virginia	20	28	48
Wisconsin	6	0	6
Wyoming	30	5	35
TOTAL (72.6% black)	1,294	3,442	4,736

INDEX

00264818452384)

0093
0026481 44 52 38 91
0026481 44 52 38 91